David Pears is Professor of Philosophy in the
University of Oxford. He is the author of *Motivated
Irrationality* (Oxford University Press, 1984),
Some Questions in the Philosophy of Mind
(Duckworth, 1975), *Ludwig Wittgenstein*
(Fontana, 1971), and *Bertrand Russell and the
British Tradition in Philosophy* (Collins, 1967).

THE FALSE PRISON

VOLUME I

THE FALSE PRISON

*A Study of the Development of
Wittgenstein's Philosophy*

VOLUME I

DAVID PEARS

CLARENDON PRESS · OXFORD
1987

Oxford University Press, Walton Street, Oxford OX2 6DP

Oxford New York Toronto
Delhi Bombay Calcutta Madras Karachi
Petaling Jaya Singapore Hong Kong Tokyo
Nairobi Dar es Salaam Cape Town
Melbourne Auckland

and associated companies in
Beirut Berlin Ibadan Nicosia

Oxford is a trade mark of Oxford University Press

Published in the United States
by Oxford University Press, New York

© David Pears 1987

British Library Cataloguing in Publication Data
Pears, David
The false prison: a study of the
development of Wittgenstein's philosophy.
Vol. 1
1. Wittgenstein, Ludwig
I. Title
192   B3376.W564
ISBN 0-19-824771-0
ISBN 0-19-824770-2 Pbk

Library of Congress Cataloging in Publication Data
Pears, David Francis.
The false prison.
Bibliography: v. 1, p.
Includes index.
1. Wittgenstein, Ludwig, 1889—1951.   I. Title.
B3376.W564P35   1987   192   87-5566
ISBN 0-19-824771-0 (v. 1)
ISBN 0-19-824770-2 (pbk.: v. 1)

Typeset by Joshua Associates Limited, Oxford
Printed in Great Britain
at the University Printing House, Oxford
by David Stanford
Printer to the University

TO JULIAN

PREFACE

THIS is the first of two volumes of a continuous study of the development of Wittgenstein's philosophy. The treatment is selective, but his investigation of the foundations of mathematics is the only topic that is left untouched. Part I starts with a brief sketch of the development of his ideas from the beginning to the end. Part II, which deals with his early system, fills the rest of Volume I. Part III, which covers his later philosophy, will appear in Volume II.

The main reason for dividing the book into two volumes was that many people study *Philosophical Investigations* without first reading the *Tractatus*, and those who do read the *Tractatus* do not always show the same interest in his later work. These tendencies are often reinforced by university courses on his philosophy. So the market seemed to demand a division.

However, it would have been unnatural to present his early system in complete isolation from what was to come later, and so without the benefit of any hindsight. For one thing, the comments, favourable and unfavourable, which he started to make in 1929 on his own earlier work could hardly be left for later consideration. Also, many of his earlier ideas reappear in the second phase of his philosophy nearly always transformed, but often easier to appreciate in their new form. So the line between Parts I and II does not divide the completion of the *Tractatus* from everything that came after it.

I first read the *Tractatus* when I was an undergraduate. I did not understand it and after my final examination it was one of the books that drew me into further work in philosophy. Like many other people, I was fascinated by its austerity and by its intimations of a perfect structure behind the disorder of the world.

Part II is based on work done for lectures at Oxford University and for a course given at the University of California, Los Angeles. I hope that it will convey some of my original feeling for the *Tractatus*, but with more understanding. I have learned much from some of the many articles and books published by others in the last forty years and from discussions with my pupils.

I take this opportunity to thank Elsie Hinkes for turning my manuscript into a legible text and Gavin Lawrence for reading it and removing many errors.

D.F.P.

CONTENTS

ABBREVIATIONS

CLI   *Wittgenstein's Lectures, Cambridge, 1930—32*, ed. D. Lee, Blackwell, 1980.

LWVC   *Ludwig Wittgenstein and the Vienna Circle: Conversations Recorded by Friedrich Waismann*, ed. B. McGuiness, tr. J. Schulte and B. McGuinness, Blackwell, 1979.

Works by L. Wittgenstein

NB   *Notebooks 1914—1916*, ed. G. H. von Wright and G. E. M. Anscombe, tr. G. E. M. Anscombe, Blackwell, 1961.

NLPESD   'Notes for Lectures on 'Private Experience' and 'Sense-data'', *Philosophical Review*, Vol. 77, No. 3, 1968. [The notes taken of these lectures by R. Rhees are published in the journal *Philosophical Investigations*, Vol. 7, No. 1, Jan. 1984.]

PG   *Philosophical Grammar*, ed. R. Rhees, tr. A. Kenny, Blackwell, 1974.

PI   *Philosophical Investigations*, tr. G. E. M. Anscombe, Blackwell, 1953; 3rd edn., Macmillan, 1958.

PR   *Philosophical Remarks*, ed. R. Rhees, tr. R. Hargreaves and R. White, Blackwell, 1975.

TLP   *Tractatus Logico-Philosophicus*, tr. C. K. Ogden, Routledge, 1922, and tr. D. F. Pears and B. McGuinness, Routledge, 1961.

My work has extended from the foundations of logic to the nature of the world.

Wittgenstein

We shall not cease from exploration
And the end of all our exploring
Will be to arrive where we started
And know the place for the first time.

T. S. Eliot

PART I

INTRODUCTION

I

Wide-angle View

OPEN any of Wittgenstein's books and you will realize immediately that you are entering a new world. The impression that you get will be quite different from the impression usually given by the writings of philosophers. You will not feel that, though the presentation may be new, the ideas merely repeat one of the familiar patterns of western thought. This landscape is quite different not only in general composition but also in the things that it contains. If the book belongs to the second period of his philosophy, which began in 1929, the biggest surprise will be the absence of theories. There will, of course, be arguments, but not the kind that we have learned to expect. They will be arguments with strange shapes, not designed to connect explicit premises with judicious conclusions, like those of other philosophers. It will not even be easy to separate them from one another and say where one ends and another begins. The usual marks will not be there to guide us and it is going to be difficult to find our way around in this unfamiliar world and even to construe what we see in it.

It is, therefore, prudent to start with a sketch of the general layout of Wittgenstein's philosophy. It will have to be an approximate sketch and it will necessarily take a lot for granted. The over-simplifications can be corrected later and arguments for interpretations which are first stated dogmatically can be added at leisure. A rough guide is better than no guide at all.

The simplest general characterization of his philosophy is that it is critical in the Kantian sense of that word. Kant offered a critique of thought and Wittgenstein offers a critique of the expression of thought in language. The human intellect is a limited instrument and philosophy's task is to turn it back on itself and to make it discover its own limitations and then mark them in a self-abasing but salutary way. Philosophy's old, ill-defined partnership with science was broken up long ago, but its attempt to set itself up in the rival business of dogmatic metaphysics still has to be blocked. Since there is no higher discipline set above philosophy, this can only be achieved by self-criticism. Philosophy must draw the line that limits the legitimate uses of the intellect, including its own rather special brand of thought.

This is already too simple to stand unqualified. It is true that dogmatic metaphysics imitates the voice of science and that the natural reaction to the works of the great system-builders of the past is to ask how they thought they knew so much about the structure of reality. However, there is an alternative to dogmatic metaphysics. A metaphysician does not have to be so overweening. He does not have to extend our concepts beyond the limits of their legitimate use, because he can avoid questions about the ultimate structure of reality and confine himself to reality as it is apprehended by us, the so-called 'phenomenal world'. For example, instead of arguing that there must be a first cause of everything that exists, he can argue that causality is a necessary ingredient in the mixture taken in by our minds. To put the point in Kant's way, he may offer a metaphysic of experience instead of a dogmatic metaphysic.

So the straightforward opposition of critical to metaphysical philosophy is really too simple for an understanding of the history of ideas in the last two hundred years. It is also too simple to serve as a key to Wittgenstein's thought. For post-Kantian Idealism did much to shape his ideas, especially in the first period of his philosophy, which ended with the publication of his *Tractatus Logico-Philosophicus* in 1921. In that book the Kantian distinction between speculative metaphysics and metaphysics deduced from experience is clearly marked. It contains no speculations about a world of things-in-themselves behind the phenomena. Wittgenstein is concerned only with *The World as I found it*.[1] True, he offers some deep metaphysical conclusions about the structure of this world, but he does not offer them as a contribution to speculative metaphysics. On the contrary, he makes it quite clear that they are not intended as a kind of super-science. They belong to an entirely different mode of thought which cannot properly be expressed in factual language. For example, he argues that the world must consist of simple objects in immediate combination with one another, like the links of a chain.[2] This is a conclusion deduced from the nature of phenomena and so it is restricted to the world as we experience it. Nevertheless, it is a metaphysical conclusion, because it is not a piece of science and it cannot

[1] L. Wittgenstein: *Tractatus Logico-Philosophicus* (henceforth *TLP*) tr. C. K. Ogden, Routledge, 1922, and tr. D. F. Pears and B. McGuiness, Routledge, 1961, 5.631.
[2] Ibid., 2.03.

even be properly expressed in the factual language that is appropriate to science.

If this conclusion is not factual, what exactly is its status? It is not much help to be told that it is part of a metaphysic of experience. And why does Wittgenstein present it in factual language if it is not really factual? These questions express the irritation felt by most people when they first reach the point in the *Tractatus* at which he denies the factuality of his own metaphysical conclusions. It looks like a superficial shuffle.

But perhaps that is unfair. Let us give Wittgenstein the benefit of the doubt for the moment while we try to work out where he stands. Kant is not the only German Idealist whose influence can be felt in the *Tractatus*. Schopenhauer's ideas have also left their mark on the book. At the basis of Schopenhauer's system there is a thesis in speculative metaphysics: we do have a resource which allows us to discern the nature of the reality behind the phenomenal world; we have our experience of our own agency. According to Schopenhauer, when we act, our knowledge of our own agency is neither scientific nor the result of any other kind of discursive operation of the intellect. It is direct, intuitive, inside knowledge of our own strivings, and he believed that it gives us our only glimpse of the true nature of reality. Thus his metaphysic was an expression of the heart rather than the head, not in the banal sense of wishful thinking—he was not the man for that—but in a deeper sense: he took human desire, striving, and achievement to be a small-scale model of the essence of the whole world.[3]

Wittgenstein was fascinated by this romantic metaphysic of the will, and, no doubt, it started his own abiding interest in agency. However, he never accepted Schopenhauer's vision of the world as a manifestation of will. On the other hand, though he did not take over the substance of this metaphysic, he did take over its spirit. He shared Schopenhauer's contempt for scientism and his conviction that our apprehension of reality cannot find its complete expression in factual reports of sensory input. So the *Tractatus* conveys a strong sense of the mystery of the world beneath the surface skimmed by factual discourse. There really are things that cannot be expressed in that way.

What, we may ask, are they? The main one, already mentioned, is the composition of the phenomenal world—simple objects in immediate combination. Another thing with the same mysterious status

[3] See below, pp. 178 and 186–7.

is the division of objects into types which determine the ways in which they can be combined with one another, their natural affinities. Wittgenstein saw the underlying structure of reality as a kind of grid of possible states of affairs, with objects at the nodal points, and it is the natures of the different types of objects which determine the way in which the grid is put together. Now, according to him, this grid imposes a constraint on all factual languages: they can describe reality only in so far as they conform to it in their own underlying structure. So though different factual languages vary in superficial ways, they all have the same deep structure in common, the structure of the ultimate grid.[4] That is the gist of the metaphysic of the *Tractatus* and Wittgenstein maintained that it is not itself expressible in factual language.

There are two differences between this metaphysic and Schopenhauer's. First, Wittgenstein is only concerned with the phenomenal world. It is true that what he says about it is deep and abstruse, but he never transgresses into speculations about a world behind the phenomena. Second, his metaphysic has nothing to do with agency. The argument which he uses to establish it starts from the existence of factual language. We evidently do succeed in using this language to describe the world, but how is it done? His answer is that we succeed only because there is a fixed grid of possible combinations of objects to which the structure of our language conforms. The grid must exist and connections must be made with it if language is going to work. But it clearly does work and so the metaphysical conclusions follow.

Wittgenstein's metaphysic is an affair of the head rather than the heart, or, to put it in Schopenhauer's terms, it is deduced from the world as idea. However, the spirit of it and the sense that it gives of the mystery of the world are more appropriate to a metaphysic derived from human aspirations. In fact, when he was working out these ideas in the journal that he kept during the First World War, he tried to connect them with some of Schopenhauer's ideas about the will.[5]

Someone who finds his denial of the factuality of his metaphysical conclusions baffling will not get much enlightenment from a study of Schopenhauer's influence. Schopenhauer offers a thesis in speculative metaphysics, and so he has no scruples about expressing it in factual language. In the *Tractatus* Wittgenstein offers only a metaphysic of

---

[4] *TLP* 6.124.

[5] See. L. Wittgenstein: *Notebooks 1914—1916*, ed. G. H. von Wright and G. E. M. Anscombe, tr. G. E. M. Anscombe, Blackwell, 1961 (henceforth *NB*), 11 June, 5 July, 21 July, 29 July, and 4 Nov. 1916.

experience deduced from the existence of factual language, but not expressible in it. What we need to know is why this deduction of his metaphysic prevents us from expressing it as a very general factual truth. Why is it impossible for factual language to express the fundamental condition of its own existence? This is a difficult question.

It sends us to the theory of language of the *Tractatus*. A short answer to it would go like this: if factual language could contain an analysis of the conditions of its own application, the language in which it analysed them would itself depend on further conditions, which would still remain to be analysed, and so on to infinity. Wittgenstein used the analogy between factual sentences and pictures to drive the point home.[6] A portrait does not depict the geometry which makes it a projection of a certain face, and, if it did include such a diagram in a corner of the canvas, that would only be another picture with its own method of projection still remaining to be analysed. Factual sentences, like pictures, present a view of the world, but they do not present a view of what made the original view possible, and, if they did start doing that, they could never finish the task.

This is hardly a sufficient explanation of Wittgenstein's picture theory of sentences, but it may serve to indicate its general orientation. It is a theory which bases the possibility of saying some things on the actuality of other things which cannot be said. Since the saying belongs to factual discourse, this thesis is, in one important respect, Kantian: science rests on a basic metaphysics which is not an extension of science.

There are, however, some striking differences between Wittgenstein's early system and Kant's. One difference is that Kant felt no scruples about presenting his philosophy in factual language, but Wittgenstein was more rigorous: if philosophy is not just a more general and abstract development of science, then its results cannot properly be expressed in factual language. This is connected with the sense of the mystery of the world which Wittgenstein shared with Schopenhauer. Now it may seem surprising that Wittgenstein's philosophy should be permeated by a sense of mystery. Such a feeling may seem appropriate for Schopenhauer who spoke of a world transcending the phenomena, but not for Wittgenstein who confined himself to the world as we find it, or, to put it in Schopenhauer's terms, 'the world as idea'. If this world is a joint product of the mind

[6] He developed the analogy in the picture theory of sentences. See below, pp. 13, 29, and ch. 6.

and the raw material presented to it, there seems to be less cause for wonder. People do not see much mystery in things with which, in John Locke's phrase, they have 'mixed their labour'.

However, Wittgenstein's attitude to the phenomenal world is not inexplicable. There are, in fact, two features of his treatment of it which show why the tone of his philosophy is more that of an artist than a scientist. Part of the explanation is that his theory about the phenomena and factual language in which we describe them is a deep theory. Although he confines his conclusions to the phenomenal world, they have the depth that is characteristic of transcendent theories. There is also another aspect of his early system which plays a role at this point, the *Tractatus* is basically realistic in the following sense: language enjoys certain options on the surface, but deeper down it is founded on the intrinsic nature of objects, which is not our creation but is set over against us in mysterious independence.[7]

Given the basic realism of the *Tractatus* it is too simple to call Wittgenstein's early philosophy 'critical'. It is true that it is concerned with the world of phenomena, but he sees a depth in the phenomena, and, beyond a certain point, an independence which a really critical philosophy would have questioned. So though his later philosophy is entirely critical, his early system is only semi-critical.

He himself emphasizes the critical aim of the *Tractatus* in his Preface and barely alludes to its metaphysic, but this emphasis is corrected in the main body of the book. This is what he says in the Preface:

The book deals with the problems of philosophy, and shows, I believe, that the reason why these problems are posed is that the logic of our language is misunderstood. The whole sense of the book might be summed up in the following words: what can be said at all can be said clearly, and what we cannot talk about we must pass over in silence.[8]

He means, of course, 'what we cannot talk about factually'. So the critical business is to be done by applying the test of expressibility in factual discourse in much the same way that Kant applied the test of possible experience, and the metaphysic fails the test.

However, in the main body of the book his metaphysical theses are treated with respect, in spite of their lack of semantic success. So when

---

[7] See *NB* 8 July 1916: 'The world is *given* to me, i.e. my will enters into the world completely from outside it as into something that is already there. . . . There are two godheads: the world and my independent I.'

[8] *TLP* Preface, p. 3.

he ends it by saying that silence is what they really deserve he leaves us with the impression that this is a paradox concealing a real problem.[9] There seems to be something wrong with a Kantian critique that is not pushed through to its logical conclusion. It may be that there is more to be said about the attachment of names to objects. Also the original exaltation of plain factual discourse was perhaps a mistake. Why should science be the measure of all things?

This was the point of tension in his early philosophy, the coiled spring which, once released, would drive him forward to the position that he occupied in his second book, *Philosophical Investigations*, when criticism had overrun the last remaining territory of realism. However, that transition was going to be complex, because it had to pass through several stages. So it too will be introduced now with a rough sketch, to which the details and qualifications can be added later.

In the *Tractatus* the beginning of language is the naming of objects. Objects are set in a fixed grid of possible states of affairs, which is in no way dependent on any contribution made by our minds. This grid allows us certain options in developing our grammar and syntax, but, once we have exercised those options, it imposes the consequences on us with a necessity not of our making.[10] There are really two reasons for calling this doctrine 'uncritical realism'.

First, nothing is said about the way in which we manage to go on using a name correctly after its original attachment to an object. The assumption is that, if that problem arises, the nature of the object will take care of it. True, we would have to respond to its nature if we encountered the object again, but our response is assumed to be entirely passive, a kind of inert receptivity. Our minds contribute nothing positive at this point and there is no admixture of intellectual labour. Now the objects of the *Tractatus* are the only ultimate constituents of the world, and so this account of the way in which they acquire and keep their names is intended as a general explanation of the attachment of language to the world. It is wholly un-Kantian,[11] a clear paradigm of uncritical realism.

The second reason for this diagnosis of the *Tractatus* is concerned not with the original attachment of sentences to real possibilities, but with liaisons between the sentences themselves, which represent

---

[9] See his letter to L. Ficker, quoted below, ch. 8 n. 3.

[10] *TLP* 6.124. cf. 3.342. See pp. 23–5 for a discussion of these two remarks.

[11] Of course, Kant never considered extending his Copernican revolution to naming. The point is only that in the *Tractatus* Wittgenstein might have allowed that the user of a name makes a more active contribution.

necessities. When we construct a language founded on the adherence of names to objects, we find that there are two different kinds of relation between its sentences. Some pairs of sentences are connected in a way that evidently depends entirely on us, because we can annul the connection by changing the meaning of a descriptive word without any fundamental change in the structure of the language. However, there are other pairs of sentences that are connected in a way that does not depend entirely on us. In these cases the connection is marked by a logical word, and, though we have certain options when we assign meanings to logical words, we must produce a logical system with a fundamental structure that reflects the fixed grid of possible combinations of objects. This is another, equally important aspect of Wittgenstein's uncritical realism.[12]

It is easier to follow his gradual abandonment of this position if we start with the attachment of sentences to real possibilities rather than with logic. The uncritical realism of the *Tractatus* is, of course, in both its aspects, the doctrine that is usually called 'Platonism' nowadays. The idea is that in all our operations with language we are really running on fixed rails laid down in reality before we even appeared on the scene. Attach a name to an object, and the intrinsic nature of the object will immediately take over complete control and determine the correct use of the name on later occasions. Set up a whole language in this way, and the structure of the fundamental grid will inexorably dictate the general structure of the logical system. The first of these two aspects of uncritical realism is evidently easier to understand than the second one, because part of it is the familiar idea that there are independent universals which determine the correct use of general words.[13]

When these ideas disintegrated the compact system of the *Tractatus* was transformed into the more diffuse philosophy of *Philosophical Investigations*. The first and most obvious objection to the early ideas was that the fixed rails are a fantasy. Many philosophers had expressed this objection before Wittgenstein. His original contribution was an argument about the demand that Platonism makes on the mind of a person using an ordinary descriptive word.[14]

[12] See *TLP* 6.124.

[13] The other part is its application to particulars.

[14] See L. Wittgenstein: *Philosophical Investigations*, tr. G. E. M. Anscombe, Blackwell, 1953; 3rd edn. Macmillan, 1958 (henceforth *PI*), I. §§ 137–242.

His argument starts from the observation that the Platonic metaphysic would be no help to such a person unless he had in his mind some representation of the infinite line dividing all the things to which the word would apply from all the things to which it would not apply. For example, if he were acquainted with the universal *red*, the inner expression of his acquaintance would have to be something strictly contemporary, an image perhaps, or a formulation of the essence of the colour. But, Wittgenstein argues, anything that he had in his mind now could be applied later in more than one way. To this a Platonist might reply that, in order to pin down the correct application now, the word-user also needs to have in his mind instructions for the application of his image or for the use of his formula. But, Wittgenstein retorts, he would encounter exactly the same difficulty again when he asked himself how he ought to interpret the instructions. In short, Platonism makes an impossible demand on the word-user's mind: it is required to contain something which is both strictly contemporary and also a self-contained, unambiguous representation of the infinite line dividing positive from negative instances. The impossibility of meeting this demand shows up in the infinite regress that it generates.

This is evidently a development of an idea which has already been introduced as the centre of the picture theory of sentences: language cannot contain an analysis of the conditions of its own application. However, there is a difference in the use that Wittgenstein is now making of the idea. In the *Tractatus* he exalted it as a mystery at the heart of factual discourse, but the conclusion that he now draws is that the application of words to things is a sustained practice, and that the mystery is, at least, diffused if, instead of staring into the view presented by a factual sentence, we shift our attention to the practice of using it and look at its place in human life.

There could hardly be a clearer example of the extension of critical philosophy into the territory that had been occupied by uncritical realism in the *Tractatus*. What makes the example so striking is that the extension exploits an idea that was already an essential part of the early system. The change to the new philosophy came about when Wittgenstein looked more closely at something that he had simply taken for granted, the adherence of names to the things to which they were originally attached. It immediately became clear that this constancy is not the automatic result of a quick christening. It is a laborious achievement requiring a sustained contribution from our minds. The meanings of our words are kept constant not by Platonic universals but by the stability of our own practices.[15] So critical philosophy completes its advance and the original mystery at the heart of factual discourse is diffused over ordinary human activities.

It is difficult to avoid exaggerating this change, and it is worth recalling Nestroy's remark, used by Wittgenstein as the motto of *Philosophical Investigations*: 'It is characteristic of progress that it appears to be much greater than it really is.' There are several ways in which the later works are apt to produce a false impression of this kind. First and most important, the contrast between the world's contribution to our view of it and the contribution made by our own minds can be misleading. Our view of the world is expressed in our language, and we begin, very sensibly, with the distinction between its optional and its mandatory features. Now in the *Tractatus* the latter are said to be imposed on us by the structure of reality, while the former are freely chosen. So we naturally go on to suppose that, when the territory of uncritical realism is overrun and the metaphysical source of the mandatory features of language vanishes, we must be left with a freedom of choice so extended that it excludes the possibility of any reasons for taking one option rather than another, as happens in the moral philosophy of Sartre.

But if we stop to reflect on what is really happening here, we can see that this all-embracing, arbitrary conventionalism is an illusion, a bogy invented by the realist who is alarmed by the visible shrinking of the territory on which he stands. The theme of *Philosophical Investigations* is not that our view of the world owes nothing to its nature. That would be absurd. Wittgenstein's point is only that, if we try to explain our view of the world by saying something about its nature, what we say will necessarily belong to our view of it. We have no independent standpoint from which to assess the relation between our usual standpoint and the world. Our usual point of view is our only point of view, not because we cannot develop it or criticize it, but because we cannot altogether abandon it for another.

Philosophical systems, even when they are constructed to rigorous intellectual standards, are often shaped by the imagination. The *Tractatus* is a clear example of this dual control. It is dominated by the Kantian picture of the mind, the world, and the products of their interaction. Ordinary knowledge is seen as a probe which cannot reach beyond the joint products of mind and world. But there must be

---

[15] But what now counts as stability? This question produces the characteristic intellectual giddiness of withdrawal from Platonism.

a world, must there not? So the mind seems to need a special way of knowing its partner in production, and metaphysical theories spring up to meet the apparent need. There is the Kantian idea that the elusive partner is the world of things-in-themselves, or it is the volitional essence of Schopenhauer's world.

Wittgenstein carefully avoided any theory of this kind and he always restricted his enquiry to phenomena. This is an important difference, but it is one that is easy to miss, because the critical account that he gave of phenomena really does sound very like a typical piece of metaphysical speculation. This illusion is reinforced by a rather unusual feature of his account. He did not think that he was in a position to identify the simple objects that fix the essence of the phenomenal world, and so he could only argue for their existence indirectly, and his indirect arguments sound very like a contribution to speculative metaphysics. There is, however, a crucial difference: he did not believe that simple objects are in principle inaccessible, like things-in-themselves in Kant's system.

However, he did hold an uncritical belief about the phenomena, which he later abandoned: he believed that language is shaped by the intrinsic nature of the underlying simple objects. The weakness of this thesis was that there is no independent standpoint from which it could be established or refuted. It may seem strange that he should dismiss speculative metaphysics in the *Tractatus* and yet adopt such an uncritical view of the application of language to the world, but the explanation is not far to seek. It is comparatively easy to see that we have no standpoint from which to assess the relation between the phenomenal world and a reality which is supposed to lie behind it. But it is far less easy to see that we have no standpoint from which to assess the relation between our words and the things to which we apply them. The second achievement is so near home that it looks as if it must be something that we can manage.

It is worth developing the contrast between these two insights. The easy one is that there is no standpoint from which we can set up the distinction between ordinary phenomena and metaphysical reality. That leaves us with the phenomena, but with the phenomena no longer contrasted with anything behind them. The painter depicts what he sees in the one and only world, including, perhaps, himself seeing it, like Vermeer. If we choose to call what he sees 'phenomena', the word will have lost its implication of 'second best'. When the territory on which the realist stands shrinks to nothing, he is no longer in a position to use the 'subjectivity' of his adversary's view as a bogy.

The other insight is far more difficult to attain, and Wittgenstein certainly did not attain it in the *Tractatus*. The reason for its elusiveness is not even easy to state precisely. The kind of uncritical realism about the nature of objects which is expressed in the *Tractatus* seems to be so much a part of our lives that we find it difficult to detach it and hold it up for inspection. It is a self-reinforcing illusion.

What we have to realize is that we cannot possibly justify our factual language by appealing to facts which can only be stated in it. In order to justify it, we would need to stand outside it and assess its appropriateness to phenomena specified in some entirely different way. But an independent specification of the phenomena is precisely what we lack. However, we do not notice the need for it when we are assessing factual language, because we find it peculiarly difficult to see that we cannot use this language to justify itself. We feel like protesting, 'Why shouldn't we use it? What on earth is wrong with it?' But we forget that nobody is saying that anything is wrong with it. The objection is only that uncritical realism pretends to prove that the system is all right, without making the move outside the system which such a proof would require.

The contrast with the other insight is striking. Anyone can see that speculative metaphysics tries to add an extension to the phenomenal world without adding a standpoint from which that extension could be viewed and the relation between appearance and reality assessed. But uncritical realism about the application of language is more insidious. Nothing is added, and the claim is simply that we can remain at our ordinary standpoint and, without making any move, achieve the following remarkable result: the justification of our factual language *in its own terms*.

The best way to see that this is impossible is to take a simple example. Our colour vocabulary divides up the field by using a different word for each colour, and when we apply one of these words, we are apt to think that we are following a line laid down by the nature of the particular colour. So if someone rejects that explanation of our practice, it may look as if he is advocating pure conventionalism, which, we object, cannot be right. The necessities and impossibilities that hedge us in when we are using colour words surely come from the colours themselves. Deny that, and you will be left standing in an existentialist void, with no reason for using the words in one way rather than another. It would be like the rule that you must drive on the right of the road. There is nothing in the nature of roads to support the choice of that particular rule and so a completely arbitrary convention is required. If our use of colour words were not guided by rails laid down in reality, the requisite conventions would be equally arbitrary. Or so the Platonist claims.

Wittgenstein objects that this dilemma is founded on an illusion. It seems to us that we have to choose between Platonism and pure conventionalism only because we have allowed ourselves to be persuaded that Platonism really would provide us with a satisfactory explanation of the stability of our colour language, if we could believe it. But would it? If the central argument of *Philosophical Investigations* is convincing, the trouble with Platonism is not only that its fixed rails are a fantasy. Even if they were palpable, we could not be guided by them unless our minds received self-contained, unambiguous representations of their infinite continuations. But that is not possible. Or so Wittgenstein claims.

If he is right, the rejection of Platonism does not force us to adopt any other single explanation. In fact, its elimination does not even reduce the field, because it was a theory with no explanatory power, a non-starter. Anyway, it could hardly reduce the field to a single competitor, conventionalism when the explanatory power of conventionalism was drawn from a contrast with realism. If realism is pushed to its extreme point, Platonism, it loses all its explanatory power and it automatically inflicts the same loss on its opposite number, conventionalism.

Wittgenstein's objection to the realist's false dilemma can be put in another way. There is a sense in which explanations appealing to the natures of things go deep, while explanations appealing to arbitrary conventions remain on the surface. The contrast is clear in the case of the rules of the road. There is something about the topology of roads which makes the adoption of a uniform convention necessary, but nothing which gives us the slightest reason for choosing one of the two conventions rather than the other. Here we think of the real need for some convention as a deep explanation of our practice, while the explanation of the particular choice remains on the surface and does not put down any roots in reality. Wittgenstein's objection is that this contrast evaporates when the deep explanation is pushed to the extreme point at which it loses all its explanatory power, and simultaneously, the superficial explanation suffers a similar fate. Therefore, the dilemma should be rejected.

Why, then, did it look so convincing? Here he takes another leaf out of Kant's book and treats the question as one about the pathology of metaphysical thinking. His answer is that there are certain forms of explanation which work very well so long as they are used as they were originally intended to be used in everyday life or in science. An appeal to the nature of a thing is often explanatory, but it must be possible to go on to say what its nature is. The trouble with Platonism is that it appeals to the natures of things without any possibility of meeting that proviso. For if it tries to meet it by specifying their natures, it will only be using more words, which will raise the same problem again. Thus an explanation which works quite well within its own limitations loses all its power when it tries to explain everything. If the opposite theory, that the rules governing the use of descriptive words are purely conventional, oversteps its own limits, it suffers a similar fate. It follows that these two extremes are not really theories at all, but aspects of the one and only truth polarized by the prism of philosophy.

This is how he puts it:

We have a colour system as we have a number system.

Do the systems lie in *our* nature or in the nature of things? How are we to put it?—*Not* in the nature of numbers or colours.

Then is there something arbitrary about this system? Yes and no. It is akin both to the arbitrary and to the non-arbitrary.

It is immediately obvious that we aren't willing to acknowledge anything as a colour intermediate between red and green.

. . . but has nature nothing to say here? Indeed she has—but she makes herself audible in a different way.

'You'll surely run up against existence and non-existence somewhere!' But that means against *facts*, not concepts.[16]

These are late remarks but they echo the theme of the picture theory of sentences: the possibility of saying some things depends on the actuality of other things that cannot be said.

Wittgenstein's later philosophy is misunderstood by those who read it as pure conventionalism. There is also another connected false impression that it sometimes gives. His dismissal of Platonism is a typical example of his reaction to such theories. When the metaphysician tries to find the right words to express his vision of reality, Wittgenstein reminds him, rather meanly, of the ordinary use of those words and of their place in human life. Worse, he points out that,

---

[16] L. Wittgenstein: *Zettel*, ed. G. E. M. Anscombe and G. H. von Wright, tr. G. E. M. Anscombe, Blackwell, 1967, §§ 357–9 and part of 364.

when they are transplanted, they will not necessarily take their meanings with them and may even end up without any meanings at all. These moves sometimes create the impression that his later philosophy is entirely negative, a tedious examination of ordinary language instead of an adventure among ideas.[17] But this too is a false impression, however difficult it may be to resist.

It is worth tracing this false impression to its source. It is connected with the pattern of ideas which makes it difficult to resist the impression that Wittgenstein's later philosophy is pure conventionalism. The point was made earlier, that people do not find much mystery in things with which they have 'mixed their labour', and that a sense of wonder at the world is more appropriate when the world is set over against us as something independent of our minds, as an 'object' or 'Gegenstand', in the full etymological sense of those words. Consequently, it looks as if Wittgenstein must have lost that sense when his critique overran the last remaining territory of pure realism. However, this explanation works only when the contributions made by mind and world can be separated from one another; and that requires us to be able to say what the material supplied by the world would be like in its raw state; and that would need a viable empirical test. In short, the explanation works and sets a limit to the sense of the mystery of the world, only when there is an assessable difference between the specific contributions made by mind and world to their joint product.

In *Philosophical Investigations* this condition is no longer met. So the sense of wonder is set free from its vanishing object and diffused over the whole range of human life and consciousness. This sense is the original source of all philosophy and in the *Tractatus* it finds an attenuated traditional expression in the precarious metaphysic of independent objects. The exposition of this ontology is notoriously difficult to follow, a last message from a vanishing world, barely articulate, because it is spoken in such a strangled voice. In the later writings the feeling has been liberated and it is diffused over all the ordinary modes of human thought and activity.

This explains the extraordinary attraction of the later works. Philosophy has been brought back from its self-imposed exile and focused on to ordinary aspects of life, without losing its original sense

---

[17] e.g. Russell says, 'The later Wittgenstein . . . seems to have grown tired of serious thinking and to have invented a doctrine which would make such an activity unecessary.' *My Philosophical Development*, Allen & Unwin, 1959, p. 217.

of the mystery of things. In fact, the achievement of the new philosophy is its demonstration of the strangeness of the ordinary. Such things are so close to us that we hardly notice them in daily life and it takes a philosopher's perception to pick them out and describe them. The method is a careful juxtaposition of familiar things but the result is a new understanding of them.

There have been philosophers who studied ordinary language not for the light that it throws on the traditional problems of philosophy, but indiscriminately, because they believed that devotion to those problems diverts attention from other equally important questions about thought and language. Wittgenstein's later writings have often been associated with the work of such 'ordinary language philosophers', and rejected because of the supposed affinity.[18] However, that is a mistake produced by neglect of an equally important lack of affinity. Suppose that the critics are right in their contention that the undirected study of ordinary language is dreary and profitless. Even so, the criticism would leave Wittgenstein's later work untouched. His interest in ordinary language is always controlled by concern with a philosophical problem. Of course, he did not think that all philosophical problems had already been posed, but, rather, that it would be a mistake to ignore the traditional ones, because they are the natural by-product of well-established patterns of thought. So beneath the surface of his later investigations of language the pull of deep philosophical problems can always be felt.

Finally, there is the suggestion that his later philosophy is negative. There is some truth in this. In *Philosophical Investigations* he poses this question:

Where does our investigation get its importance from, since it seems only to destroy everything interesting, that is, all that is great and important? (As it were, all the buildings, leaving behind only bits of stone and rubble.)

His answer is:

What we are destroying is nothing but houses of cards and we are clearing up the ground of language on which they stand.[19]

He does not go on to put up new theories on the ground that he has cleared. Philosophy, he thinks, is not like science, because its task is

---

[18] e.g. by Russell: loc cit., and by Ernest Gellner: *Words and Things*, Gollancz, 1959, pp. 134–53 and 254–60.
[19] *PI* I § 118.

not to theorize but only to describe. The understanding that philosophers seek can never be caught by a theory, but only by a description which makes us see the familiar phenomena in the right way. Philosophy is like art.

This is, of course, half negative and half positive. The philosophy of the past modelled itself on science and its theories became more and more remote from life as it is lived, an exile not to be repeated. The new philosophy comes back from the desert with a different message: describe the familiar in the right way, and you will understand it. The task is extraordinarily difficult, because philosophy has no point of view of its own and there is no mechanical formula for discovering which ordinary point of view will be the right one. It may even be that the task is misconceived. But there is no longer any possibility of pretending that it is obviously necessary that philosophy should continue to be cast in the old mould.

2

Close-up:
The Early System

WHEN Wittgenstein's philosophy is put in a Kantian frame, most of its main lines stand out clearly. However, this way of looking at it does bring out its form rather better than its content. The material that he casts in that form is more variegated than has yet been indicated. In fact, one of the main difficulties of understanding him is to see how the details fit into the general pattern. Even when his treatment of a particular topic gives the impression of a strong underlying structure, it is often not at all obvious what it is.

So the description of his philosophy that has been given so far may not correspond to what people get first from his works. The discussions of particular topics stand out immediately but the general pattern only emerges gradually. That was often the way in which his ideas actually developed. For example, the work that went into the *Tractatus* did not begin as an attempt to fix the limits of language. That was a later development, which gave the book its final shape. The original problem was posed by logic. He was searching for a theory of meaning which would explain the necessary truth of logical formulae.

Similarly, his later work in the philosophy of mind was not undertaken in order to show what is wrong with Platonism. His interest in the mind did not even originate entirely in his investigations of language. There is also another line of development, which started from the treatment of solipsism in the *Tractatus*, moved on to sensations and the way we manage to communicate about them, and finally opened up a new way of looking at all mental phenomena. The traditional view had made the contents of each person's mind inaccessible to others, and, in the case of the ego, inaccessible even to the person himself. Wittgenstein's new view avoided these unacceptable consequences without toppling over into behaviourism, in something like the way in which his new view of language avoided pure realism without toppling over into arbitrary conventionalism. So here in the philosophy of mind is another example of two opposed polarizations of a single concrete phenomenon, neither of which struck him as acceptable as a theory.

To start again at the beginning, the *Tractatus*, as its full title implies, is a philosophical treatise on logic. It was the foundations of logic that presented the problem, because, though we all know how to establish ordinary contingent truths, it is not clear how the familiar necessary truths on which we rely in everyday arguments are established. It is no good saying that we prove them, because anyone who has looked into Euclid knows that you cannot prove anything from nothing. Axioms and rules of inference are always needed, but then their status too can be questioned.

Much of the preliminary work for the *Tractatus* is in Wittgenstein's *Notebooks*. The text, as we now have it, opens with a memorable sentence: 'Logic must take care of itself.'[1] In other words, logic is a self-contained system which can be validated only from within. Its formulae, therefore, must be completely different from factual sentences, which have to measure up to something outside them-selves, the contingent layout of the world. This is a simple contrast, but the conclusions that he draws from it are far-reaching. If he is right, Russell's axiomatization of logic in *Principia Mathematica* was mistaken in more than one way.

His main criticism of Russell's system is that it is not self-contained. When the need arises, Russell helps himself to additional axioms which, Wittgenstein argues, are, at best, only contingently true. Now a conclusion cannot be any stronger than the weakest of the premisses from which it was drawn. Therefore, after the point at which Russell adds contingent truths to his axioms, the theorems or formulae that he proves will all belong to science rather than to logic. But that violates the fundamental distinction between logical formulae and factual sentences.

Another criticism that he makes of Russell is the one that occurs to everybody. Even if none of the axioms were contingent, they would all remain unproven, and so the task of proving the theorems from them was not worth undertaking. However strong your rope, you cannot hang anything on it unless it is attached at the other end, and then what you can hang on it will depend on the strength of that attach-ment. Schopenhauer makes this criticism of Euclid and goes on to argue that, if we found a method for validating the axioms—and we really need to find one—we could use it for validating the theorems

[1] *NB* 22 Aug, 1914.

directly. So Euclid's axiomatization of goemetry was not only un-completable, because the axioms hung in the air, but also unnecessary, because the theorems never needed any proof in the first place.[2] Axioms and theorems alike stand on the same level and they are all equally in need of direct validation. This point is made against Russell by Wittgenstein,[3] but, of course, with a difference: Schopenhauer's direct method of validation in geometry was pure spatial intuition, while in logic Wittgenstein's was to test for tautology.

Whatever its merits, this test certainly occupies an interesting position in the system of the *Tractatus*. If logical formulae are tautologies, logic really does take care of itself, because tautologies do not depend on anything that happens in the world. They are not hostages to contingency. Factual sentences make claims and they get a grip on the world, which then verifies them or falsifies them. Tautologies make no claim and they ride loosely on the world, being neither supported nor let down by any contingency. They levitate because they say nothing. Logical formulae are radically independent when their necessary truth is explained in this way. Each of them can be validated directly without any help from the others. There is, therefore, no need to string them together in a calculus, giving some of them the role of premisses and proving others as con-clusions.

If this is what logic is like, it is very unlike anything to be found in factual discourse. It is not a system of connected truths, like science: it is not even a medley of independent truths, like the ordinary record of what goes on around us. In the *Tractatus* Wittgenstein spends a lot of time on these differences between the formulae of logic and factual sentences, but people read this part of the book rather rapidly, because they are already converted. They ought to pause and ask themselves how he saw the point which strikes them as so obvious. He saw it as a deep difference. It is not only that logic does not cover the same ground as factual discourse: it does not cover its own ground in the same way—or, rather, it does not cover *any* ground. Its formulae do not express knowledge of any subject. They merely reveal connections between different forms of sentences, and so between different forms of facts. But these forms do not belong to another world, to be explored *after* the world of facts, as it were, on a separate

---

[2] Schopenhauer: *The World as Will and Idea*, tr. R. B. Haldane and J. Kemp, Routledge and Kegan Paul, 1883: 9th impression 1950, Vol. 1 pp. 90ff.

[3] *TLP* 6.126–6.127.

expedition. That was Russell's idea,[4] and Wittgenstein was completely opposed to it. However, it did seem to him to be a natural and, therefore, a prevalent misunderstanding of logic, and that is why he spends so much time saying what logic is not like.

The system of the *Tractatus* is built on an idea that is the exact opposite of Russell's idea: the forms revealed by logic are embedded in the one and only world of facts and, therefore, in the language that we use to describe it. If Russell's view was Platonic, this view is approximately Aristotelian. Logic is immanent in factual discourse from the very beginning, and it emerges when we take factual sentences and combine them in various truth-functional ways—that is, in such ways that the truth or falsehood of the combinations will depend entirely on the truth or falsehood of what went into them. Most of the combinations will make factual claims about the world and, if we want to find out exactly what claims they make, we must identify the sentences that were originally combined in them and discover what claim each of them makes on its own. When we do this, we shall find that some of the combinations make no claim about the world. These are tautologies. They always come out true and so they are the limiting case, the boundary of factual discourse, not part of it.

If tautologies reveal the connections between the forms of factual sentences, they must show us something about those forms. For if two sentences of given forms can be combined by a logical connective to produce a tautology, that must be the result of the forms themselves. It is rather like chemistry, where the properties of a compound can be entirely explained by the properties of the components that went into it. This is how Wittgenstein puts the point:

It is clear that something about the world must be indicated by the fact that certain combinations of symbols—whose essence involves the possession of a determinate character—are tautologies.[5]

Now tautologies are the formulae of logic. So this revelation about the world is a revelation made by logic. The quoted sentence occurs in a lengthy remark which begins with these words:

The propositions of logic describe the scaffolding of the world, or rather they represent it. They have no 'subject-matter'. They presuppose that names have meaning and elementary propositions[6] sense; and that is their connection with the world.

4 See Russell: *Theory of Knowledge, 1913*, Pt. I ch. 9 and Pt. II ch. 3, in *The Collected Papers of Bertrand Russell*, Vol. 7 ed. E. Eames and K. Blackwell, Allen & Unwin, 1984.
5 *TLP* 6.124.   6 i.e. fully analysed propositions.

This is not an easy passage to interpret and two questions about it
need to be answered. What exactly does logic reveal about the world?
And how is its revelation made?

The answer to the second question is implicit in Wittgenstein's
anti-Platonic view of logic. Whatever logic conveys about the world, it
does not convey it in anything like the way in which factual sentences
convey information. It conveys it in a way that he calls 'showing', and
'showing' is almost a technical term in the *Tractatus*. Among the things
that can be shown but not said[7] he includes everything that can be read
between the lines of factual discourse, or, to put his point in another
way, everything that is expressed by logic. He calls logic 'the great
mirror',[8] and, when we read his account of it, we feel that we are
standing within a limited structure which reflects the ground on which
it was built. Each elementary possibility supports the sentence that
reflects it, and the load-bearing lines are carried upwards and
combined in many different ways. The limiting case is tautological
combination but tautologies are the outline of the structure, not part
of it.

The *Tractatus* presents one possible view of the nature of logic. It is
an anti-Platonic view, because it denies that logic is something that we
bring back from the exploration of a second world, and treats it,
instead, as a peculiar extract from the results of exploring the one and
only world of facts.

But what exactly is it that logic conveys to us about the world? That
was the other question that needed to be answered. A short reply
would be that logic reveals the essence of the world of facts rather than
the existence of another world. This is made very clear in the
continuation of the quoted passage. After saying that 'something about
the world must be indicated by the fact that certain combinations of
symbols . . . are tautologies', he continues:

This contains the decisive point. We have said that some things are arbitrary
in the symbols that we use and that some things are not.[9] In logic it is only the
latter that find expression: but that means that logic is not a field in which *we*
express what we wish with the help of signs, but rather, one in which the

---

[7] *TLP* 4.12–4.1212.

[8] Ibid., 5.511.

[9] This refers back to 3.342, which draws the distinction between the optional and the
mandatory, discussed in ch. 1 (p. 10 and pp. 15–16). 'Although there is something
arbitrary about our notations, *this* much is not arbitrary—that *when* we have determined
one thing arbitrarily, something else is necessarily the case. (This derives from the
essence of notation.)'

nature of the absolutely necessary signs speaks for itself. If we know the logical syntax of any sign-language, then we have already been given all the propositions of logic.

That answers the question, but in doing so it raises others. Logic reveals the essence of the world, but what is that? And is there really any difference between this view of logic and Russell's Platonic view of it? If this view connects logic with the basic ontology of the *Tractatus*, which is uncritically realistic, it looks as if there is not much difference at this stage between Wittgenstein and Russell on the foundations of logic. Surely the real difference only begins later, when Wittgenstein's critical philosophy overran the last remaining territory of realism?

A short answer to the first question about the essence of the world, revealed by logic, is that it consists of elementary possibilities which are either realized or not realized, with no third contingency. Now there is often a third contingency at the level of ordinary factual discourse. To use one of Wittgenstein's examples in the *Notebooks*,[10] if someone says 'My watch is on the table,' it may or may not be on the table, but there is also a third contingency, that he has no watch, in which case the possibility, that it is on the table, is not there to be realized. Wittgenstein's point is that this third contingency is excluded at the level of completely analysed factual discourse. Or, to put it in the terms used in the previous chapter, at the ultimate level there is a grid of simple possibilities, each of which is either realized or not realized, and we cannot go below that grid to ask what things would have been like if its possibilities had not been there to be realized. The grid is ultimate and any speculation that purports to go beyond it is senseless.

A short answer to the question about the relation between Wittgenstein's view of logic in the *Tractatus* and Russell's contemporary view is that they really were opposed to one another. Russell believed that the logician's task is to carry out a survey of 'logical objects', some of which are forms while others are the real counterparts of logical connectives.[11] Wittgenstein's view was that there are no logical objects,[12] forms cannot be investigated and described like things,[13] and logical connectives do not stand for anything in the world and are, therefore, utterly unlike names.[14]

[10] *NB* 15 and 16 June 1915.
[11] See above, n. 4. [12] *TLP* 4.441.
[13] Ibid., 2.172 [14] Ibid., 4.0312.

These are real differences between the two philosophers. It is one thing to say that logical connectives stand for a special kind of object and quite another thing to say that they do not stand for anything, but merely indicate different ways of producing truth-functional combinations of the sentences that they connect. It is one thing to say that the form of a sentence is a special kind of component, and quite another thing to say that it is nothing of the sort but, rather, the possibility of a structure.[15] Indeed, the latter view of form is essential to the picture theory of sentences: the form of a fact is a possibility projected into the sentence that depicts it.[16] So this is not a case of two philosophers 'agreeing to have a battle'. It may look like that, if we ask whether sentential forms exist in a transcendent world of their own or are merely immanent in this world. For how can we answer such an airy question? But we can bring it down to earth by catching it at the point of take-off and treating it as a question about the elements of semantics, which is what it really is.

It remains true that Wittgenstein's later view of logic is even further from Russell's. However, that is a distance travelled in a different direction. In his early work Wittgenstein puts logic on a realist basis, but he does not do this in the same simple way as Russell. He does not use the link between name and object as a model to which the solution of every semantic problem presented by logic has to conform. Nevertheless, at the foundation of the system of the *Tractatus* there is the grid of elementary possibilities imposing certain absolute constraints on the logical structure of any language. That is uncritical realism, and later, when he abandoned it, he moved even further from Russell's Platonism, but in a different direction. In his later writings he was not merely objecting to the way in which Russell developed his semantics: he was objecting to the whole idea that the world's contribution to the necessity of logical formulae can be separated from our contribution. This is yet another example of two opposed polarizations of a single concrete phenomenon, neither of which struck him as acceptable as a theory.

There are one or two points in the short answers to the two questions about Wittgenstein's early view of logic where immediate amplification is needed. Of course, a complete account is not the aim of this chapter, but even a passable sketch requires more than has yet been done. Wittgenstein's idea that tautologies reveal the

---

[15] Ibid., 2.033.
[16] See below, Ch. 6.

essence of the world cannot really be appreciated without more details of his argument for the existence of the ultimate grid of elementary possibilities. There are also gaps that cannot be left unfilled in the account so far given of the connection between his early view of logic and the uncritical realism of the basic ontology of the *Tractatus*. The move to his later view of logic strikes most people as the most paradoxical feature of his whole philosophy. Universals may not be independently anchored in the natures of things, but can logic too slip its moorings? It would obviously be a good idea to take a closer look at the way in which its moorings are set up in the *Tractatus*.

First, then, we need Wittgenstein's argument for the existence of the ultimate grid of elementary possibilities.[17] Now an elementary possibility is one with simple objects at its nodal points. So the question is 'What reason did Wittgenstein have to believe that ordinary factual sentences can be analysed down to factual sentences in which only simple objects are named?' His argument for this conclusion is reductive: if there were any complex things designated in the complete analyses of ordinary factual sentences, then the analysing sentences would have senses only if certain other sentences, not included in *their* analyses (they have no analyses), were true. For complex things would not be there to be designated unless it were true that their components were arranged in the way required for their existence. But, Wittgenstein argued, the sense of a sentence about a complex thing cannot possibly depend on the truth of another sentence about its components. So the analysis must go on down to the next level and include the further sentence in the sense of the original one, and this process must continue until all words for complexes have been replaced by genuine names standing for simple objects.[18]

The assumptions on which this argument is based will be examined later. The point to be made about it now is that it pushes the level of complete analysis downwards until there are no underlying facts left, but only objects devoid of internal structure. These simple objects are the pivots on which all factual discourse turns. So logic reveals the structure imposed on all factual discourse by the ultimate structure of reality. That is its connection with the world.

[17] i.e. for the thesis which Russell called 'logical atomism'.
[18] See *TLP* 2.0211–2.0212 and L. Wittgenstein: *Notes Dictated to G. E. Moore in Norway* (1912) in *NB* p. 116.

This is an audacious argument and it is easier to grasp its separate stages than to grasp it as a whole. So people often get from the *Tractatus* the message that the necessities of logic are not of our making, without Wittgenstein's much more remarkable explanation of their origin. He does not rest his case on the claim that the formulae of logic are in fact tautologies. He goes on to ask why we speak a language which throws up tautologies as by-products of its structure. His answer to this further question is that the essential structure of our language is imposed on it by the ultimate structure of reality, which is a grid with simple objects at its nodal points. If this were not so, our language would not have tautologies marking the outline of its structure. For tautologies are true in all possible contingencies, and that evidently requires their component sentences to be true or false with no third possibility.

So the picture of our intellectual predicament now needs to be modified. It is true that we stand within a limited structure which is bounded by tautologies and which reflects the ground on which it was built. However, the foundations lie deeper than at first appeared. What purport to be names designating objects in ordinary factual discourse are not genuine names and those are not genuine objects. The real designation is done at a much lower level, where everything that is designated is devoid of internal structure.

The other point that needed amplification was the relation between the view taken of logic in the *Tractatus* and two other views of it, Russell's contemporary theory and Wittgenstein's own later account of it. Here it is necessary to be very precise about the questions that were answered in the *Tractatus*. The question posed at the beginning of this chapter was 'How are the necessary truths of logic established?' The answer given in the *Tractatus* was 'By testing for tautology'. But, as has just become apparent, there is also another question asked by Wittgenstein at this point: 'Do we have to speak a language that generates tautologies?' Now realism answers these two questions by making two very different moves. It answers the first one by claiming that logic studies abstract objects in another world. This claim can take various forms, and Russell's version of it, in *Theory of Knowledge, 1913* is very different from Frege's. It is against Russell's version that Wittgenstein's main objections are directed in the *Tractatus*. The second question raises a separate issue and so the realist's answer to it takes an altogether different line; the ultimate structure of reality forces us to speak a language that generates tautologies. This time the realist is Wittgenstein. So he gives an anti-realist answer to the first question, but a realist answer to the second one.

The strategic situation on this field of controversy is complicated. It is, therefore, useful to go back to the basic realism of the *Tractatus* and take a closer look at it. It was called 'uncritical realism' in the previous chapter, because objects are the dominant partners in their relationships with names and nothing is said about any contribution made by our minds at this point. True, we attach the names and we maintain their attachment (if the need arises), but the nature and identity of each object is fixed independently of anything done by us. This is Aristotelianism rather than Platonism, because objects exist in the one and only world, but it is uncritical realism, because the question, whether we contribute anything to the constitution of that world, is not even asked.

Standing on this platform in the *Tractatus* Wittgenstein criticizes the airy acrobatics of Russell's contemporary theory of logic. There is, he argues, no need for a second world to house sentential forms and logical objects. However, in order to make good his criticism, he has to give an anti-Platonic explanation of what Russell tried to explain Platonically. Using materials drawn entirely from this world he has to explain the towering structure of logic. He did not encounter much difficulty in dealing with logical connectives once he had dealt with the problem of form. The really difficult task was to show how sentences acquire their forms from the one and only world.

The picture theory of sentences was his solution to this problem. Form is the possibility of structure and sentences pick up the forms of facts through the links between their names and the objects embedded in reality. The details will be given later, and the immediate point is only that this theory gave Wittgenstein a platform from which to criticize Russell's Platonic theory of logic. The platform is Aristotelian in this sense:[19] it brings down sentential forms from Russell's transcendent world and treats them as immanent in this world. This, as already remarked, is a real difference between the two philosophers.

At this stage the common ground between them was the mandatory character of logic. Of course, both of them believed that some features of our language are optional. There are even necessary truths which we ourselves generate by choosing to define certain non-logical words in one way rather than another. Those are connections between

---

[19] But, of course, Wittgenstein's forms, unlike Aristotle's, are sentential. It is only his view of their source that is Aristotelian.

concepts which do not have to be marked in any way in our language. But there are other features of our language which are mandatory. These are the connections which hold between sentences in virtue of their forms, and they have to be marked in our language in one way or another. Wittgenstein and Russell agreed that these logical features are mandatory. They only disagreed about their source, which Russell placed in a transcendent world, but Wittgenstein placed in this world. So Wittgenstein's problem, like Aristotle's, was to explain how we get the abstract out of the concrete.

Wittgenstein deserted this common ground in his later writings. In so doing he abandoned both kinds of realist theory of logic, Platonic and Aristotelian. This strikes almost everybody as an extremely paradoxical move. Can logic really slip its moorings in this way? The question is beyond the scope of this book. However, a few brief points, which may take some of the shock out of the paradox, can be made here.

First, it really is necessary to identify the position from which Wittgenstein started. According to the *Tractatus*, the formulae of logic are tautologies and we are forced by the one and only world to use a language that generates tautologies. It is surely not too difficult to understand how he came to abandon the second of these two theses. The move away from it would start with the reflection that it may not be the ultimate grid of elementary possibilities that forces this logic on us. It may be the other way round: we have this logic already, and looking at the world through its formulae, we think that we can see an ultimate grid-like structure supporting it. The apparent independence of the grid may be an illusion, because it may just be the shadow cast on the world by the logic that we use. And how can anything be supported by its own shadow?[20]

Second, this interpretation of Wittgenstein's move fits in very well with the anti-realist move that he made simultaneously in the theory of descriptive language. That move was introduced in the previous chapter. Instead of holding that the criteria of identity of objects and their types are simply imposed on us, he came to think that a considerable contribution is made at this basic point by our minds. However, that was not the beginning of a stampede into arbitrary conventionalism. On the contrary, he was redrawing the map without the traditional boundary between arbitrary conventionalism and pure realism. May that not be what is happening in the case of logic too?

[20] See *PI* I § 104.

We have to be careful at this point, because the line between the immanent, Aristotelian version of realism and the transcendent, Platonic version is not always easy to draw. Of course, Russell's theory, that we understand logic when we achieve acquaintance with objects of a special kind, was clearly Platonic. But was the rival theory put forward by Wittgenstein in the *Tractatus* Platonic or Aristotelian? The case for calling it 'Aristotelian' is that it represents logic as something that is forced on us by the structure of the grid that we find underlying the phenomenal world. This looks like the immanent version of realism, and it needs to be labelled in a way that will distinguish it from Russell's transcendent version.

However, a moment's reflection will show that the difference between the two theories is not really so great. According to the *Tractatus*, the nature of reality is there to be discovered in objects. If we could encounter an object, it would imprint its form on our minds. This form would give us two things, one specific, and the other more general. Specifically, it would give us an unambiguous representation of the correct use of the word in the future. More generally, it would be part of the grid-like structure of reality which forces us to hold our sentences true or false, with no third possibility and so throws up tautologies on the outer edge of language. Is it really so easy to decide whether these two results of an encounter with an object are Platonic or Aristotelian?

The point can be made in another way. Wittgenstein's move against Russell's theory of logic gave his own theory an inner momentum which would carry it to self-destruction later. After 1929, the specific aspect of the realism of the *Tractatus* would be destroyed by the 'anti-Platonic' argument of *Philosophical Investigations*,[21] which could equally well be called 'anti-Aristotelian'; and its general aspect would be destroyed by the development of logic without realism of either type.

There is, however, a difference between the liberation of logic and the liberation of descriptive language. In the case of descriptive words it is fairly easy to understand both the realism that is rejected by Wittgenstein and the effect of rejecting it. It is the kind of realism that claims that there are standards for the correct use of our descriptive vocabulary fixed independently of us, and perhaps fixed even before we arrived on the scene. When this kind of realism is rejected, the result is not that we are left wildly improvising. A contribution to stability is still made by the natures of the things to which we apply our

[21] *PI* I §§ 137–242. See above, pp. 10–11.

words. It is just that another contribution is made by the ways in which we find it natural to apply them, and the two contributions cannot be disentangled from one another.

So it ought to be the same with logic. However, though it is easy enough to *say* this, it is far more difficult to understand in the case of logic than it is in the case of descriptive words. This is not the place to deal with these difficulties. Perhaps they can all be explained as consequences of the differences between logic and factual discourse without relinquishing Wittgenstein's view, that in the end realism and conventionalism about logical necessity are two aspects of a single concrete phenomenon which can be polarized but not treated as rival theories. Or perhaps he is mistaken in this case. The only way to settle the question would be to work through the details, but that will not be done in this book.

There are, however, some general observations about the problem which can be made quickly. Suppose that we really did encounter people who seemed to follow eccentric patterns of thought instead of our logic. We ought not to protest immediately, 'The idiots! Why don't they make the inferences that we make?' That would be too like criticizing the colour vocabulary of the ancient Greeks, on the ground that they must have seen that they were really grouping together colours that were quite different from one another and separating colours that were really the same. We would have to give our eccentrics the benefit of the hypothesis that they really were thinking in a regular way.

So we would need to observe them carefully, in order to see what use they made of their thought processes. Did anything in their environment enter the strange patterns on one side, pass through them, and come out on the other side as intelligible actions? To ask the same question less obscurely, was there any real reason to call their idiosyncrasies 'a logic'? Here we must remember that Wittgenstein always regarded logic as a handy guide for moving from one ordinary truth to another, rather than as a vehicle with which to explore a transcendent world for truths of a special kind.

Now many commentators have pointed out that his dramatizations of encounters with radically eccentric thinkers are extremely thin. Is this merely because it is difficult to present such cases from our standpoint? If so, we ought to reflect that, if we were in their shoes, we would have just as much difficulty in appreciating the logic that is now ours, and we ought to show tolerance. After all, in the case of descriptive words, though we can report what eccentric speakers do, it is hard for us to accept that it is really the same kind of thing that we do. So hasty ridicule is out of place.

But this way of putting it masks a real difference between the two cases. An eccentric user of a descriptive word has his own way of applying it, and we cannot fault him on the ground that it does not serve the general purpose of descriptive language. But if the general purpose of logic is to get from true premisses to true conclusions, then, provided that we know the criteria of truth used by the eccentric thinker for his premisses and conclusions, we shall be in a position to fault him. He may, of course, reject our criticism, but, if he does so, it will look as if he is not engaged in a new kind of logical inference, but in improvisations with no attachment to the world. Even if he also uses descriptive words in an eccentric way, so that we have to pick up his criteria of truth as he goes along, there is still a resource available to us. We can give him blind tests, by asking him his reaction to each actual situation after we have made him forget the inference that he had made about it. That would put him on the spot. For if his patterns of inference would often have forced him off course, they would not count as an alternative logic, and this verdict will not be affected by the fact that the course that he steers with each descriptive word is, from our point of view, eccentric.

3

Close-up:
The Later System

A GOOD way of approaching Wittgenstein's later philosophy is to pick up a thread discarded near the beginning of the previous chapter. Starting from the treatment of solipsism in the *Tractatus* there is a line of development which runs through his two accounts of sensation-language and leads into his whole later philosophy of mind. This line can be explored in more detail.

A solipsist is a philosopher who in theory has dropped out of the world of other people and common things. If his theory is right, neither the objects of his immediate awareness nor he himself, the subject, can be located in that world or connected with anything located in it. He tries to compensate for any loss by claiming that he lives in a private world. His critics argue that he cannot detach his private world from the common world as if it had some independent basis of its own, and that he cannot conceal its deficiencies by modelling it on the common world. He replies that it is the common world that is, at least, precarious and speculative and, if he is right, does not exist.

This theory, which has haunted philosophy for centuries, is reviewed by Wittgenstein in the *Tractatus*.[1] His treatment of it has several novel features. First, he takes over an original idea of Russell's: the solipsist is setting a limit not only to his knowledge of truths but also to his acquaintance with objects, and so to his language.[2] For the scope of his meaningful discourse is determined by the range of his acquaintance with objects on which it is founded. Second, unlike Russell, he refuses to treat solipsism as a theory which might be true, but which the evidence showed to be more likely to be false. It is, he thinks, a metaphysical theory, an insight which could not really be expressed in factual language. Third, throughout his discussion, he is

[1] *TLP* 5.6–5.641.
[2] Russell: *On the Nature of Acquaintance*, in *Logic and Knowledge*, ed. R. C. Marsh, Allen & Unwin, 1956, pp. 130 and 134.

concerned with the effect of detaching the subject of awareness, rather than its objects, from the common world. Contrary to popular belief, he does not identify the objects of the *Tractatus* with sense-data, and he is not concerned with the possibility that sense-data might mark the limit of each person's awareness, so that nobody could understand a language based on physical objects. It was the detached subject that posed the problem in the *Tractatus* and it was only later that it would spread to detached objects. In fact, the solipsist who figures in the early discussion may simply be taken to be speaking about phenomena, i.e. about the world as he finds it, rather than about his own itemized sensory input.[3]

But who does he think he is? That is the question. He announces that the only things that exist are things of which he himself is aware. But how are we to understand his announcement? Or rather, since his claim is that we are not there to understand it, how does *he* understand it? He assumes that he knows who he is independently of the things of which he is aware, and that, using himself as a reference-point, he can indicate those things and claim that they alone exist. But how does he achieve the independent identification of himself from which he claims to start? It is no good his saying, 'I do not know where I am on the map, but I do know that I am here.' For what would it be that he knew? It seems that, when he thinks about himself, the subject of awareness, in this way, he loses the necessary independence of his starting-point, because the subject is then only identifiable through its objects. As Wittgenstein said later, he is like someone who constructs a clock which will not indicate the time, because he has inadvertently attached the dial to the hour-hand so that they both go round together.[4]

Here at the beginning of Wittgenstein's philosophy of mind we can see one of his most characteristic thoughts emerging and taking shape. The solipsist would succeed in saying something only if he could identify himself independently of the objects of which he is aware. However, his theory deprives him of the independent identification that he needs, because the whole point of it is that he, the subject of awareness, is neither located in the common world nor connected with anything located in it. So he begins by claiming that only things of which he is aware exist, and then, pressed for an identification of

[3] See *TLP* 5.631 and *NB* 2 Sept. 1916.
[4] See *The Blue Book* in L. Wittgenstein: *The Blue and Brown Books*, Blackwell, 1958, p. 71.

himself, he can only say that he is the subject who is aware of them.[5] This is an interesting way of losing independence and there are other examples of it in Wittgenstein's later writings. It occurs in this case because the solipsist does not have any trouble identifying himself in real life and so he assumes that it will be just as easy in his theory. However, if it is true that he can identify himself, then, however easily he does it, there must be an underlying criterion of identity. But in his theory, the only available criterion is 'the subject who is aware of these objects', and that drains all the content from his solipsistic claim.

This criticism is presented in the *Tractatus* as a criticism of ego-based solipsism, but it is equally effective against any solipsism that exploits the existence of the subject without giving it a criterion of identity that is independent of its objects. A solipsist who rejected the idea that the subject is a separate ego and adopted Hume's theory instead, would be just as vulnerable. For when he identified the subject with the sequence of its impressions and ideas, he would have abandoned all hope of giving it an independent criterion of identity. That is a very obvious case of strapping the clock-hand to the dial. The attractiveness of the solipsism discussed in the *Tractatus* is that it does seem to offer some hope of an independent criterion of identity for the subject, because it does, at least, gesture in the direction of a separate ego. But the difference is really illusory, because in the end the subject has to be defined as 'the subject that is aware of these objects', and so this kind of solipsism too is devoid of factual content.

It might be supposed that, if it is impossible to express solipsism in factual language, that is because there is nothing there to be expressed. But that was not Wittgenstein's view. He believed that the solipsist has a real point, but not the sort of point that can be expressed in sentences aimed at contingent truth. So, according to him, Russell went wrong when he took solipsism at face value and marshalled scientific evidence against it.[6] It was an insight of a different kind.

The solipsist starts from a very natural way of picturing the human predicament. Each of us, he thinks, lives out his mental life in a phenomenal bubble, the world as he sees it, attached to the world at the point where he stands in it. He looks out on to the world and, if he

---

[5] Russell describes his predicament in this way in *Knowledge by Acquaintance, Knowledge by Description*, in *Mysticism and Logic*, Longmans, 1918, pp. 211–12.

[6] See Russell: *On the Nature of Acquaintance*, pp. 134–5.

wants to know where he stands in it, he can review what he sees around him or he can look at his own body and locate it directly.

This account of the way in which we are placed in our environment may contain the seeds of many errors, but there does not seem to be anything in it so far that common sense would have to reject. The phenomenal bubble has two kinds of attachment to the common world outside it, one through the subject of awareness and the other through its objects. Paradox begins only when the solipsist misunderstands these attachments. His best known misunderstanding concerns the objects of awareness: they are, he maintains, all inside the bubble—in the crucial case of perception, they are all mental sense-data. This evidently makes it impossible for him to place his private world in the common world. However, he also misunderstands the other connection between the two worlds, the connection that goes through the subject of awareness. He turns his attention inwards and searches the phenomenal bubble for its point of attachment to the common world, and he gets a shock. He expects to find a subject of awareness, an ego, but he only finds more and more objects and never any subject. Hume established this point with devastating clarity,[7] Kant accepted it and explained why the transcendental subject can never be an object,[8] and Schopenhauer said that the subject is placed at the back of the bubble like the eye in the visual field.[9]

In the *Tractatus* Wittgenstein used these ideas in a new way. He took the solipsist to be setting a limit to his language and to the possibilities that he can express in it. This is a natural development because the scope of the solipsist's language is determined by the range of objects on which it is founded. However, his success in limiting his language is questionable. In fact, he faces two problems, one about each of the two attachments of his private world to the common world. The first problem, which is not discussed in the *Tractatus*, concerns the connection that goes through the objects of the solipsist's awareness. How are they related to objects in the common world? Is it a case of identity, because they simply *are* the common objects as seen by him? Or are there two sets of objects here, one inside, and the other outside the phenomenal bubble, but in some way connected with each other? These are questions in the philosophy of perception and knowledge, and Wittgenstein did not raise them until later.

---

[7] *Treatise of Human Nature*, I. iv. 6.
[8] *Critique of Pure Reason*, *Transcendental Dialectic*, Bk. II ch. 1.
[9] *The World as Will and Idea*, Vol. 3 p. 285.

The second problem, which monopolizes the discussion in the *Tractatus*, concerns the other connection between the two worlds. It is posed in a dramatic form by the vanishing subject. Is it not strange that I can never find the subject of all my consciousness? After all, it is an important fact that all this consciousness really is mine. So why does my ego not figure in it as an identifiable owner? How do I even know that it is I who am asking this question, if all that I am aware of is the asking of it and not *myself* asking it?

The insight for which Wittgenstein gave the solipsist due credit was that the bubble of his mental life has a subject but does not contain it. So though it is attached to the common world through its subject it does not contain within itself any aspect of that attachment. This insight then generates the solipsist's illusion; he draws the conclusion that he can set a limit to the language that he understands, using himself as a reference-point, but without actually identifying himself. He thinks that he can exploit the absence of an ego in what is so evidently his own consciousness. Is it not an absence which must be accepted by any theory? So why should his theory be criticized for acquiescing in it? But here he goes wrong. His restrictive thesis requires an identifiable reference-point, and, in default of an ego, it can only be his body. However, that is not what he wanted at all. He wanted to express his restrictive thesis entirely from inside the phenomenal bubble. Is it not obvious that, if he uses anything outside it, he will be contradicting himself? In any case, how could there possibly be anything like it outside it?

The context of the discussion of solipsism in the *Tractatus* is worth noting, because it explains both the sympathetic treatment of the original insight and the criticism of the way in which the solipsist tries to develop it. Wittgenstein has just been dealing with the question whether logic can tell us in advance what the various forms of elementary propositions are.[10] If logic could do this, it would be doing much more than giving the general form imposed on all factual discourse by the ultimate grid: it would be putting specific restrictions on the forms that are allowable. However, his verdict is that logic cannot do this, because it is not a matter that can be settled a priori. He introduces solipsism at this point, because it is another claim to limit factual discourse in a more restrictive way than he is prepared to allow. It is, of course, a persuasive claim—otherwise, why bother to assess it?—but a claim that he is not going to concede. So what we find

[10] *TLP* 5.55–5.5571.

in his assessment of it is a sympathetic account of the origin of solipsism followed by a demonstration that it cannot succeed in limiting language in its own further way. The only acceptable limit is the general one imposed by the ultimate grid.

Wittgenstein was evidently fascinated by the solipsist's picture of the world as he finds it, a world which is not only like the visual field but also includes the visual field as a part of itself. The relationship between the solipsist's world and the visual field is a complex one, because there are two distinct similarities between the two spheres: outside the boundary of the solipsist's world there is nothing more of the same kind, and inside it there is no representation of its point of attachment through the subject, and both these features are reproduced by the visual field. There is also the further complication that the solipsist's world includes the visual field as part of itself, because the objects of sight are among its objects, and so too are the objects of the other senses, though they tend to be less in evidence in his picture.

These objects are going to give trouble later, when their place in the common world is questioned, but meanwhile all the interest is focused on to the ego. Why is it so elusive? After all, my ownership of all this consciousness is important and it receives ample acknowledgement in my language. So why is it that, when I turn my attention inwards, I fail to find any trace of the owner? Wittgenstein's sympathy with this frustration is evident in the *Tractatus* and the *Notebooks*.

The failure of this search has far-reaching consequences. In the *Tractatus* Wittgenstein draws the conclusion that the extra restriction which the solipsist seeks to impose on the scope of language is empty. He wants to use his ego as a reference-point in order to draw his personally restricted boundary, but he cannot use it, because in his theory it is not independently identifiable. He is like someone who tries to use a pair of compasses to draw a circle without choosing a centre, and so the circumference remains no more than a vague aspiration. If this ego is never identified as his, it could be anybody's. It could be the collective ego of all humanity, or even of all creatures endowed with consciousness.[11] So his intended restriction vanishes in the hazy idea that a subjectivity that is sufficiently extended becomes objectivity again.[12]

In 1929 Wittgenstein pushed the investigation in a different direction. It is hardly satisfactory to show sympathy with solipsism,

[11] See *NB* 15 Oct. 1916.   [12] *TLP* 5.64.

demonstrate its emptiness, and then leave it at that. If it is worth discussing, it must raise a real problem, and, if it fails to solve it, the attempt must, at least, be interesting. We might also feel that it would not be too much to ask for the correct solution. Now it is a curious fact that the line of thought that leads to a solution of the problem is firmly marked in the *Notebooks*, but scarcely discernible in the *Tractatus*. This is because the question examined in the *Tractatus* is 'How much truth is there in solipsism?', but the real problem is the one that lies behind that one. The real problem is the ownership of the solipsist's experiences. Is it possible to explain this ownership in a way which will do justice to the extraordinary closeness of subject and object without making them lose their independence from one another?

Wittgenstein's solution to this problem can be found near the beginning of *Philosophical Remarks*.[13] It starts from the solipsist's failure to discover his ego, or any representation within the phenomenal bubble of its point of attachment through the subject to the common world. The first thing to see here is that it is just as well that he does fail in this quest. For suppose that he did discover an ego as well as a lot of sensations. He would then need to find out if one of these sensations belonged to this ego or to another one. He would be like a schoolteacher who hears a pupil at the back of his class complaining of a headache and asks the sufferer to identify himself by putting up his hand. It would evidently be absurd to suggest that the pupil who feels the pain first has to find the ego that owns it. His predicament is not an internalized version of the teacher's predicament. If he feels the pain, it is his, and that is the end of the question of ownership as far as he is concerned. The task of identifying the owner is not for him, but for the teacher. If he puts up his hand, he does not choose whose hand to put up. Of course, he could be pretending, but an unfaked groan is, for all practical purposes,[14] as closely connected with the pain as the pain is connected with his consciousness. That is how these things are wired up to one another. Putting up his hand is just a voluntary loop inserted in the original involuntary circuit.

These remarks give a different picture of the human predicament. Instead of the solipsist's phenomenal bubble, they offer us something that is unadventurous to the point of platitude. But that is deliberate. They are sober correctives, to be printed on the page that faces the

---

[13] L. Wittgenstein: *Philosophical Remarks*, ed. R. Rhees, tr. R. Hargreaves and R. White, Blackwell, 1975 (written in 1929–30: henceforth *PR*), §§ 57–66.

[14] And, therefore, perhaps, for all purposes.

solipsist's heady picture. Indeed, they are so ordinary that it is easy to miss their drift. It is, therefore, worth recalling two things, both of which have already been mentioned, but which can now be used to throw more light on what Wittgenstein was doing to solipsism in 1929. One is the fact that he took it as a theory about language, and the other is his tendency to treat apparently irreconcilable opposites, like solipsism and realism, not as rival theories, but as presentations of aspects of a single, indivisible reality, polarized by the prism of philosophy.

When the solipsist claims that the only things that exist are things of which he himself is aware, it really is not captious to ask how we are to understand his claim. We do overhear it, even if it was not intended for us, and that puts us in a position to try to understand it. So we do not have to take the impersonal viewpoint of the *Tractatus* and ask how he, whoever he may be, understands it. In fact, it can hardly be wrong to start with a room full of people, one of whom announces his solipsism while the others try to argue him out of it. Solipsism in the *Tractatus* has already travelled a long way into the outer space of an impersonal philosophy of mind and we need to start again at the point of take-off.

So we prepare ourselves by reading Wittgenstein's rather banal remarks, and this time, when the solipsist claims that nothing exists except his headache, we point out to him that the complaints which come from a mouth not chosen by him are as closely connected with his ownership of the pain as that ownership is connected with the occurrence of the pain in a consciousness which is also not chosen by him. He can, of course, pretend to be the sufferer, when he is not, but, given that someone is suffering, if it is another person, that person will not be able to operate the solipsist's mouth any more than he could get his groan to come out of the other person's mouth. That kind of faking is as impossible as 'sending' one's pain into another person's consciousness.

Naturally, this new treatment of solipsism needs to include an examination of the effects of crossing the wires of different people's nervous systems, and that too can be found in *Philosophical Remarks*.[15] The general idea is that the two aspects of ownership, the 'inner' and the 'outer', start off together. Then philosophical theories, like behaviourism or introspectionism, try to separate them simply by altering the ways in which we think and speak about them, without any change in the underlying facts. But the only effective way to separate

[15] See *PR* §§ 60 and 63.

them is to imagine bizarre changes in our nervous systems, which might actually pull them apart. If things had been different in this way or that, there might have been corresponding differences in our concept of the ownership of sensations. Mere philosophical concentration on a single aspect of things as they are can only produce the illusion of innovation.

This new treatment of the ownership of sensations is strikingly successful. If a human being were like a hydra with seven interconnected brains, he really might have something more to do when he was asked to assign a felt pain to its owner. Equally, if he chose from seven mouths the one from which to utter his groan, his audience really might have something more to do after noting the source of the groan. However, that is not the human predicament. Each of us has only one brain and a single field of consciousness which is, on the phenomenal level, unique and all-embracing. The very idea of assigning a felt sensation to one person rather than to another cannot arise on that level. It is on the physical level that the question of ownership first comes up, and, even when I say that a felt sensation is mine, my full meaning, 'mine rather than someone else's', must be rooted in the physical world.

As a philosopher, I cannot help being struck by the fact that, when I feel a pain, I do not have any trouble answering the question 'Who is in pain?' However, I ought not to forget the equally important fact that spectators do not have any trouble with the question after they have heard my groan, provided that I am not faking. These are the consequences of the simple circuitry of our nervous systems. The ownership of a pain expressed by an unfaked groan is no more speculative than the ownership of a pain in a certain field of consciousness. If ownership can be pinned on to the central events, it can also be pinned on to the peripheral events that are equally essential to the basic pattern.

There are two reasons for the striking success of this account of the ownership of sensations. One is that there is only a single line running from the stimulus into the owner's brain and then out again to his response. The other is that anything in the field of consciousness at the centre will necessarily be his, and so he does not have the further task of verifying that it is presented to his ego. Put the two reasons together and we can see why a question of ownership is so simple to answer. When someone is in pain, the sufferer does not have to choose between alternative answers to the question 'Who is it?' He does not even have to identify the line on which his consciousness lies, because that identity speaks for itself. Equally, the spectators only have to identify the source of the unfaked groan, and the earlier events in the basic pattern do not present them with a further problem.

But what happens when this treatment is extended from the ownership of sensations to the sensations themselves and their types? So far, that question has been avoided by the assumption that someone is in pain, and the only question has been 'Who is it?' But is it really pain? If we now take the ownership of the sensation as settled and apply the same treatment to its type, can we succeed in avoiding the two extremes, behaviourism and introspectionism, in this matter too? The new task will certainly be more difficult, because people are not conscious of their egos but they are conscious of their sensations. Also, if they did have egos, each person would have only one, but each person has many different types of sensation. So in this new field we are conscious of things to which we are required to react with discrimination.

In the *Tractatus* Wittgenstein avoided the task of extending the treatment of the subject to sensations and their types. He left the nature of the objects of awareness unexamined and concentrated exclusively on the nature of the subject. That was an unstable position, occupied only while he was trying to understand the 'I' of solipsism. If the detachment of the subject of awareness from the common world deprives the word 'I' of its independent reference, can the objects of awareness be detached from the common world without their names' suffering a similar loss? The question could not be postponed indefinitely, and Wittgenstein's first answer to it, given in 1929 shortly after he took up philosophy for the second time, was affirmative: each person's immediate awareness terminates not on the world as he sees it, but on his own inner objects, to which he makes independent references in complete privacy.[16] After formulating this answer, he reacted against it almost immediately and rapidly worked his way towards the carefully qualified negative answer that he gives in *Philosophical Investigations*.[17]

This development needs to be understood in the order in which it occurred, first thoughts, followed by what looks like a complete

---

[16] See *Ludwig Wittgenstein and the Vienna Circle: Conversations Recorded by Friedrich Waismann*, ed. B. McGuinness, tr. J. Schulte and B. McGuinness, Blackwell, 1979 (henceforth *LWVC*), pp. 49–50. Cf. *PR* § 59.

[17] *PI* §§ 243 ff.

reversal. First, we are told that it is possible to make independent references to sensations and their types privately, and then we are told that it is impossible. Commentators usually look back on this journey from its destination in *Philosophical Investigations*. That is already to see it in the wrong perspective. They then make matters worse by treating the second answer as self-evidently true and the first one as an obviously absurd piece of Cartesianism. The truth is that this is an extremely difficult topic and both Wittgenstein's treatments of it were guided by the same purpose. He was trying to give an account of sensations and their types, and, more generally, of all mental phenomena, which would avoid both behaviourism and introspectionism. His task was to take the two aspects of our mental lives which other philosophers had diffracted and to bring them together again. This may look an easy task, because it ends where it originally started, with the familiar concrete reality. In fact, he found it fantastically difficult, because he had to return to the starting-point with a full understanding of its complexity. It was as if he had to pick up shafts of coloured light in his fingers and weave them back into clear daylight.

The extreme difficulty of the task becomes apparent when we follow the development of his ideas forwards from the successful solution of the problem of the ownership of sensations. There are two things, both already mentioned, which make the problem of the sensations themselves and their types much more difficult to solve. First, a person's ego does not figure among the objects of his awareness, but he is aware of his sensations and their types. Consequently, though an introspectionist account of the inner owner of sensations is absurd, a similar account of the sensations themselves is not absurd. Second, the question that a person's ego was supposed to help him to answer was whether a felt sensation is his, and that is a question that he can simply answer 'Yes' or 'No', and when the ego vanishes without leaving any trace in his consciousness, that does not make it any more difficult for him to answer the question. He merely needs to know whether the sensation occurs on his line, and he will always know that it does as soon as he feels it, and that it does not if he does not feel it. But his sensations come in a variety of different types which he has to discriminate, and even if 'introspection' is the wrong name for the way in which he discriminates them, it is a name for something real and familiar which cannot be conjured away. In short, even if the introspectionist's account of the subject's awareness of different types of sensation is not true, or at least, not the whole truth, it is not absurd.

So the spectacular success of the balanced account of ownership cannot be exactly repeated for sensation-types. The next stage of the journey between the two opposed misconceptions, behaviourism and introspectionism, runs along a narrow ridge with no firm footholds.

Wittgenstein's first move was to try to found each person's primary language on his own sensations, and yet to preserve intercommunication between them in their secondary languages. A person A issues direct reports of his own sensations in his primary language—e.g. he is in pain and he simply says so—but he describes the pains of another person B indirectly as 'sensations of the type which are sandwiched between the same kinds of stimulus and response as my pains'. These indirect descriptions belong to A's secondary language, which is a derivative of his primary language, and the two languages together express his view of the world, a view which is unavoidably centred on himself. This was not a perverse excursion into Cartesianism, but a genuine attempt to pull together the 'inner' and the 'outer' aspects of our mental lives. The stratification of language was intended to achieve for sensations and their types the recombination of diffracted components which had already been achieved for the owner.

It did not work, because it failed to explain how A and B can communicate with one another. A starts by making an independent reference to his own pain, but B does not get the reference, because he does not share A's direct awareness of the sensation. So A realizes that it is no good behaving like an Englishman abroad and that he must speak to B in a secondary language. But which secondary language ought he to use? If he speaks his own secondary language, how will B know which sandwich of stimulus and response is in fact filled by A's pains? If B is baffled by A's direct references to A's pains, he will be equally baffled by A's specification of the particular sandwich of stimulus and response that he means when he says 'the kind of stimulus and response between which my pains are sandwiched'. B is in the position of a waiter who is asked to bring a certain kind of sandwich to the only person in the world who can tell what is inside it.[18]

It follows that A has to make a further concession to B's limited powers of understanding. He has to use B's secondary language and he must begin by saying 'I am having a sensation of the type that occurs in the same sandwich of stimulus and response as your pain.'

---

[18] Cf. *PI* I § 293, on the beetle in the box.

But now *A*'s trouble will be that he does not understand *his own* words, because he does not share *B*'s direct awareness of *B*'s sensations and so he does not know which sandwich of stimulus and response he means. Evidently, *A*'s attempt to translate his primary report of his pain into *B*'s secondary language runs into a further case of the very difficulty that it was designed to avoid. If *B* never knows what type of sensation *A* is having, he cannot tell what kind of sandwich of stimulus and response *A* means when he specifies that kind in a way that makes an essential reference to *A*'s pains. But if *A* tries to avoid this difficulty by speaking to *B* in *B*'s secondary language, he removes *B*'s handicap only by taking it over himself. In short, the difficulty is symmetrical and cannot be avoided by speaking to the other chap in his lingo.

What can be done about it? Before we look at Wittgenstein's answer, it is necessary to understand what the question means. It is not asking what *A* and *B* have to do next in order to achieve communication about their sensations. If I am *A* and you are *B*, we are already in a position to understand each other's communiqués in fine enough detail for me to get you the medicine that your pain indicates that you need. The question means 'What has gone wrong with Wittgenstein's first explanation of this achievement?'

So much is obvious. What is not so obvious is that there is no independent standpoint from which the achievement can be explained, and so it must be understood exactly as it actually occurs in our lives. No extra resources are going to be needed for its explanation and none are available. This is not a scientific problem and we cannot hope to find an independent source of factual information which will show us how we manage to do something which would otherwise be inexplicable. For example, it would not help if a psychologist told us that infants and their parents do have some direct awareness of each other's sensations, and that this gives us all the necessary bridgehead in another person's consciousness, which we then proceed to expand by using ordinary inductive arguments. However much empathy there may be in such cases, we know that that is not how we achieve communication with one another about our sensations. No parent would say 'I simply cannot get through to this child, and so I do not really know what type of sensation is sandwiched between its injury and its screams.' It is not even like water-divining, where those who can do it react to an effect of the presence of water without necessarily knowing that the tell-tale effect is change in the local magnetic field.

There is nothing more that we need to know about intercommunication in sensation-language and nothing relevant that science could tell us. We just need to understand what we already know, which is that what *B* gathers about *A*'s pain is neither speculative nor reducible to *A*'s circumstances and behaviour.

The trouble with Wittgenstein's first attempt to solve this problem is that the independent references to sensation-types which *A* and *B* make in their primary languages do not really play any role in their communications with one another. He evidently thought that they did play a role, because *A*'s message to *B* is that the sandwich of stimulus and response in which *B*'s sensation is occurring is the kind which in *A*'s case is filled by pain. But since *B* cannot understand the end of this message, all that he gathers is that in *A*'s case this particular sandwich always has the same filling. It follows that in the secondary languages of both *A* and *B* it is really the kind of sandwich that is dominant and it is quite hollow to claim that each of them derives his secondary language from a primary language in which he makes independent references to his own sensation-types. The truth is that, when *A* and *B* confer with one another, the actual types of their sensations drop out of consideration in something like the way in which the ego dropped out of consideration when ownership was in question.[19] However, there is a very important difference between the two cases: the ego dropped out at the start, when the subject was talking to himself, because it is a pure fantasy, but sensation-types are real enough and they drop out only when he begins talking to someone else in the way suggested by Wittgenstein in 1929. The problem of other minds is not the problem of other people's egos, because one's own ego is problematical, but it is the problem of other people's sensations.

Direct, independent references, made by each of us to his own sensations and their types, cannot possibly support a common language in which we communicate with one another about them. This theory puts too much weight on isolated sensation-types and they

---

[19] It is worth looking at Wittgenstein's later comments on the collapse of his 1929 account of sensation-language. See *PI* I §§ 273–80, and *Zettel*, § 87. Cf. R. Rhees's notes of Wittgenstein's 1936 lectures on 'private experience' and 'sense-data' (Wittgenstein's own notes are published as *Notes for Lectures on 'Private Experience' and 'Sense-data'*, see below, n. 29.): 'There is then the temptation to think "I ought to have two words for my toothache—the one which I use to myself, the other to someone else." For someone else gets only the skeleton of my toothache, not the real timbre of it.' (*Philosophical Investigations*, Vol. 7 No. 1, Jan. 1984.)

drop through the floor. On the other hand, behaviourism, which does not even try to tie them into the system, is obviously unacceptable. So there ought to be a more subtle way of adapting the successful treatment of the owners of sensations so that it will work for their types. That success had been achieved by abandoning the idea of detached mental ownership and treating the subject as essentially physical as well as mental, because the criterion of personal identity combined both aspects. But was it possible to give a similar account of the criteria of identity of sensation-types?

The adaptation of the treatment of the ownership of sensations to their types proved difficult. Wittgenstein's leading idea was that the mind is not really like a theatre.[20] Or, to put his point in the terms used by the solipsist, it is not really true that each of us lives out his mental life in a phenomenal bubble. We must go back to the beginning of this inquiry and reject the picture that the solipsist put up on the blackboard before the discussion began.

But how can anyone reject a picture that fits the human predicament so well? At this point we must be careful. If we start with the platitude, that *A* cannot have *B*'s sensations, add the comment that, therefore, he cannot be directly aware of them, and then adopt the picture of the phenomenal bubble as a perfect illustration of this situation, we shall be likely to assume that anyone who rejects the illustration must also be rejecting the whole of the accompanying text. Knock over the last domino and the whole line will collapse backwards on itself. So it will seem that Wittgenstein must either be denying the platitude or mitigating its consequences by giving reports of sensations a paradoxical behaviourist interpretation.

However, it is a mistake to assume that we have to take or leave a package deal at this point. Wittgenstein can reject the introspectionist's original picture, not because it is wholly inappropriate to our predicament—it is not—but because it makes us misunderstand the very things that it seemed to illustrate so well. In fact, it is precisely because it is a persuasive picture accepted right at the beginning without argument, almost subliminally, that it can mislead us so insidiously. So we must be careful here. We must not assume that in rejecting the picture Wittgenstein is denying everything conveyed by it, including the obvious. We must find out exactly why he does not buy it.

---

[20] Hume's ironical analogy. See *Treatise of Human Nature*, I. iv 6.

We already know half the answer to this question. The elimination of the ego has removed half the analogy between mind and theatre or phenomenal bubble. But it is not so easy to see what he found wrong with the other half of the analogy, the array of phenomenal objects. Let us begin again with a review of what happens when someone gets hurt. There is a neural path leading from the point of injury into his brain and then out again to his response. In the middle of this sequence of events the person feels pain. At this point the introspectionist produces his picture of the expansion of consciousness. He thinks that the only way to show what is unpleasant about the whole process is to put the pain on the inside of the skin of the phenomenal bubble. There is, of course, no man within to scan it, but perhaps that does not matter, because all pain is felt pain. What, according to him, is essential is that at this point in the three-act drama, stimulus, consciousness, and response, the sensation should actually be on stage—or, perhaps, appear on the screen.

When Wittgenstein objects to this, introspectionists, believing it to be the only way of getting pain into the picture, accuse him of behaviourism. That is a common misunderstanding of his treatment of this topic in *Philosophical Investigations*. But, though it is a mistake to equate introspectionism with common sense and to assume that anyone who rejects the introspectionists' picture is a paradoxer, it is, of course, necessary for Wittgenstein to explain what is wrong with their picture.

Consider once more the problem of the ownership of the pain, which served as a guide for the treatment of the sensation itself and its type. The ownership of the pain makes itself evident at all three points on the neural path. It reveals itself physically to the spectator when he notices the stimulus and the response, and it forces itself mentally on the sufferer. We have seen that it is unnecessary and impossible to model what happens at the mid-point on what happens at the two end-points. The sufferer need not and cannot identify his ego in the way in which the spectator can, and must identify his body. The process simply goes through the sufferer and the pain is unmistakably his.

Wittgenstein tries to destroy the other half of the analogy between mind and theatre or phenomenal bubble in a similar way. Because the process goes through the sufferer, what he has is immediately and unmistakably a pain. He need not and does not inspect an impression inside the skin of the bubble in order to assign it to its type. That is what the spectator does with the stimulus and the response, but it is a mistake to model the sufferer's awareness of his sensation and its painfulness on the way in which the spectator notes the stimulus and the response and classifies them. The pain is too close to the sufferer for that and the introspectionists' picture, which tries to distance it from him by putting it on an inner screen, is misleading. The mind is unlike a theatre not only because it contains no ego but also because it contains no inner spectacle. That it not the way to picture sensations.

It is not even quite right to say that the pain is too close to the sufferer for him to be able to regard it in the way in which the spectator regards the stimulus and the response. That is an understatement of the difference between a pain and an object in the physical world. It would be truer to say that the sensation is part of the sufferer, because he does not sit back and take it in like a spectacle, but lives through it. So the fusion which explains why the subject cannot be encountered as a separate ego also explains why its objects cannot be treated as detached apparitions on an inner screen. It is not even true that the pain is confined to the second of the three acts of the drama, the phenomenal act. It is a spreading structure, with its roots in the stimulus and its ramifications in the subject's reponses.

When sensations are looked at in this way, the two difficulties mentioned above certainly become less formidable. One was that sensation-types are genuine objects of awareness, unlike the ego, and the other was that they are many and various, again unlike the ego, so that they have to be discriminated by the person who has them. Naturally, Wittgenstein agrees that sensations and their types are objects of awareness, but not in the way in which physical objects are. As for the subject's ability to discriminate various types of sensation, that too is something that he takes on board and explains as a development of the resources available to the subject before he acquired language.

It is a striking feature of his account of sensation-language that first-person reports are incorrigible because sensation-types are unmistakable to the subject. Wittgenstein rates our ability to discriminate them as high as it could possibly be, and, according to him, this is another important difference between sensations and objects in the physical world, because, of course, it is always possible to make a mistake when one is describing a physical object. He tries to explain this difference by connecting it with the way in which sensation-language is learned. But, before anything is said about that, a word of warning is needed.

The line that has been followed so far has led from the treatment of solipsism in the *Tractatus* through the 1929 account of sensation-language to the very different account of it given in *Philosophical Investigations*. It is a line of thought which was not confined to sensations and their owners, and it opened up a new way of looking at all mental phenomena. For Wittgenstein's later philosophy of mind was a development of the idea that we all live in the unique common world from which it is quite impossible for each of us to cut out a miniature world of his own. However, that does not mean that he treated all mental phenomena in the same way. Even in the case of sensations, the automatic expression of pain is not something that can be matched across the whole range of sensation-types. Sometimes a sensation needs to be carefully described. Emotions too may not always find immediate expression; they can be more elusive, and introspection may be needed to pin them down. Even one's own beliefs and intentions can be poker-faced. So when the new philosophy of mind rejected the idea that the mental is a world apart, detached from the physical world, and, by way of compensation, modelled on it, it put the first emphasis on the differences between the mental and the physical, but naturally it did not treat everything mental in the same way. That would have been implausible.

Two of the differences that Wittgenstein saw between sensations and objects in the physical world have now been mentioned. First, sensations are part of the subject and he cannot distance himself from them as if they were physical objects. Second, his reports of their types are incorrigible. These two differences must now be connected with his repudiation of his 1929 account of sensation-language and his adoption of the new account of the way it is set up and maintained. That will complete this selective sketch of the development of his philosophy.

The fault in his 1929 account of sensation-language was that independent references made by each person to his own sensation-types proved to be incapable of supporting a common language in which people could communicate with one another about them. There is not much room for a philosopher to manœuvre at this point and it seems that there are only two possible moves. One would be to hold on to the idea that each person makes independent references to his own sensation-types and to admit that on this level of language they cannot communicate with one another. Then, since they obviously do succeed in talking to one another about their sensations, the next step would be to explain this achievement by letting sensation-types drop out of the common language, and to represent *A* and *B* as talking to one another about 'whatever sensation-type fills this particular sandwich of stimulus and response in my case', and 'whatever sensation-type fills it in your case'.[21] This is a desperate remedy, because it is so far from what we think we mean when we confer with one another about our sensations. It is also vulnerable to the objection that, if *A* could not extend his concept of 'pain' to *B*, then he could not even extend his concept of 'sensation-type' to *B*.[22] For the very phrase 'filling of the sandwich' carries unjustifiable implications of inner similarities between what *A* has and what *B* has.

The other move is to drop the whole idea of independent private references to one's own sensation-types. Certainly, we refer to them, but our references are made in a physical setting on which they depend. It may have seemed obscure to say above that 'a sensation is a spreading structure, with its roots in the stimulus and its ramifications in the subject's responses'. For that makes it sound as if the subject bases his sensation-reports impartially on all three acts of the drama, and does not attach special weight to the central phenomenal episode. And would that not be absurd?

But that was not the implication. The implication was only that we exploit the physical context when we are learning the common language for sensations, and, thereafter, when we are attributing them to others, but not when we are reporting our own. Once we have learned the language, we discriminate our sensation-types immediately, without needing to make any contemporary use of their physical context, though, of course, it is always available if a check is wanted. In fact, the word for the sensation-type sometimes replaces a piece of behaviour which is already linked by nature to the type itself.[23]

This last way of taking language into our lives is important, because it relies on the fact that our sensations were part of the drama before we began to talk about them or theorize about them. The physical roots and ramifications of sensation-types are an intelligible part of

---

[21] This is the line taken by R. Carnap in *The Unity of Science*, Kegan Paul, 1934, pp. 76–92 and by M. Schlick in 'Meaning and Verification', in *Readings in Philosophical Analysis*, ed. H. Feigl and W. Sellars, Appleton-Century-Crofts, 1949, pp. 161–70 (reprinted from *Philosophical Review*, 1936).

[22] See *PI* I § 261.

[23] See *PI* I § 244.

their pre-theoretical structure, and infants use these physical links in order to capture the sensation-types in the net of their language. They soon find that their verbal reactions become immediate, and, according to Wittgenstein, if they are normal pupils, incorrigible. This is not surprising, because, before they acquired language, the natural drama already contained three essential acts, and language insinuated itself into the second act only by basing itself on the first and third acts.[24]

It was very difficult for Wittgenstein to put across this new way of looking at sensations and sensation-language. So many things conspire to produce misunderstandings of his delicately balanced description of our predicament as sentient, social beings. In philosophy there is the persuasive picture of 'foundations', which gets such a grip on our imaginations. How can the basic references to sensation-types be tied into the superstructure? Who would build a house like that? Also, in daily life there is the daunting opacity of other people. They often conceal their thoughts and feelings, don't they? So why shouldn't nature have concealed their sensation-types? These pressures push people into misunderstandings of what Wittgenstein says about sensation-language in *Philosophical Investigations*. Either he is taken to be that rare thing, a genuine behaviourist, who entirely omits the heart of the matter, 'this damned pain'; or else he is taken to be a fellow-traveller with behaviourists, on the ground that, though he allows *A* and *B* to refer to their sensation-types, they refer to them only in the remote way described in the first attempt to improve his 1929 account, 'the sensation-type that in my case fills this particular sandwich of stimulus and response'.[25]

His new idea was that references to sensation-types are tied into their physical setting more closely than that from the very beginning.[26] The idea was difficult to put across, because the more completely he tried to capture the actual sensation-type, the more uncapturable it seemed to be to his misinterpreters. So his strategy was to argue not merely that we do not make independent private references to our sensation-types, but that we *could not* do so. If this further argument could be made good, it would demonstrate that, when his critics try to point to something that his context-linked references to sensation-types fail to catch, they are not really pointing to anything. They

---

[24] This can be put in terms of criteria.

[25] i.e. the theory adopted by Carnap and Schlick.

[26] To put it crudely, the filling of the sandwich 'is not a *something*, but not a *nothing* either'. See *PI* I § 304.

would, perhaps, be pointing to something that he had failed to catch, if there were, in fact, another way of catching it besides his way. But, he argues, there is no other way, because it is not possible to make context-free references to sensation-types. It is not possible in real life, and philosophy has no access to an independent stand-point from which such references would become possible. This is evidently a late and subtle application of his old thesis about the limits of language: language captures the one and only world and there is no way of cutting out of that world another miniature world in which language could start all over again.

But why exactly are context-free references to sensation-types impossible? Wittgenstein's answer is given in the 'private language argument' of *Philosophical Investigations*.[27] The argument is ambitious and its interpretation controversial. Evidently, he is not just contending that a language with context-free references to sensation-types would not be our sensation-language, because ours is a language in which we do succeed in communicating with one another about our sensations. That hardly needs argument, and he had rightly taken it for granted in 1929. His point now is that context-free references to sensations would not make a language of *any kind*, not even a language for interior monologue. The performance might sound and look like a use of language, but it would not really be one.

But why not? Why are contexts necessary for succesful reference, and so for genuine language? And if they really are necessary, why should they not be provided by recurrent patterns of sensations, which would be available in a system like Berkeley's or in modern phenomenalism? Or if sensational contexts could not provide the necessary frame for successful reference, is that only because they are not good enough for us, given the way in which we learn descriptive language? Or is it because they are absolutely inadequate?

These are the questions that need to be answered by anyone interpreting Wittgenstein's 'private language argument'. They are too complex to be answered in this introduction, but a rapid survey may help to locate the main issues, explain their interconnections, and give some idea of his line of thought.

Imagine an infant, living in its physical environment, interacting with it, and, of course, unable to afford the luxury of doubting its existence. There will be many circuits connecting stimulus, consciousness, and response already set up in this creature by nature, and

[27] *PI* I §§ 243 ff.

perhaps also some set up by training. Language, which has not yet been acquired, will be laid on top of all this. It will, of course, be an artificial overlay and the meanings of the words that are imparted must be tied down by the methods used in teaching their use. If the word 'pain' replaces natural responses to the sensations, their type can hardly be as elusive as it is made to appear by Carnap and Schlick.

But, it will be objected, this appeal to our methods of teaching a sensation-vocabulary simply assumes that the pupil is not making an independent reference to his own sensation-type at the very moment when he is being told the word for it. How do we know that that is not what is going on? It is against this possibility, or apparent possibility, that Wittgenstein develops his 'private language argument'. If the argument is valid, it is impossible to make independent references to one's own sensation-types, and so, when the objector suggests that that is precisely what is done by anyone learning a sensation-vocabulary, Wittgenstein can retort that it is not done because it cannot be done. The objector, he maintains, cannot split the sensation-type down the middle, so that half of it may be captured by the criteria used by the teacher, while the other half remains impossible to capture by anything except an independent reference made by the pupil.[28]

At this point we must ask the first of the three questions posed above. Why did Wittgenstein think that references to sensation-types need a context? Fortunately, the answer to this question is uncontroversial. He started from the assumption that to apply a word to a sensation-type is to exercise an acquired skill, and nobody could set out to acquire a skill unless he had some way of telling whether he was succeeding or failing in his early attempts. Indeed, if he had no way of telling, what could he be trying to do? Even if the skill had been innate, he would still have needed a criterion of success. For the exercise of a skill is an intentional performance, and so, even if he did it perfectly by natural endowment, he would still need a check on what he was doing. It would not be enough that he should have the impression of using the word correctly. He must know what would count as a *correct* impression of correct use, and that requires an independent criterion.[29]

---

[28] He counters the objection in this way in *PI* I §§ 273–80 and *Zettel*, § 87. See above, n. 19.

[29] See *PI* I §§ 258–60. Cf. L. Wittgenstein: 'Notes for Lectures on 'Private Experience' and 'Sense-data'', *Philosophical Review*, Vol. 77 No. 3, 1968 (henceforth *NLPESD*), p. 297, penultimate paragraph. Two kinds of independent criterion are mentioned in *NLPESD*, one based on standard objects and the other based on the judgements of others (p. 306).

So far, many philosophers would agree with Wittgenstein, but the next hurdle is the second question posed above. Why should the word-user not check his use of the word for the sensation-type by waiting to see if the pattern of further sensations that usually follows it follows it this time? A phenomenalist would say that that is all that anyone ever does when he checks his use of any descriptive word. This is a tricky objection to answer, because it adopts Wittgenstein's tune and plays it in a different key.

However, there are two ways in which he might counter this move. First, he might argue that anyone who sets out to learn descriptive language must learn it at the interface between himself, body and mind, and his immediate environment. He cannot set up tests for himself internally, and check whether he passes or fails them internally. The phenomenalist will, of course, retort that the learner's immediate environment makes an impact on him only as sensory input, so that his whole performance *can* only be internal.

But here we must remember that it is the phenomenalist who is the innovator making the philosophical move. He is trying to cut his miniature world out of the common world. But is he *really* doing this or only pretending to do it? Perhaps the genuine isolation of a private world could be achieved only by severing every connection between a sensation and its physical cause, however described. Certainly, there is an air of pretence about merely *calling* the cause of a sensation 'a sequence of further sensations'. That does not seem to be what was meant by 'a private world'.

Here we run into the general problem of worlds within the world. It may be that there is no short way of determining whether we can or cannot set them up. Certainly, there must be a difference between seceding into a miniature world and imagining oneself in it from the start, but the trouble with this controversy between Wittgenstein and his adversary is that it moves to and fro on the borderline between these two intellectual enterprises. Perhaps we cannot settle the matter until we have completely understood what is wrong with solipsism.

Wittgenstein has a second resource that he can use at this point. He can criticize his opponent's over-intellectualization of the process of learning descriptive language. The phenomenalist assumes that this process begins on an empty stage with the first application of a single world to a sensation-type. That is supposed to be done without any check. Then a second sensation-type is picked out and named, and soon there is a group of them, which will, with luck, cohere with one another, so that at last the language-user will be in business.

But it is just not true that the process of acquiring language begins in such an abstract, intellectual way. Language is a late arrival on a busy scene of long-established activities. There are already many strands running through the learner and linking stimuli, sensations, and responses, and so he already has a pre-theoretical head start in his acquisition of language. The purely intellectual feat ascribed to him by the phenomenalist may not be absolutely impossible, but Wittgenstein's account of the way in which language is acquired is, at least, more realistic.

Finally, there is the third question posed above. When he rejects the phenomenalist's account of the achievement of successful reference to sensation-types, is his point that the proposed checks are not good enough for us, given the way in which we have actually learned descriptive language? Or is his point that they are absolutely inadequate, and the feat, as described, absolutely impossible? This question takes us back to the general problem of worlds within the world, because we really do learn descriptive language at the interface between ourselves, bodies and minds, and our immediate environment, even if we prefer to describe the process phenomenalistically. It will be left unanswered for the moment because enough has been said to introduce the topic of 'private language', and the discussion will be continued in Chapter 7 and in Volume II.

Two further points are needed to complete this sketch of the main strategy of Wittgenstein's later philosophy of mind. First, something should be said about his tendency to treat sensation-types as unmistakable to the subject who has them, because it may seem inconsistent with his refusal to equate success and impression of success. Second, there is evidently a connection between the structure of his 'private language argument' and the structure of the anti-Platonic argument which precedes it in *Philosophical Investigations*, and it might be useful to establish what the connection is.

First, then, the apparent inconsistency of treating sensation-types as unmistakable to the subject is not a real inconsistency. There is a clear difference between the correctness of a claim made about a physical object and the speaker's impression of correctness. But if he merely reports the sensations that it gives him, there is, according to Wittgenstein, no difference on that level between his impressions of correctness and actual correctness. This is not an inconsistency, because Wittgenstein's idea is that the difference must exist not only on the basic physical level but also on the phenomenal level while sensation-language is being learned. It is only when the speaker graduates in sensation-language that the difference vanishes on the phenomenal level and his sensation-types become unmistakable to him.

It might even be thought that Wittgenstein was forced to take this line about sensations, because if he treated them as objects about which the subject might be mistaken, he would be well on the road to treating them as independent objects. However, it was not really necessary for him to insist on the unmistakability of all types of sensations. If he had taken the view that unmistakability lies at the end-point of a scale on which the incidence of mistakes steadily increases as we move away from it, he would not have been committing himself to the possibility of referring to sensations as independent objects. On this view, the limiting case would be ownership of a sensation claimed by the subject. If it were a pain, its painfulness would lie very close on the scale of increasing liability to mistake, but for an entirely different reason: any alternatives to his ownership of it would be inconceivable, whereas alternatives to its painfulness would only be excluded by his proficiency in the use of the word 'pain'. There are, of course, descriptions of sensations that are harder to apply, and in those cases we would not require such a high standard of proficiency before allowing that someone had learned the meanings of the words. No doubt, the introspectionist's notion, that sensations are objects inside the phenomenal bubble, leads to an exaggeration of the possibility of the subject making mistakes about their types, but, if we reject that picture, we can cut back this possibility to the right size, which may not be zero.

The second point needed to complete this sketch was a point about the structure of Wittgenstein's 'private language argument'. There is a pattern of thought that runs very deep in his philosophy and manifests itself not only in this argument but also in the anti-Platonic argument which precedes it in *Philosophical Investigations*. Its earliest appearance is in the treatment of solipsism in the *Tractatus*. Two things, which in reality are independent of one another, are clamped together by a definition in some philosophical theory and the result is rigid immobility where there ought to have been movement and interaction. These are vague words but they exactly fit the collapse of solipsism, as it is present in the *Tractatus*.

The solipsist starts with the idea that he can model his metaphysical thesis on an ordinary empirical claim: 'The only good restaurants in Oxford are ones that I have tried.' However the guide picked out by the word 'I' must be identifiable if this is going to be informative, even to him. Now it may not be easy to identify him, but one thing is certain: he will not merely be introduced by definition as the person who has tried the only good restaurants in Oxford. Guides need to be discovered, not invented. Similarly, when the solipsist says, 'The only things that exist are things that I have encountered', the explorer needs to be identified, and this need is just as real when he does not claim to have stepped outside his own phenomenal bubble as it would be if he were talking about 'the world as he found it'. Unfortunately, when he searches for the point of origin of his egocentric map, he necessarily fails to find it, and so it has only been introduced by definition, as the geometrical point from which the privileged things can be viewed.[30] If nothing more is done, this ego will not be tied to a particular person and it could even be the collective ego of all humanity. Therefore, the solipsist's claim remains uninformative. A philosopher's definition has deprived two things of the independence that they needed. The clock-hand has been strapped to the dial, so that they both go round together.

Wittgenstein's anti-Platonic argument, mentioned in Chapter 1,[31] exhibits the same pattern. The problem in that case was posed by the fact that people use descriptive words with constant meanings. How do they do it? Wittgenstein's answer was that, having learned the meaning of a descriptive word, a person finds it natural to continue in a certain way, to apply it in this case and to withhold it in that one. The Platonic answer is that this kind of reliance on human nature would lead to a breakdown of law and order, and so what is needed is a fixed standard of correct usage, already laid down in reality and waiting for us to conform to it.

Wittgenstein's objection to Platonism starts from the observation that the fixed rails on which we are supposed to be running when we use a descriptive word are a fantasy. He then argues that, in any case, they would be no use, because the speaker's mind would have to contain something—an image, perhaps, or a formula—which would be both strictly contemporary and also a self-contained, unambiguous representation of the infinite line dividing positive from negative

[30] See *The Blue Book*, pp. 63–4, and *NLPESD* pp. 298–9.
[31] See above, pp. 10–11.

instances; which is impossible. Finally, he claims that Platonism destroys the distinction between obeying a rule and disobeying it. For human nature makes an essential contribution to what counts as obedience, and when this contribution is excluded by Platonism, the result is the collapse of the *concept* of law and order, because we are left free to choose to regard any continuation as one that fits the formulation of the rule, or to choose to regard it as a misfit. In fact, we would find either that the continuation was natural or that it was unnatural. But if we were not allowed to listen to those promptings, there would be nothing to fix the correct continuation.

This objection to Platonism is another example of the same pattern of thought. The question is 'How are we to describe the contents of the mind of a person who has mastered the use of a word?' Instead of describing them as they really are, the Platonist clamps them by definition to a standard of correct use, pictured as already laid out on fixed rails. A sober account of the contents of his mind and the use that he makes of them would show how he himself contributes to laying the rails on which he is running. He is really a groper, but a groper so effectively inspired that he is hardly aware of his own contribution. If the contents of his mind are defined in the Platonist's idealizing way, they are lifted out of the real world and frozen in a world of fantasy.

Finally, Wittgenstein's 'private language argument' is yet another example of the same pattern of thought. This time the crippling definition has been set up in the opposite direction. The correct use of a sensation-word is attached by definition to the user's impression of correctness. His mind then no longer makes measurements of the world which are required to lead to substantial results. It becomes a capricious measuring instrument which is answerable only to itself.

PART II

INSIDE THE EARLY SYSTEM

4

Logical Atomism

'LOGICAL atomism' is Russell's name for the theory that there is a limit to the analysis of factual language, a limit at which all sentences will consist of words designating simple things. He supposed that these simple things would be particulars, qualities, and relations, and he called the propositions expressed by the corresponding, completely analysed sentences 'atomic'. His theory of knowledge led him to claim that the only simple particulars that we know are sense-data, and that the only simple qualities and relations that we know are certain qualities and relations of sense-data. Their simple qualities and relations are those with which we have to achieve acquaintance in order to understand the words designating them. This fixes the character of his logical atomism. It is a version of empiricism and it uses a criterion of simplicity based on the exigencies of learning meanings. We could not learn the meanings of the logically proper names which designate particular sense-data without acquaintance with the sense-data themselves, and we encounter the same constraint when we try to learn the meanings of certain words designating their qualities and relations. This doctrine of forced acquaintance is the foundation of Russell's logical atomism.[1]

The brief description of Wittgenstein's logical atomism in Chapter 2 gave it a very different character.[2] The most striking difference was that Wittgenstein did not argue like Russell that the analysis of factual language can be discovered to terminate at a level at which our only resource for learning the meanings of words is acquaintance. He argued that factual sentences have senses only because there is a level at which words would designate things devoid of internal structure. These words would be genuine names of objects, but there is no suggestion in the *Tractatus* that we ever operate at that level, nor is the criterion for simplicity or lack of internal structure supposed to be that, if we did operate at that level, we would be forced to rely on acquaintance in order

[1] See Russell: *The Philosophy of Logical Atomism*, in *Logic and Knowledge: Essays 1901–1950*, ed. R. Marsh, Allen and Unwin, 1956, pp. 193–5.
[2] See above, p. 25 and p. 27. Cf. *TLP* 4.211

to learn the meanings of the names that would be used down there. Wittgenstein's criterion for simplicity is quite different: a thing is simple, and so what he calls 'an object', if and only if its nature does not generate any necessary connections between a sentence in which it is named and any other sentence belonging to the same level. So his logical atomism is not a version of empiricism: he did not use an empiricist criterion of simplicity based on the exigencies of learning meanings, nor did he rely on the empirical claim that analysis soon uncovers the atomistic foundations of factual discourse. He argued a priori from the existence of factual sentences with senses to the existence of an underlying grid of elementary possibilities, with simple objects at the nodal points.

Given these differences, it may seem misguided to introduce Wittgenstein's logical atomism with a thumb-nail sketch of Russell's version of the theory. If Wittgenstein believed that his objects were not the same as Russell's logical atoms, and that their existence and character were not even established by the same kind of argument, would it not be better to give a completely independent description of his system? That, of course, is something that could be done, because it stands on its own feet. However, here, as in the case of his picture theory of sentences,[3] he reacted against Russell's views without totally abandoning them. It is, therefore, historically and intrinsically explanatory to record the similarities between them as well as the differences.

The historical continuity must be important, because many of his views about the nature of logic and the nature of things developed out of Russell's views originally through actual discussions with Russell.[4] Consequently, it would be very surprising if the comparative description of his system were not intrinsically apt. There is also a special reason for adopting a comparative approach to the two versions of logical atomism. When Wittgenstein compiled the *Tractatus* from material in his notebooks, he did not claim to be able to give any examples of objects,[5] and that makes his version very abstract and difficult to understand; but he does use sense-data and their properties at least as illustrations,[6] and that implies that his version and Russell's were not too far apart.

---

[3] See above, pp. 7, 11, and 29.

[4] See R. W. Clark: *The Life of Bertrand Russell*, Jonathan Cape and Weidenfeld and Nicolson, 1975, ch. 7.

[5] See N. Malcolm: *Ludwig Wittgenstein, a Memoir*, 2nd edn., Oxford, 1984 p. 70, cf. *LWVC*, pp. 41–2 and 182–4.   [6] e.g. *TLP* 2.0131.

But how much did they really have in common? There is a wide range of answers to this question. At one extreme, there is the suggestion that the objects of the *Tractatus* simply were sense-data, which were, therefore, introduced not as rather remote illustrations but as actual examples.[7] At the opposite extreme there is an interpretation of Wittgenstein's early system which denies that it is based on independent references to objects, and claims that it is not even a generalized version of Russellian realism, with objects of some other, unspecified kind substituted for sense-data and their properties.[8]

It will be evident that the view taken in Part I lies somewhere between these two extremes. For Wittgenstein's early system was described as 'basic realism',[9] and one of the advances made in his later system was said to be the abandonment of the idea that, when a name is attached to a thing, the nature of the thing takes over and dictates its subsequent use.[10] Another, connected idea, that we carve up phenomena by making independent references to their various types, was also said to be abandoned later. However, phenomena need not be taken to be sense-data, and the identification of the objects of the *Tractatus* with sense-data was rejected. Wittgenstein's treatment of solipsism was then interpreted as a treatment of an ego-based solipsism rather than a solipsism based on sense-data.[11]

However, the theses which were put forward in Part I were not supported by much argument. The intention was only to give a sketch of the general layout of Wittgenstein's philosophy, leaving the details of the suggested interpretations and the arguments for them to be added later. That is what now needs to be done, and the first step must be the exposition of Wittgenstein's argument for his version of logical atomism. Russell's argument for his version is easy to follow: in the analysis of factual language we are supposed to reach words which we can understand only through acquaintance with the things that they designate. But Wittgenstein argues a priori from the existence of factual sentences with senses to the existence of an underlying grid of elementary possibilities, and it is not so easy to follow his line of thought.

---

[7] See J. and M. Hintikka: *Investigating Wittgenstein*, Blackwell, 1986, ch. 3.

[8] See H. Ishiguro: 'Use and Reference of Names', in *Studies in the Philosophy of Wittgenstein*, ed. P. Winch, Routledge, 1969, and B. McGuinness: 'The So-called Realism of the *Tractatus*', in *Perspectives on the Philosophy of Wittgenstein*, ed. I. Block, Blackwell, 1981.

[9] See above, pp. 8–10.

[10] See above, pp. 11–13 and 30–1.

[11] See above, pp. 34–9.

It is best to start from the sketch given in Part I of his logical atomism and of the way in which he argued for it.[12] He formulated his version of the theory in the following way: ordinary factual sentences can be analysed down to factual sentences in which only simple objects are named. He called these sentences 'elementary', and their distinctive feature is that they never contradict one another.[13] This is because the objects named in them are devoid of internal structure.

In order to prove that ordinary factual discourse must be analysable in this way, he used a reductive argument. If there were any complex things named in the complete analyses of ordinary factual sentences, then the analysing sentences would have senses only if certain other sentences, not included in *their* analyses (they have no analyses), were true. For complex things would not be there to be named unless it were true that their components were arranged in the way required for their existence. But the sense of a sentence about a complex thing cannot possibly depend on the truth of another sentence about its components. So the analysis must go on down to the next level and include the further sentence in the sense of the original one, and this process must continue until all words for complexes have been replaced by genuine names standing for simple objects.

In Part I two passages were cited in support of this interpretation of his argument. One was *Tractatus* 2.0211–2.0212:

> If the world had no substance, then whether a proposition had sense would depend on whether another proposition was true.
> In that case we could not sketch any picture of the world (true or false).

The other passage was a single sentence in *Notes Dictated to G. E. Moore in Norway*:[14]

> The question whether a proposition has sense (Sinn) can never depend on the *truth* of another proposition about a constituent of the first.

These two passages certainly give some support to the suggested interpretation of Wittgenstein's argument for his version of logical atomism, but more evidence will be needed to corroborate it. If it is right, his view of logical analysis is much less perspicuous than Russell's view, and it might be useful to show how the two views are related to one another. There is also something else that needs to be

---

[12] See above, pp. 24–8.
[13] *TLP* 4.21–4.211.
[14] *NB* p. 116.

done. The suggested interpretation assumes that Wittgenstein's early system is based on independent references to objects, an assumption which is rejected by those who adopt the extreme view that it is not even a generalized version of Russellian realism. It is, therefore, necessary to show what, if anything, is wrong with that extreme view. Finally, there is the view which stands at the other extreme, that the objects of the *Tractatus* were intended to be sense-data, and that view too will have to be eliminated, if the interpretation that is being proposed here is going to be established.

This is a long list of tasks and they need to be carried out in some sort of logical order. The proposed interpretation stands on the middle ground between the two extremes, and it can be defended either on its intrinsic merits or by criticism of the two extremes. It is evidently best to begin with its intrinsic merits, because that will make it clear from the start what theses are being attributed to Wittgenstein, and how they fit into the general pattern of the development of his ideas. The examination and rejection of the two extreme interpretations can be left to the next chapter.

The first thing that is needed is a commanding view of the scene in which the logical atomism of the *Tractatus* is set. The eye is so easily caught by inessential details and the general pattern so easily missed. One way of achieving a commanding view is to compare Wittgenstein's logical atomism with Russell's doctrine. The baffling feature of Wittgenstein's doctrine is its extreme abstractness. No definite examples of objects are given and this makes it hard to identify the conclusion that he took his argument to establish. All that we are told is that objects are devoid of internal complexity, and so, when their names occur in propositions, their natures do not generate any necessary connections between them. He calls such propositions 'elementary' but gives no examples of them. Evidently, propositions like 'This is red' and 'This is green', which are necessarily incompatible with one another, do not count as elementary propositions.[15] This is interesting but baffling, because it tells us what objects are not like without telling us what they are like. They must not have any internal complexity, but we are left to guess how they manage without it. It is like the *via remotionis* in theology: God is described by listing the properties that he does *not* possess. However, this move of Wittgenstein's does allow us to draw a clear line across the whole landscape, separating Russell's logical analysis which terminates on

[15] See *TLP* 6.3751.

familiar, identifiable things from the logical analysis of the *Tractatus*, which terminates on things that have not yet been identified. This dividing line is the most prominent feature in a confused scene. On one side of it Russell operates with a criterion of simplicity which allows him to identify logical atoms as things with which we are familiar, namely sense-data and their properties. His criterion is an empiricist's criterion, forced acquaintance. Also, a separate point, his argument for the existence of logical atoms is empirical: he claims that as a matter of fact we find things that satisfy his criterion, but there was no necessity that this should be so, and he says that it is arguable that logical analysis might never reach logical atoms.[16] His empiricist criterion of simplicity is, of course, less demanding than Wittgenstein's logical criterion. It does not require logical atoms to be devoid of internal complexity: it only requires them to lack the kind of internal complexity which would make it possible for someone who was not acquainted with them to learn the meanings of the words that designate them. So Russell, unlike Wittgenstein, allowed that determinate shades of colour are simple.[17]

The logical atomism of the *Tractatus* is clearly placed on the other side of the dividing line. Wittgenstein's a priori requirement, that objects should be entirely devoid of internal complexity, drove his analysis of factual discourse beyond the terminus that satisfied Russell. Objects might even turn out to be things that no philosopher had ever suggested as the ultimate targets of reference. Indeed, they would have to be new and strange, because nothing with which we are familiar could get past his total embargo on internal structure.

He was well aware of this dividing line and in the *Notebooks* he showed some reluctance to cross it.[18] This is not because he was unwilling to move so far from empiricism. He never used an empiricist criterion of simplicity, and his reluctance came from

---

[16] See *The Philosophy of Logical Atomism*, p. 202. The remark is made by Russell in the discussion at the end of Lecture II. He must have meant that logical analysis *might have gone* on interminably, because he says 'I do not think it is true [sc. that it goes on interminably].' This was in 1917. Later, when he became aware of Wittgenstein's a priori argument for his different version of logical atomism, he was evidently attracted by it, because he said things which are not appropriate to the version that he develops in *The Philosophy of Logical Atomism*, and some of which cannot even be reconciled with it; e.g. 'Logical Atomism' (in *Logic and Knowledge*) p. 337, and *My Philosophical Development*, pp. 221–3. Cf. his Introduction to the *Tractatus*, p. xiii.

[17] See *The Philosophy of Logical Atomism*, pp. 193–5.

[18] See the entries on 16, 17, and 18 June, 1915. Cf. A. Kenny: *Wittgenstein*, Penguin, 1973, pp. 80–4.

a different source: it seemed paradoxical to him that the complete analysis of an ordinary factual sentence should be so remote from anything that its user could say if he were asked what he meant. This is not the paradox of analysis, because the surprising thing is not just that the user of the sentence does not know its analysis, but, rather, that he has no idea what kind of thing would be mentioned in its analysis, and might even find that he was not familiar with that ultimate kind of thing when he was told what it was. In the *Notebooks* Wittgenstein evidently feels misgivings about this extreme view of logical analysis, and he says things that betray a strong inclination to pull back the terminus to a point that is not so remote from the consciousness of ordinary speakers.[19] Could he really rely on his austere criterion of simplicity to carry him across the dividing line into the unknown?[20]

His first move away from the system of the *Tractatus* was to abandon the requirement that objects should be devoid of internal complexity, and so to allow that 'This is red' and 'This is green' are elementary propositions in spite of their logical incompatibility.[21] Since it was always clear to him that his total embargo on internal structure would drive logical analysis to a remote and unfamiliar terminus, it may seem surprising that he maintained it for so long. However, the *Tractatus* doctrine of logical analysis is not unparalleled. The analysis of words for natural kinds proposed by Kripke and Putnam allows for the possibility that the users of such a word might believe that it could be analysed in scientific terms, although they could not carry out the analysis themselves and, perhaps, did not even know what sort of thing would be mentioned in it.[22] There is, however, a difference between the two cases. When the analysis of a word like 'measles' goes beyond the familiar symptoms, it is guided by scientific knowledge; whereas in the *Tractatus*, when logical analysis is pushed across the line into unexplored territory, no guidance is offered and the description of the destination does not help us to locate it.

[19] See *NB* 17 June 1915: 'All I want is only for *my meaning* to be completely analysed.'
[20] In 1931 he criticized the *Tractatus* not only for its dogmatism about objects, but also for its assumption that later it would be possible to discover what kind of thing they are. See *LWVC*, pp. 182–4.
[21] See L. Wittgenstein: 'Some Remarks on Logical Form', *Aristotelian Society*, Suppl. Vol. 9 pp. 162–71: reprinted in *Essays on Wittgenstein's Tractatus*, ed. R. Beard and I. Copi, Routledge and Kegan Paul, 1966, pp. 31–7.
[22] H. Putnam: 'The Meaning of Meaning', in *Collected Papers*, Vol. 2, Cambridge, 1981, and S. Kripke: *Naming and Necessity*, in *Semantics of Natural Language*, Reidel, 1972, reprinted by Blackwell, 1980.

There is another vantage-point from which a commanding view of this complicated scene can be obtained, and, before we plunge into details, it is worth trying to exploit it. Wittgenstein's argument for logical atomism starts from the evidently true premiss that 'we picture facts to ourselves',[23] or, in other words, that we have thoughts and express them in sentences.[24] He then argues reductively that these achievements would be impossible if there were no objects. Now what we really need is a perspicuous way of representing his argument, because it certainly does not make an irresistible appeal to intuition. Why can the sense of one sentence never depend on the truth of another? Why does each sentence have to stand alone with its sense reaching as far into the nature of things as any language could possibly reach? Why should our use of ordinary, factual sentences depend on the existence of things which we may never have heard of before, and which even now Wittgenstein cannot identify for us? It would be hard to imagine a more counter-intuitive argument.

However, there is a way of making it accessible to intuition, and we can at least share his vision of far-reaching senses, even if we do not accept its validity. If a sentence is like an ordinary picture, for example a painting of a room and its contents, then we ought to be able to pick up from its words alone everything that it is telling us, just as we can see in the picture itself everything that it is telling us about the room.[25] But how much does the sentence tell us? In the case of the picture, all is set our clearly on the surface of the canvas, but that is not true of a typical factual sentence.[26] When we raise the question of the analysis of such a sentence, and try to bring all its implications to the surface, it is not obvious how deep we have to trawl and what the limits of our search ought to be. That is the problem.

The picture theory suggests a way of finding a solution. One thing that the picture of the room cannot do is to present a view of the geometry that made its view of the room possible. The parallel limitation for the sentence is that the possibility of its saying what it does say depends on the actuality of other things which it cannot say.[27] Now suppose that we introduce the idea of a 'total demand': there is a total demand made by the picture on the world, everything that has to be the case if it is true, and there is a similar total demand made by

[23] *TLP* 2.1.
[24] *TLP* 3 and 3.1.
[25] See *TLP* 4.02–4.023.
[26] See *TLP* 3.262 and 4.002.
[27] See above, p. 7.

the sentence on the world. But if either the picture or the sentence is going to be true, it must already have a sense.[28] Therefore, we ought to be able to draw a line through their total demands separating the sense-conditions from the truth-conditions.

On the face of it, the sense of a sentence attributing a quality φ to a particular a depends on five things: the existence of φ, the existence of a, their combinability, the attachment of the name 'φ' to φ and the attachment of the name 'a' to a. The sixth element in the sentence's total demand, that φ and a should be arranged in reality as it says that they are arranged, is the element on which its truth depends. The difficulty begins when the question of analysis is raised. For suppose that 'a' is found to designate a complex thing, b-in-the-$relation$-R-to-c. Then there will be a further sentence 'bRc' whose truth must be placed in relation to the line dividing the total demand of the original sentence into sense-conditions and truth-conditions. Is the truth of this further sentence a condition of the sense or of the truth of the original sentence?

We know Wittgenstein's answer: it is a condition of the truth of the original sentence, because it is part of what the original sentence is saying. What we want to know is why he gives this answer to the question, and what would be wrong with answering that the truth of the further sentence is a condition of the sense of the original sentence.

His reason for rejecting this answer is connected with his views about the limits of language.[29] He believed that the possibility of the original sentence's saying what it does say depends on the actuality of other things which it cannot say. He also believed that no sentence could say those other things, because sense-conditions are ineffable. But what the further sentence 'bRc' says is evidently not ineffable. Therefore, the truth of 'bRc', which is certainly part of the original sentence's total demand, should be counted among the truth-conditions of the original sentence and not among its sense-conditions.

This is not a complete explanation of his reason for taking the crucial step in his argument: 'The question whether a proposition has sense (*Sinn*) can never depend on the *truth* of another proposition about a constituent of the first.'[30] For we now want to know why he held

---

[28] See *TLP* 4.064.
[29] See above, pp. 7–8 and p. 27.
[30] See above, p. 66.

that sense-conditions are ineffable. Why did he count them among the things that can only be shown, not said?[31] However, the explanation of that thesis will have to wait until Chapter 6, which will deal with the picture theory in detail.

Meanwhile, we have at least located the force which carried the logical analysis of the *Tractatus* across the line that separates the familier from the unknown. Everything that is sayable in a sentence's total demand is actually said by it, and logical analysis has to bring it to the surface. When that has been done, we shall be able to read off from the analysis the complete message conveyed by the original sentence, just as we can read off the picture's complete message from the disposition of the flecks of paint on the canvas.

We also have a clearer view of the connection between Wittgenstein's far-reaching analysis of factual sentences and his views about logic. In Chapter 2 his far-reaching analysis was described in the following way: it pushes the level of complete analysis downwards until there are no underlying facts left, but only objects devoid of internal structure.[32] In other words, all the factual implications in a sentence's total demand are brought to the surface and included in what it says. The simple objects that remain, when logical analysis has been completed, are the pivots on which all factual discourse turns. This is directly connected with his view of logic. He says that all necessity is logical necessity, reducible to the tautological combinability of sentences.[33] This view would have to be abandoned if it turned out that some necessary connections were embedded in the unanalysable natures of things. For if that were the situation, the properties on which these exceptional necessary connections depended could not be extracted and their names could not be included in the analyses of sentences mentioning the things that possessed them, and so the connections themselves could not be represented tautologically.[34] It is from this point of view that we should see his refusal in the *Tractatus* to treat colours as simple objects.[35] If colour-words could not be analysed, the undeniable incompatibilities between colours would force him to retract his sweeping claims about necessity. In 1929 he gave up the thesis that colour-words are analysable and allowed

---

[31] See *TLP* 4.022 and 4.1212.

[32] See above, p. 27.

[33] See *TLP* 6.1 and 6.37.

[34] See my article, 'The Logical Independence of Elementary Propositions', in *Perspectives on the Philosophy of Wittgenstein*, ed. I. Block, Blackwell, 1981.

[35] *TLP* 6.3751.

them to occur in elementary sentences.[36] That amounted to an abandonment of the sweeping claims made about necessity in the *Tractatus*, and his more subtle account followed later.

Convincing or unconvincing, his early vision of the relation between language and the world is powerful and penetrating. What is needed next is more evidence for interpeting the *Tractatus* in this way, and the remainder of this chapter will contain the further evidence and an evaluation of it. One of the most revealing pieces of evidence will be his 1929 retractation of his earlier extreme logical atomism. It is worth remarking incidentally that his own self-criticisms often provide the necessary key to his earlier views. He was a thinker who saw the way ahead with exceptional clarity and so covered the intervening distance with a rapidity that makes it difficult to be sure which way he has gone until we read his later retractations. The remaining evidence will now be reviewed in detail and then the next chapter will move off the middle ground and examine the two extreme interpretations of his logical atomism.

So far, only one of the premisses of Wittgenstein's argument has been given: 'We picture facts to ourselves.'[37] But there are other premisses which have not yet been identified. One is the principle of representation:[38] 'The possibility of propositions is based on the principle that objects have signs as their representatives.'[39] Another is the postulate of definiteness of sense: 'The requirement that simple signs be possible is the requirement that sense be determinate.'[40] It may not be immediately obvious that any use has been made of this postulate, but in fact its role has been essential. For if the sense of the sentence 'φa' were not definite, the sense of the further sentence 'bRc' which analysed the complexity of a, might be ambiguously placed: before this step in the analysis had been taken, it might lie outside the sense of 'φa', waiting to be roped in after the step had been

---

[36] See 'Some Remarks on Logical Form'.

[37] See above, n. 23.

[38] 'Vertretung', which in G. E. M. Anscombe's translation of *NB* is rendered 'going proxy for'.

[39] *TLP* 4.0312.

[40] *TLP* 3.23. The German word is 'Bestimmt'. The idea is Frege's: a concept 'must have a sharp boundary' and its definition must 'unambiguously determine, as regards any object whether or not it falls under the concept' (*Grundgesetze der Arithmetik, begriffschriftlich abgeleitet*, Vol. 2 § 56). It follows that the implications of a sentence must all lie in it from the beginning, and we cannot improvise new implications as we go along. Frege's idea is criticized in Wittgenstein's later review of the system of the *Tractatus* (*PI* I § 71), and that review leads into the anti-Platonic argument sketched above, pp. 10–11 and 59–60, and below, p. 104.

taken. That was not Wittgenstein's view. His argument relied on the
assumption that the entire sense of the sentence, stretching out to the
limit of the sayable in its total demand, is already attached to it.[41]
Finally, there is a fourth premiss which must not be forgotten, 'All
things are complex.' This occupies a special position, because he is
trying to reduce it to absurdity, whereas, of course, the other
premisses are accepted by him and used as the basis of his reductive
argument.

Let us look at these premisses more closely. The principle of representation (*Vertretung*) is the core of the picture theory. In a pointillist
picture each dot of paint on the canvas is correlated with a minute
fragment of the actual scene, and, similarly, each referential element
in a sentence is correlated with a thing:

[A picture] is laid against reality like a ruler.
Only the end-points of the graduating lines actually *touch* the objects to be
measured.
So a picture, conceived in this way, also includes the pictorial relationship
which makes it into a picture.
The pictorial relationship consists of the correlations of the picture's
elements with things.
These correlations are, as it were, the feelers of the picture's elements, with
which the picture touches reality.[42]

The heavy emphasis on actual contact between pictorial elements and
things marks the importance of the principle of representation, but it
is not immediately clear how Wittgenstein is using it in his reductive
argument.

There are two main problems of interpretation. First, the referential
elements in sentences are names, and Wittgenstein makes a caution-
ary remark about names:

[41] This is made quite clear in *NB* 18 June 1915: 'We might demand definiteness in
this way too: if a proposition is to make sense, then the syntactical employment of each
of its parts must be settled in advance. It is e.g. not possible *only subsequently to come upon*
the fact that a proposition follows from it. But e.g. what propositions follow from a
proposition must be completely settled before that proposition can have a sense.' Cf.
L. Wittgenstein: *Prototractatus*, ed. B. McGuinness, T. Nyberg, and G. H. von Wright,
tr. D. F. Pears and B. McGuinness, Routledge and Kegan Paul, 1971, 3.20101–3.20103.
Someone who finds it paradoxical that the sense of an ordinary factual sentence should
be so far-reaching may object that the sentence 'This is a case of measles' in earlier
centuries carried no implication that the familiar symptoms were caused by a specific
virus. See H. Putnam, op. cit., above, n. 22.
[42] *TLP* 2.1512–2.1515.

Only propositions have sense: only in the context of a proposition does a name have meaning.[43]

Does this imply that the contact between name and things is not established first, or does it merely imply that the contact is maintained only so long as the name occurs in a proposition with a sense? This is an important question of interpretation, because the answer will indicate the distance between the account of factual language given in the *Tractatus* and the account given in *Philosophical Investigations*. To put the matter very approximately, Wittgenstein's destination was the idea that meaning is use, but how far back did he start? In the beginning did he try to extract everything that is needed for sense from the contact between names and things, or was that contact always qualified and hedged about with stipulations concerning use?[44]

This question will be answered dogmatically here, and supporting arguments will be given in the next two chapters. Yes, Wittgenstein did always qualify the contact between name and thing by making it conditional on the correct use of the name in sentences. The condition on which he insisted was that sentences in which the name occurs must present real possibilities for the named thing. If this condition is not met, contact is broken and the name no longer represents the thing.[45] This does not mean that the question 'Which thing does this name represent?' can be answered in the following way: Find out in which sentences the name makes sense and you will know which thing it represents. That method would be circular, because it is only through its name–thing contacts that a sentence acquires its sense.[46] The condition imposed by Wittgenstein *qualifies* name–thing contact, but does not *replace* it. The thing, with its independent nature, is the dominant partner in the association, and if the name does not remain faithful to the possibilities inherent in the thing, the association is annulled. So representation (*Vertretung*) requires an initial correlation followed by faithfulness to possibilities intrinsic to the thing with which the initial correlation was made.

The geometry of a picture of a room will show how this qualified correlation works. A particular dot of paint is correlated with a

---

[43] *TLP* 3.3. Here the German word translated as 'meaning' is 'Bedeutung', which can be translated as 'reference'. 'Context' is C. K. Ogden's translation of 'Zusammenhang'.

[44] The question is discussed by H. Ishiguro: 'Use and Reference of Names', and by B. McGuinness: 'The So-called Realism of Wittgenstein's Tractatus'. Their answer to it, the second of the two extreme views mentioned above, p. 65, will be examined in ch. 5.

[45] See *NB* 4–5 Nov. 1914.

[46] Ibid. 20–1 Nov. 1914.

particular point in the actual scene. The dot is placed on the canvas and, when the painting is finished, it will be part of a message. The content of the message will depend on painting in other dots each of which will be correlated by projective geometry with its own point out there. Now the qualification works like this: the painted dots must present real possibilities for the points out there. If this qualification does not seem to add anything in this case, it is worth recalling Escher's impossible perspectives.

The second question about the interpretation of Wittgenstein's principle of representation is less difficult. Does the principle apply only to elementary sentences or does it also apply to ordinary sentences before they have been analysed? This is a question that does not arise for a painting, because everything that a painting tells us is set out clearly on the surface of the canvas. Wittgenstein's answer can be gathered from two remarks in the *Tractatus*:

> The essence of a propositional sign is very clearly seen if we imagine one composed of spatial objects (such as tables, chairs, and books) instead of written signs.
> Then the spatial arrangement of these things will express the sense of the proposition.[47]

And later:

> It is obvious that a proposition of the form '*aRb*' strikes us as a picture. In this case the sign is obviously a likeness of what is signified.[48]

So even before sentences are analysed, their referential elements are correlated with things.

However, these things will be complex, and

> A complex can be given only by its description, which will be right or wrong. A proposition that mentions a complex will not be nonsensical, if the complex does not exist, but simply false.
> When a propositional element signifies a complex, this can be seen from an indeterminateness in the propositions in which it occurs. . . . [49]

So if *a* is complex, the correlation of the word '*a*' with it is only a provisional and makeshift arrangement, typical of ordinary language.

---

[47] *TLP* 3.1431. Cf. *NB* 29 Sept. 1914: 'In the proposition a world is as it were put together experimentally. (As when in the lawcourt in Paris a motor-car accident is represented by means of dolls, etc.)'

[48] Ibid., 4.012.

[49] *TLP* 3.24, second paragraph and the beginning of the third paragraph.

The appropriate way to signify a complex is to give its analytic description, which in the example used earlier was '*b-in-the-relation-R-to-c*'. Of course, it would be tedious to refer to complexes in such an elaborate way in daily life and so we use a word like '*a*' instead:

> The contraction of a symbol for a complex into a simple symbol can be expressed by a definition.[50]

That is how the principle of representation comes to be applied to sentences before they are analysed, in spite of the fact that its primary application is to elementary sentences.

What is not so easy to understand is the way in which the two applications of the principle of representation work in Wittgenstein's reductive argument. The difficulty begins when we ask how ordinary factual sentences, like 'The watch is on the table' or 'The broom is in the corner', are supposed to get their senses. Wittgenstein evidently accepts the obvious fact that they get them in a provisional and makeshift way in daily life, because we simply attach the referential sign '*a*' to the complex thing. Now this seems to make the sense of '*φa*' depend on the truth of '*bRc*', e.g. it seems to make the sense of 'The broom is in the corner' depend on the truth of 'The brush is attached to the broomstick'. However, he explicitly says that 'A proposition which mentions a complex will not be nonsensical if the complex does not exist, but simply false.'[51] That shows that he accepts Russell's theory of definite descriptions, according to which 'The King of France is bald' is false if there is no such person.[52] So his argument, interpreted in the way proposed here, appears to be incoherent. What is more, the apparent incoherence occurs at its cardinal point: the

---

[50] *TLP* 3.24, last paragraph. Cf. *NB* 5 Sept. 1914: '*φ*(a), · *φ*(b), · aRb = Def*φ*[aRb]', cf. also *PI* I § 60, where the sentence 'The broom is in the corner' is analysed into 'The broomstick is fixed in the brush and the brush and the broomstick are in the corner.' Cf. *TLP* 2.0201 and *Notes on Logic*, p. 99. The convenience of definitional contractions is mentioned in *Prototractatus*, 3.2021 11 and in *TLP* 4.002.

[51] *TLP* 3.24, quoted above, p. 76.

[52] The connection with Russell's theory is not quite so straightforward as it looks. There are two reasons for this. First, Russell's analysis uses quantification and variables, whereas Wittgenstein's uses names, as in '*bRc*'. However, Wittgenstein certainly allows for the possibility that someone might be unable to use names when he moved down to the next level of analysis. See *NB* 17 June 1915: 'If generalizations occur, then the forms of the particular cases must be manifest . . .'. E.g. someone might know that measles is caused by a virus without being able to identify the culprit. The second reason why it is none too easy to appreciate the connection with Russell's theory is that in his popular expositions of the theory, Russell quantifies over things at the same level but, when he uses the theory in logical analysis he quantifies over things at the next level down, namely sense-data.

dependence of the sense of 'φa' on the truth of 'bRc' is irreconcilable with his claim that 'bRc' is really part of the analysis of 'φa', and so gives a truth-condition of 'φa' and not a sense-condition.

It would be implausible to credit anyone with the ability to make such a gross mistake at the central point of a short argument. So either the interpretation of Wittgenstein's argument that is being defended here must be abandoned, or else it must be shown that the apparent incoherence is not really there.[53]

This can in fact be shown. The illusion of incoherence begins when we tell ourselves that the rough and ready attachment of 'a' to the complex thing a makes the sense of 'φa' depend on the truth of 'bRc'. That is not so. Wittgenstein can allow for the attachment of 'a' to the complex without conceding that it makes the sense of 'φa' depend on the truth of 'bRc'. He merely has to point out that 'φa' need not have packed up its sense in this rough and ready way, and so its sense does not require the existence of the complex and, therefore, does not depend on the truth of 'bRc'. The existence of the complex simply gave 'φa' a short cut to its sense, which really depends on the existence of the simple objects mentioned in its complete analysis.

Then what, if anything, *would* make the sense of 'φa' depend on the truth of 'bRc'? Here we have to remind ourselves that Wittgenstein's argument is reductive and his fourth premiss, 'All things are complex', is the one that he is trying to reduce to absurdity. This gives us the answer to our question. *If* all things really were complex, then, whatever the level of analysis at which 'φa' acquired its sense, it would always be necessary for certain sentences to be true at the next level down, namely those that analysed the complexity of the things exploited by 'φa' when it acquired its sense by a short cut. So this dependence of sense on truth is only a consequence of the hypothesis which Wittgenstein is trying to reduce to absurdity. It is, therefore, not surprising that it cannot be reconciled with his own view of the matter, and this irreconcilability can hardly be used against the interpretation of his argument that is being defended here. Indeed, it would be worrying if the two views were reconcilable.

[53] The interpretation proposed here is, or was, fairly generally accepted, and it can be found, in one form or another, in G. E. M. Anscombe: *Introduction to Wittgenstein's Tractatus*, Hutchinson, 1959, M. Black: *A Companion to Wittgenstein's Tractatus*, Cambridge, 1964, and A. Kenny: *Wittgenstein*. H. Ishiguro, op. cit., pp. 42–4 argues that the apparent incoherence is real, and that the interpretation proposed here must be rejected.

If we now take a closer look at Wittgenstein's third premiss, we shall be able to see even more clearly why logical analysis in the *Tractatus* crosses the line into the unknown. His third premiss is the postulate of definiteness of sense: 'The requirement that simple signs be possible is the requirement that sense be determinate.'[54] This postulate was criticized in *Philosophical Investigations* after it had been abandoned.[55] When it was in force, it seemed to give a clear and compelling view of what lay on the far side of the line at which Russell's kind of logical analysis terminated. Everything that was sayable in the total demand made by a sentence on the world would be set out clearly in its complete analysis. Until that point was reached, the analysis would be driven forward not by the need for scientific micro-explanation, but by the need for logical micro-explanation. The idea was that if we set out to define everything definable, we would be following a track that led to indefinable words representing simple objects. These logical atoms would provide the true explanation of the existence of factual discourse. If we do not push the cutting edge of definition forwards to the limit, we will get a sort of explanation, but it will be makeshift and provisional, because sense will reach beyond it.

Although the general line of thought is clear enough, Wittgenstein's exposition is very compressed and not obviously coherent. On the one hand, he maintains that ordinary factual sentences have definite senses. He says this briefly in the remark already quoted, and at greater length later:

If we know on purely logical grounds that there must be elementary propositions, then everyone who understands propositions in their un-analysed form must know it.

In fact, all the propositions of our everyday language, just as they stand, are in perfect logical order. That utterly simple thing, which we have to formulate here, is not an image of the truth, but the truth itself in its entirety.[56]

When the definite sense of an ordinary factual sentence is given in elementary sentences, that is not an ideal sense to which the sentence aspires but its actual sense. So he continues:

(Our problems are not abstract, but perhaps the most concrete that there are.)[57]

---

[54] *TLP* 3.23. Cf. *NB* 18 June 1915, quoted above, n. 41.
[55] *PI* I §§ 60–71. See above, n. 43.
[56] *TLP* 5.5562–5.5563, first paragraph. The translation has been changed slightly.
[57] *TLP* 5.5563, last paragraph.

On the other hand,

> When a propositional element signifies a complex, this can be seen from an indeterminateness in the propositions in which it occurs. In such cases we *know* that the proposition leaves something undetermined. (In fact the notation for generality *contains* a proto-type.)[58]

A prototype is an expression composed wholly of variables like 'ξx'.[59] So what he is saying here seems to be that sense need not be determinate. How can he have it both ways?

There is not much room to manœuvre at this point. He can hardly have contradicted himself in the space of a few lines, and there seem to be only two other possibilities. Either he must be allowing that some elementary propositions contain quantification and variables instead of names, or else, if he is ruling that out, the point that he is making must be that there is an indeterminateness in the *expression* of a proposition mentioning a complex but not in its sense.

There cannot really be any doubt that the second interpretation is the correct one. It invokes a contrast between determinate sense and indeterminate expression of sense which perfectly explains the sequence of his thoughts in 3.23 and 3.24. We might complain that the contrast is not drawn in very perspicuous terms, but he does say that we can see from a certain indeterminateness in the propositions that a complex is signified, and that does suggest that the indeterminateness is in the signs.[60] His idea is that the details of the determinate sense of a proposition about a complex are contracted into a single word or phrase like 'The broom', and that this makes the expression of the proposition indeterminate in another, quite different way: it is vague.[61] This interpretation is corroborated by the final parenthesis of 3.24, which alludes to the predicament of someone who is not in a position

---

[58] This is the third paragraph of *TLP* 3.24, part of which was quoted above, p. 76. The fact that it follows so closely on the postulate of definiteness of sense in 3.23 is striking.

[59] See *TLP* 3.315.

[60] See *TLP* 3.12: '. . . a proposition is a propositional sign in its projective relation to the world.' Cf. 3.32.

[61] i.e. it is a vague expression *of its own sense*. This is not the usual criterion of vagueness. It is usually in relation to the facts that a statement is judged to be vague. Wittgenstein mentions that possibility *NB* 16 June 1915, paragraph 11: 'So a proposition may indeed be an incomplete picture of a certain fact, but it is ALWAYS *a complete picture*.' Cf. *TLP* 5.156. A proposition always has a complete or determinate sense, but it may not do justice to the facts, and—a different possibility—its expression may not do justice to its sense.

to use names at the next level of analysis, and so is reduced to using quantification and variables.[62]

The alternative interpretation, according to which he is allowing that some elementary propositions contain quantification and variables instead of names, faces two objections. First, it makes it almost impossible to explain the sequence of his thoughts in 3.23 and 3.24. Can he really be alluding to another way in which the determinate sense of a sentence might be set out at the level of complete analysis? Second, even if it had been appropriate to mention another kind of complete analysis at this point, had he believed in it, he could not have believed in it, because it would contradict his explicit and frequently emphasized doctrine, that all factual sentences are analysable into elementary sentences consisting of names.[63]

However, there is one remark in the *Tractatus* which might seem to support the suggestion that he envisaged a second kind of elementary sentence, containing quantification and variables:

We can describe the world completely by means of fully generalized propositions, i.e. without first correlating any name with a particular object.

Then, in order to arrive at the customary mode of expression, we simply need to add, after an expression like, 'There is one and only one x such that ...', the words, 'and that x is a'.[64]

But the fully generalized propositions are not logically equivalent to the propositions containing names and the sentence that is added, 'This x is a' says something which might not have been the case. So we cannot argue that, if the propositions in 'the customary mode' are elementary, then the fully generalized propositions will be elementary too. It would be better to assume that the fully generalized propositions belong to the penultimate level of analysis.[65] Certainly there is nothing in this passage that goes against that assumption.

---

[62] Like the doctor who knows that measles is caused by a virus which he has not yet identified. See above, p. 69.

[63] See *TLP* 3.2–3.203 and 3.25–3.261.

[64] *TLP* 5.526. This remark is interpreted in a different way by H. Ishiguro, op. cit. She does not argue that it shows that Wittgenstein envisages a second kind of elementary proposition containing quantification and variables. She argues that it is the so-called 'penultimate stage' that contains quantification and variables, and that what the remark shows is that the business of logical analysis is completed at that stage, and that the substitution of names for bound variables at the next stage adds nothing. Her view, much of which is shared by B. McGuinness, (op. cit.), will be examined in Ch. 5.

[65] See above, pp. 68–9 and n. 52.

However, this does involve a complication. Although such a fully generalized proposition will belong to the penultimate level of analysis, it will not actually be a stage in the analysis. This is easily seen. Suppose that, contrary to what was assumed earlier, [66] the sentence '*bRc*' had not belonged to the final level of complete analysis. Then '*bRc · φb · φc*' would be a stage in the analysis of 'The broom is in the corner', because these two sentences and the complete analysis would all be logically equivalent to one another. But, if we delete the names in '*bRc*' and use quantification and variables, what we get will not be a stage in the analysis but something non-equivalent on a sideline that leads no further. [67]

That completes the review of the premises of Wittgenstein's reductive argument for his extreme version of logical atomism. Most of the emphasis has been on the long reach that it ascribes to the senses of factual sentences. But the theory also has another equally striking feature, its separatism. It isolates each factual sentence and looks for the roots of its sense in its own patch of reality. The two features are connected in a way that has already been explained: [68] if two things produce a logical connection between two sentences in which they are named, the connection is taken to be rooted in their natures, and it is assumed that further analysis will unearth something which is included in the nature of one of them, but excluded from the nature of the other. These assumptions drive the analysis forwards until it reaches a level at which every sentence will be logically independent of every other sentence. That is the connection between far-reaching sense and the logical independence of elementary sentences, each of which is supposed to be linked to its own bit of reality.

The examples used earlier to illustrate this separatism were colours. In the *Tractatus* the logical impossibility of attributing two colours, like red and green, to the same physical point was taken to indicate that further analysis was needed. [69] The idea was that the sentence 'This is red' would be discovered to require the presence of something whose absence was required by 'This is green'. Or to put

---

[66] See above, pp. 71–2.

[67] Wittgenstein never worked out exactly how the logical analysis of the *Tractatus* would get from ordinary factual propositions to elementary propositions consisting of names. So the suggestion, that formulae containing quantification and variables do not lie on the main line of analysis is conjectural.

[68] See above, pp. 67 and 72–3.

[69] *TLP* 6.3751.

the point entirely in terms of sentences, it would turn out that there was some sentence *p* which 'This is red' required to be true, while 'This is green' required it to be false.

The example is important for several reasons. First, it is the only case mentioned in the *Notebooks* or the *Tractatus* which shows us clearly why Wittgenstein believed that analysis must continue until it reaches sentences that are logically independent of one another. It is, of course, a case of two contrary qualities in the same range. It might also be possible to illustrate his account of analysis with an example of two complex particulars which produced a logical connection between two sentences in which they are named, but it is not so easy to think of an example of this kind. Two brooms *a* and *b* cannot both occupy the same space, but that is not something to be explained by an analysis of their individual natures: the explanation is to be found in their common nature as solid objects. Perhaps a closer analogue would be two brooms composed of one handle and two brushes, so that they could not both exist at the same time. The example has to be far-fetched, because particulars do not lend themselves to this sort of thing. But qualities readily generate incompatibilities of this kind, and so they reveal more clearly the driving force behind the logical analysis of the *Tractatus*.

Another reason why this much discussed example is so important is that it is one of the points at which Wittgenstein began to change his mind in 1929. When he started to work out the implications of the logical atomism of the *Tractatus*, he soon realized that they were unacceptable. So he retraced his steps and modified the two linked features of his early theory of language, far-reaching sense and separatism.

There are several texts which explain in detail why he changed his mind.[70] The fundamental reason was that colours, velocities, electrical charges, temperatures, and pressures[71] all exhibit variations on a scale on which one degree is intrinsically incompatible with every other degree. When he wrote the *Tractatus* he realized that this is true of colours, but thought that they might be analysable in terms of the velocities of particles. However, if velocities exhibit the same pattern,

---

[70] L. Wittgenstein: *Some Remarks on Logical Form*, *PR* § 8 and p. 317, and L. Wittgenstein: *The Big Typescript* (item 213 in G. H. von Wright's list, *Philosophical Review*, Vol. 78, October, 1969, Special Supplement; see A. Kenny, 'From *The Big Typescript* to the *Philosophical Grammar*', in *Essays in Honour of G. H. von Wright*, ed. J. Hintikka, *Acta Philosophica Fennica*, Vol. 28, Nos. 1-3, 1976), pp. 473–85.
[71] This list is given in *PR* § 81.

and, more generally, if nearly all qualities and relations belong to ranges of intrinsically incompatible specifications, there was really no hope of analysing ordinary factual sentences into the logically independent elementary sentences of the *Tractatus*. Why, then, had he been so confident that such an analysis could be carried out? He says that he had relied on his a priori argument for his extreme version of logical atomism and expected the details to be discovered later.[72] In particular, he says that he had assumed that the ascription of a colour to a thing would be analysed as a conjunction in which one of the conjuncts would be the negation of the ascription of an incompatible colour; for example, 'This is red' would be analysed as the conjunction of some sentence p and 'This is not green'. This would have the same effect as the slightly less simple assumption attributed to him above,[73] that 'This is red' would be analysed as '$p \cdot q$', where q entails 'This is not green'.

But why had he made such an implausible assumption? That is the interesting question and his answer throws much more light on the logical atomism of the *Tractatus* than anything that he said at the time. He says that he was aware that an ascription of a certain degree n of a quality to a thing meant not only that it had at least n degrees of the quality, but also that it had no more than n degrees of it. But that in itself is enough to rule out any conjunctive analysis of the statement that the thing has n degrees of the quality, because '$p \cdot q$' does not mean '$p \cdot q \cdot nothing\ else$'. There is an implied completeness in the original statement which is lacking in the conjunction. In any case, the proposed analysis is in even worse trouble with the statement that the thing has at least n degrees of the quality. For mere conjunction cannot cope with the effect of adding one degree to another. This is easily seen if we suppose that 'Ba' ascribes one degree of brightness to a light. Then '$Ba \cdot Ba$' will still give it one degree, because the repetition will not signify addition.[74] If our reaction to this failure is to tag the letter 'B' with subscripts to indicate which degree of brightness

----

[72] As if this were science. See *LWVC* pp. 182–4.

[73] See above, p. 83.

[74] The reason why a conjunctive analysis cannot cope with addition is explained in the following way in *The Big Typescript*, pp. 473–85. Let 'Q_1r' ascribe one quantity of the colour red, and 'Q_2r' another greater quantity of it. Then there will be no contradiction between these two, if 'Q_1r' does not imply 'no more than Q_1r'. Now his idea in the *Tractatus* had been that 'Q_2r' must be a conjunction of 'Q_1r' and some other proposition, p. So p must ascribe the difference between Q_1 and Q_2. But what analysis of p will show how it manages to do that?

is meant—, first, second, or third, and so on—, we run into a worse difficulty. We write '$B_1a \cdot B_2a$' to indicate that the thing has two degrees of brightness, but now our conjunctive analysis no longer satisfies the obviously necessary condition of such analyses—that the conjuncts must have a sense when they occur on their own.[75]

This recantation shows very clearly what was wrong with the logical atomism of the *Tractatus*. It was a theory which crossed the line into the unknown, confident in the assumption that qualities and relations belonging to ranges of incompatible specifications could be analysed in terms of things which had not yet been identified. These things need not be altogether new or unfamiliar, and in the case of colours they might be degrees of saturation. The analysis would be conjunctive, and it would treat the degrees, or whatever played the same role, exactly like particulars. To use Wittgenstein's example,[76] the two sentences, 'The brush is in the corner' and 'The stick is in the corner' are logically independent of one another (given enough room in the corner), and they have senses when they occur on their own. This was his model for the things mentioned in each of the conjuncts in the analysis of an ascription of a colour, and it did not fit.[77] For though it is not implausible to imagine a level of analysis at which no particulars generate any logical connections between the sentences in which their names occur, it is impossible for qualities and relations to achieve this independence without a drastic impoverishment of language. He explains what had gone wrong and how he changed his mind in a conversation with Waismann in 1929:

I once wrote: 'A proposition is laid like a yardstick against reality. Only the outermost tips of the graduation marks touch the object to be measured.' I should now prefer to say: a *system of propositions* is laid like a yardstick against reality. What I mean by this is: when I lay a yardstick against a spatial object, I apply *all the graduation marks simultaneously*. It's not the individual graduation marks that are applied, it's the whole scale. If I know that the object reaches up to the tenth graduation mark, I know immediately that it doesn't reach the eleventh, twelfth, etc. The assertions telling me the length of an object form a

---

[75] So what he says in *Some Remarks on Logical Form* (p. 35) is: 'We assume two different units of brightness; and then, if an entity possesses one unit, the question could arise, which of the two . . . it is; which is obviously absurd.' Cf. *The Big Typescript* pp. 473–85, where this kind of conjunctive analysis of ascriptions of colours is criticized on the ground that the conjuncts do not have senses when they occur on their own.

[76] *PI* I § 60.

[77] See my 'The Logical Independence of Elementary Propositions'.

system, a system of propositions. It's such a whole system that is compared with reality, not a single proposition.[78]

He says that, when he wrote the *Tractatus*, he was on the verge of this discovery. For he compared names with co-ordinates fixing the senses of sentences,[79] and he mentioned the necessity that a visual object should possess one colour out of the range of possible colours,[80] but he did not take the next step and treat the colour itself as a co-ordinate with a range of possible values.

> In my old conception of an elementary proposition there was no determination of the value of a co-ordinate; although my remark that a coloured body is in a colour-space, should have put me straight on to this.
>
> A co-ordinate of reality may only be determined *once*.[81]

So logical analysis in the *Tractatus* remained atomistic and the decisive step towards the later holism came later.

However, here as elsewhere in Wittgenstein's philosophy, the subsequent development is foreshadowed in the early work. For the *Tractatus* does emphasize many holistic features of language; for example, the remarks about co-ordinates in 3.4 and 3.41, are immediately followed by this:

> A proposition can determine only one place in logical space: nevertheless, the whole of logical space must already be given by it.[82]

There are also several passages in the book which mention different kinds of systematic connection between propositions.[83] In fact, it would hardly be an exaggeration to say that the natural tendency of Wittgenstein's mind was towards holism, and that the atomism of the *Tractatus* was the consequence of his early preoccupation with logic and the influence of Russell. Anyway, his theory of logical analysis remained stubbornly separatist in his early work.

His 1929 recantation was a move in the direction of his later account of language, a small move, it is true, but a very significant one. The assumption behind his early theory was that all the logical properties of an ordinary factual sentence are the product of its far-reaching

---

[78] *PR* p. 317.

[79] *TLP* 3.4–3.411.

[80] *TLP* 2.013–2.0131.

[81] *PR* § 83.

[82] *TLP* 3.42. See Max Black's comments on this in his *Companion to Wittgenstein's Tractatus*, pp. 154–8.

[83] e.g. *TLP* 5.475, 5.555, and 6.341.

sense, and so logical analysis would simply forge ahead without looking to right or left, a kind of tunnel vision. His later account of language was based on the naturalistic assumption that the logical grammar of an ordinary sentence is a function of its place in a system whose features all lie on the surface. Consequently his later investigations are always lateral and they often rely on the description of miniature systems or language-games.

5

The Basic Realism of the Tractatus

IF the interpretation of the *Tractatus* proposed in the previous chapter is correct, Wittgenstein's early system is basically realistic. Any factual sentence can be completely analysed into elementary sentences which are logically independent of one another because they name simple objects. At that basic level all languages have the same structure, dictated by the structure of reality. True, different languages incorporate that structure in different ways, and so they exhibit considerable variation on the surface, but in the final analysis there are no options.[1] The superstructures vary, but the foundations are necessarily identical. Once a name has been attached to an object, the nature of the object takes over and controls the logical behaviour of the name, causing it to make sense in some sentential contexts but not in others.

This system, like Russell's, is the product of reflection on the attachment of language to the world, and it was certainly influenced by Russell's ideas. So the method of interpretation used in the previous chapter was to compare the two systems with one another, noting their similarities and their differences. The result, to summarize it vaguely, was that Wittgenstein's early system was placed somewhere on the middle ground between general acceptance of Russell's ideas and general rejection of them. Before this interpretation was defended, two others were mentioned, one minimizing, and the other maximizing his distance from Russell. According to the first extreme interpretation, the objects of the *Tractatus* are sense-data and their properties, while, according to the second one, they cannot be identified with any kind of independently specifiable thing, because Wittgenstein turned Russell's semantics upside down, and, instead of making elementary propositions depend on the objects named in them, made the objects named in them depend on the elementary propositions.[2]

These two extreme interpretations now need to be examined in some detail. Wittgenstein's version of logical atomism is elusive, and

[1] See above, pp. 10, and 24–5. Cf. *TLP* 6.124.   [2] See above, p. 65 and Ch. 4, n. 64.

even the essential features of the complete analyses envisaged in the *Tractatus* are controversial. The middle ground interpretation, which has so far been defended only on its intrinsic merits, would get further confirmation if its two main rivals could be shown to be mistaken. There is also another advantage in making an attempt to refute them: the basic realism of the *Tractatus* has not yet been completely characterized, and, though a lot of details have been extracted from Wittgenstein's argument for logical atomism, there are still some unanswered questions: for example, what kind of thing did he take objects to be? And did he really think that in the complete analysis of factual discourse they would be identified by name? If so, would the introduction of their names make it possible at that level to say things that could not have been said without them? Or would it be possible to use quantification and variables to express everything that could ever be said about objects? If their names really would add to the sayable, when they were introduced, what exactly would they add and how would they do it? Would they channel the essences of their objects into the senses of sentences? Or perhaps it is all the other way round— first the senses of sentences and then the identity of the objects named in them? These are fundamental questions of interpretation, because the answers given to them will determine how far back Wittgenstein started, and so how far he had to travel before he arrived at the position that he occupies in *Philosophical Investigations*.[3]

The question, 'What kind of thing did he take objects to be?'[4] is often made to appear simpler than it really is. Commentators usually ask whether he took them to be material points (point-masses) or sense-data. The *Notebooks*, which record exploratory work, canvas both possibilities, and in the *Tractatus*, where he might have been expected to make up his mind and choose between them, he does not do so, and does not even formulate the question to which of the two categories objects belong.[5] Now in the interpretation of his writings it is a golden rule to treat as peripheral the questions that he himself treats as peripheral. He always goes straight to the heart of any matter, as he sees it, and pushes inessential questions to one side. That is the wonderful thing about his philosophy, the characteristic stamp which it exhibited from the start and retained to the end. So it is tempting to

[3] See above, pp. 30–1 and 75.
[4] From now on his usage will be followed and 'object' will mean 'simple object', as it always does in *TLP*.
[5] See D. Keyt: 'A New Interpretation of the *Tractatus* Examined', *Philosophical Review*, Vol. 74 no. 2, 1965.

conclude in this case too that, since there is very little argument in the *Notebooks* about the merits of the two categorizations of objects and the *Tractatus* is entirely non-committal, he must have thought the question unimportant. His a priori argument for the existence of objects of some kind was what really mattered, and the question 'What kind?' could be postponed. Certainly, this is the attitude that he attributed to himself later, when he looked back at his early philosophy from his later standpoint.[6]

However, though this would not be the wrong conclusion to draw, it would be very misleading to leave it at that. For there are really more than two possible answers to the question 'What kind of thing did he take objects to be?' or, to get rid of the attribution of dogmatism, 'What kind of thing did he suppose that they might be?' If they were not material points it may have seemed to him possible that they should belong to the world as we find it[7] without being Russellian sense-data and their properties. This third possibility would fit very well into the Kantian framework of the *Tractatus*, which is an investigation of the relation between language and the phenomenal world.

It is, of course, a vaguely formulated possibility, but it is none the worse for that. Its advantage is that it does not draw on recondite scientific knowledge, and at the same time it avoids the identification of objects with the itemizable sensory packets offered by Russell. If Wittgenstein's logical atomism really was just like Russell's, it would follow that his objects were essentially private and it would be hard to believe that his treatment of solipsism in the *Tractatus* was not concerned with their privacy. It would also be difficult to understand why the problem of other minds, which this categorization of objects would obviously make unavoidable, was not posed by Wittgenstein until 1929.[8] How could the implications of privacy have remained dormant for so long?

At this point it will be useful to pick up some points that were made earlier. That will make it clear that it is, at least, possible to attribute to Wittgenstein the idea that objects might belong to the world as we non-scientists find it without being Russellian sense-data and their properties. In the previous chapter two things were said about the obstacles which stand in the way of reading the *Tractatus* as a treatise

---

[6] See above, p. 64 and p. 69.

[7] *TLP* 5.631.

[8] Russell alludes to this problem in 1917 in *The Philosophy of Logical Atomism* (pp. 195–6).

about the foundations of empirical knowledge. First, it was pointed out that Wittgenstein's criterion of simplicity was not an empiricist's criterion: he did not hold that a thing is simple if and only if acquaintance with it would have to be achieved by anyone who was going to learn the meaning of its name.[9] Second, he did not argue for his logical atomism empirically: that is, he did not argue that, if philosophers began to analyse an ordinary factual sentence stage by stage, they would soon reach a point where they would find that they could go no further.[10] However, these two negative points do not imply that he was not concerned with the foundations of empirical knowledge. They still leave it an open possibility that that was his concern in the *Tractatus*. True, his approach would be entirely different from Russell's: it would be an a priori deduction of the essential structure of empirical knowledge, in the style of Kant. Nevertheless, the *Tractatus* would still be about empirical knowledge and its main thesis would be that objects belong to the world as we find it.

Is that really so? Before the evidence is reviewed, it is necessary to eschew all preconceived opinions. The trouble is that this question has become a sectarian battleground in which the finer details have long since been trampled out of recognition. This unusual state of the subject has more than one cause. First, the *Tractatus* was published long before the *Notebooks*, and so people read it and puzzled over it for many years without any knowledge of its essential background.[11] Of course, *Philosophical Investigations* too stood for several years in magisterial isolation, and even now there are lacunae in the supporting works which give an exaggerated impression of its independence.[12] However, the public life of the *Tractatus* suffered from the handicap of isolation not only for a longer time but also more severely, because Wittgenstein was studiously agnostic about any features of objects that would make no difference to the occurrence of their names in logically independent elementary propositions. That left a vacuum which commentators felt obliged to fill with dogmatic interpretations, and so

---

[9] That was the criterion of forced acquaintance used by Russell. See above, pp. 63–4.

[10] That was Russell's argument, but he did not press it with much determination, because he admitted that there might be no such terminus. See above, Ch. 4 n. 16.

[11] *NB* appeared in 1961, forty years after *TLP*.

[12] See e.g. A. Kenny: From the '*Big Typescript* to the *Philosophical Grammar*', in *Essays on Wittgenstein in Honour of G. H. von Wright*, ed. J. Hintikka, in *Acta Philosophica Fennica*, Vol. 28 Nos. 1-3, 1976, pp. 41–3.

there was a proliferation of exegeses offering to unlock the secrets of the ontology of the *Tractatus*.

Some commentators simply took advantage of the vacuum to assimilate Wittgenstein's logical atomism to Russell's. That is hardly likely to be right, because the two systems are based on arguments so different from one another that their conclusions ought to differ too. However, it is not at all obvious what the differences are. So in their zeal to establish the distance between the two systems, commentators of the opposite school exaggerated it. The exaggeration came all the more easily to them because they saw the connections between Russell's *Philosophy of Logical Atomism* and the writings of another group of philosophers from which, they felt, for similar reasons, that the system of the *Tractatus* needed to be distanced as far as possible. This was the work done in the late 1920s and the 1930s by the philosophers of the Vienna Circle, many of whom claimed to be inspired by the *Tractatus* and actually to be developing its leading ideas. So the shortest way to dismiss an interpretation of Wittgenstein's early system was to label it 'empiricist', and it did not seem necessary to ask exactly what the word meant. The evidence does not provide support for either of these two opposed views.

Consider, first, the evidence for assimilating Wittgenstein's logical atomism to Russell's. It is true that on more than one occasion in 1929 and 1930 Wittgenstein said that he used to believe that there were two languages, 'the everyday language that we all usually spoke and a primary language that expressed what we really knew, namely phenomena'.[13] It is also true that in one of these passages he said that the phenomenological language was not about physical objects but about sense-data.[14] However, before we concluded that the objects of the *Tractatus* were Russellian sense-data, we would have to establish two further premises: first, that in these passages, he really was referring to the *Tractatus*, and, second, that he was implying that his view of phenomena had been the same as Russell's.

The first of these two premises is rejected both by the editor of *Philosophical Remarks*[15] and by the editor of *Ludwig Wittgenstein and the*

---

[13] *LWVC* p. 45. This is taken from a conversation dated 22 Dec. 1929. Cf. *PR* §§ 1, 11, 47, and 57.

[14] *PR* § 57.

[15] R. Rhees, who suggests that Wittgenstein's remarks about phenomenological language may refer to an 'earlier view' which he had expressed in his paper *Some Remarks on Logical Form* (*PR* p. 349).

Vienna Circle.[16] Now they may be right in suggesting that Wittgenstein did not *develop* the identification of the objects of the *Tractatus* with sense-data until 1929, but it is surely beyond belief that he did not consider it a *possibility* when he put the book together. The moderate hypothesis that he believed the identification to be a possible one, is supported by a lot of evidence not only in the *Notebooks* and the *Tractatus* itself,[17] but also in the criticisms of the *Tractatus* that he made in the very period in which he wrote most extensively about his former belief in a phenomenological language.[18] Now though this moderate hypothesis does not amount to very much, it is the furthest point to which the assimilation of Wittgenstein's logical atomism to Russell's could possibly be pushed. For nothing that Wittgenstein said later about the *Tractatus* could count against the evident fact that the possibility of a different identification of objects, with material points, was also discussed in the *Notebooks*, alluded to in the *Tractatus*, and rejected in neither. In any case, his later admissions, that he had not claimed to know what objects were like, obviously rule out any dogmatic characterization of them at the time when he compiled the *Tractatus*.

The second questionable premiss required by those who assimilate the logical atomism of the *Tractatus* to Russell's version of the theory is that the word 'phenomena' was being used by Wittgenstein in 1929 to mean Russellian sense-data. This is not sufficiently supported by the textual evidence. It is true that in an early passage in *Philosophical*

---

[16] B. McGuinness, who says, 'Here Wittgenstein no doubt refers to earlier manuscript volumes in which some of the *Philosophical Remarks* may have occurred for the first time' (*LWVC* p. 45 n. 8).

[17] See above, n. 5.

[18] 1929–30. These criticisms simply take it for granted that the *Tractatus* had exaggerated the potential of the truth-functional analysis of phenomenal qualities. See above, pp. 82–7. Now phenomenal qualities need not be taken to be qualities of Russellian sense-data. However, there is a later discussion of the *Tractatus* in which he says: 'Formerly I myself spoke of a "complete analysis", and I used to believe that philosophy had to give a definitive dissection of propositions, so as to set out clearly all their connections and remove all possibilities of misunderstanding. I spoke as if there was a calculus in which such a dissection would be possible. I vaguely had in mind something like the definition that Russell had given for the definite article, and I used to think that in a similar way one would be able to use visual impressions, etc. to define the concept, say, of a sphere . . .' L. Wittgenstein: *Philosophical Grammar*, ed. R. Rhees, tr. A. Kenny, Blackwell, 1974 (henceforth *PG*), (p. 211). It is true that this was written later, probably in 1936, but it comes from a passage in which he is explicitly criticizing the *Tractatus*. If there were not such strong evidence on the other side, it would be hard to resist the conclusion that he had unequivocally identified the objects of the *Tractatus* with sense-data.

Remarks in which he is discussing his former views he says that phenomenological language is not about physical objects but about sense-data.[19] But the implication, that sense-data are private, is not developed, and nothing is said about the problem of other minds. So it is more plausible to take him to be saying that the *Tractatus* was concerned with phenomena in the Kantian sense of the word, or, to put it in the terminology of Schopenhauer, it was concerned with the world as idea.[20] This is, of course, the empirical world and it floats in a space of possibilities which extends to the limits of the scope of factual discourse. It is the world as we find it, and in the discussion of solipsism it is not presented as a world of Russellian sense-data:

> If I wrote a book called *The World as I found it*, I should have to include a report on my body, and should have to say which parts were subordinate to my will, and which were not, etc. . . .[21]

This is the world as idea and, though it is the phenomenal world, here, at least, he is evidently not treating it as a world of mental sense-data.

Solipsism is introduced for a reason which was explained in Chapter 3: if language is limited, one question that obviously needs to be asked about it is whether I could draw its limits in a personal way.[22] This does not mean 'Could I use my own sense-data as the baseline for drawing the limits of language?' It means 'Could I draw them using my ego as the point of origin?' If I could do this, 'empirical reality', which is limited by 'the totality of objects',[23] would be personally restricted, because they would be the objects presented to my ego. However, that is a restriction which turns out to be impossible.

It does not amount to very much to say that the world as idea is the empirical world. But it does gain a little more substance if we ask what is being *denied* by a philosopher who calls it 'empirical'. In Wittgenstein's case the answer is that he is denying that there is a world of things-in-themselves beyond phenomena, and not denying that phenomena are more than sequences of sense-data. To put the point

---

[19] *PR* § 57.

[20] Or if *TLP* could be read as an attempt to found language on sense-data, that would only be because sense-data and physical objects are not rivals. See *Wittgenstein's Lectures, Cambridge 1930–32*, ed. D. Lee, Blackwell, 1980 (henceforth *CLI*), p. 68: 'There is no need of a theory to reconcile what we know about sense-data and what we believe about physical objects, because part of what we mean by saying that a penny is round is that we see it as elliptical in such and such conditions.' Cf. ibid., pp. 81–2.

[21] *TLP* 5.631.

[22] See above, pp. 38–9.

[23] *TLP* 5.5561.

in another way, he is writing in the tradition of Kant and Schopenhauer and not in the tradition of Locke and Berkeley. It is, therefore, not surprising that he sometimes borrows the terminology of Russell's theory of perception[24] without even raising the problem of privacy. What interests him at this stage is the relation between language and the one and only phenomenal world.

His Kantian orientation is conspicuous in the *Tractatus*, but it can also be discerned in some of the work that he did in 1929–30. There is a particularly clear example near the beginning of *Philosophical Remarks*:

That it doesn't strike us at all when we look around us, move about in space, feel our own bodies, etc. etc., shows how natural these things are to us. We do not notice that we see space perspectively or that our visual field is in some sense blurred towards the edges. It doesn't strike us and never can strike us because it is *the* way we perceive. We never give it a thought and it's impossible we should, since there is nothing that contrasts with the form of our world.

What I wanted to say is it's strange that those who ascribe reality only to things and not to our ideas move about so unquestioningly in the world as idea and never long to escape from it.

In other words, how much of a matter of course the given is. It would be the very devil if this were a tiny picture taken from an oblique, distorting angle.

This which we take as a matter of course, *life*,[25] is supposed to be something accidental, subordinate; while something that normally never comes into my head, reality!

That is, what we neither can nor want to go beyond would not be the world.

Time and again the attempt is made to use language to limit the world and set it in relief—but it can't be done. The self-evidence of the world expresses itself in the very fact that language can and does only refer to it.

For since language only derives the way in which it means from its meaning, from the world, no language is conceivable which does not represent this world.[26]

This passage expresses a rejection of things-in-themselves beyond the phenomena and not a denial that the phenomena possess the objectivity which Kant and Schopenhauer attributed to them.

The point that is being made here must not be exaggerated. It is not that Wittgenstein's standpoint in the *Tractatus* made it unnecessary for

[24] E.g. *NB* 6 May 1915 and *TLP* 2.0131.
[25] Cf. *TLP* 5.621: 'The world and life are one', discussed below, p. 174.
[26] *PR* § 47.

him to distinguish sense-data from objective phenomena, or unnecessary for him to ask for the criteria of identity of sense-data and to
raise the question of their privacy. The point is only that his Kantianism kept all these problems in abeyance while he dealt with the
general question of the relation between language and the one and
only phenomenal world.[27]

This explains something which would otherwise be very puzzling.
As already mentioned, he canvasses two specifications of objects in
the *Notebooks*, material points and sense-data, and he does not choose
between them in the *Tractatus*. This would scarcely be intelligible in a
philosopher preoccupied with the problems of Locke and Berkeley, as
Russell was. But Wittgenstein's early Kantianism explains the wide
tolerance of his indifference. However, it was inevitable that the
claims of sense-data would make themselves increasingly felt. After
all, he was familiar with Mach's work[28] as well as with Russell's. So,
when he looked back on his early writings from the point that he had
reached in 1929 and 1930, he came near to implying that the objects of
the *Tractatus* had been sense-data. But he did not go all the way. For
though he sometimes used sense-data and their properties as
examples when he was explaining his early system,[29] he still did not
raise the question of their criteria of identity or pose the problem of
their privacy. His slow progress towards the crisis which was
eventually produced by these difficulties would be unintelligible if his
starting-point had not been Kantian.

It is imprecise to say that he came near to implying that the objects of
the *Tractatus* had been sense-data, and something more needs to be
said about his terminology. The trouble is that there is a certain
ambiguity in the phrase 'phenomenological language' as he uses it. Its
basic meaning is 'language concerned with phenomena', and the main
endeavour of the *Tractatus* was to show how ordinary factual language
might be analysed in a way that would perfectly reflect the nature of
phenomena.[30] The language in which this analysis was expressed
would not be an ideal alternative to everyday factual language, but an
ideal actually realized by it.[31] At the beginning of *Philosophical Remarks*

---

[27] This is really the most fundamental mistake that he made in his early work. He
ought not to have postponed the consideration of all these problems. See below, p. 194;
Cf. *LWVC* pp. 182–4.

[28] E. Mach: *Die Analyse de Empfindungen*, 2nd edn., Jena, 1900.

[29] See *CLI* p. 120.

[30] See *TLP* 6.124.

[31] See *TLP* 5.5563.

he calls this language 'phenomenological' and he says that he no longer believes it necessary to discover it. He is evidently not concerned with the special problem of private sense-data. His point is that he now thinks that he can separate what is essential from what is inessential in ordinary language without extracting from ordinary language the perfect mirror which he formerly took to be hidden deep within it. The further element in the meaning of the phrase 'phenomenological language', the implication that it would be about private sense-data, is still latent.

The passage is worth quoting because it expresses his change of view very clearly, and it does so without mentioning sense-data:

> I do not now have phenomenological language, or 'primary language' as I used to call it, in mind as my goal. I no longer hold it to be necessary. All that is possible and necessary is to separate what is essential from what is inessential in *our* language.
>
> That is, if we so to speak describe the class of languages which serve their purpose, then in doing so we have shown what is essential to them and given an immediate representation of immediate experience.
>
> Each time I say that, instead of such and such a representation, you could also use this other one, we take a further step towards the goal of grasping the essence of what is represented.
>
> A recognition of what is essential and what inessential in our language if it is to represent, a recoginition of which parts of our language are wheels turning idly, amounts to the construction of a phenomenological language.
>
> Physics differs from phenomenology in that it is concerned to establish laws. Phenomenology only establishes the possibilities. Thus, phenomenology would be the grammar of the description of those facts on which physics build its theories.[32]

Here the emphasis is on the basic meaning of the word 'phenomenological'. Phenomenology penetrates to the essential nature of the world as we experience it and describes the underlying possibilities. So its task is exactly the same as the task assigned to logic in the *Tractatus*,[33] and it is equated with grammar in the 'The Big Typescript'[34] and in many other texts.[35] What Wittgenstein is retracting in

---

[32] *PR* § 1. This should be compared with *TLP* 4.5, 5.472, and 6.124.

[33] See *TLP* 2.0121, third paragraph: '(Nothing in the province of logic can be merely possible. Logic deals with every possibility and all possibilities are its facts)'.

[34] See *The Big Typescript*, pp. 437–40.

[35] Especially in L. Wittgenstein: *Remarks on Colour*, ed. G. E. M. Anscombe, tr. L. McAlister and M. Schattle, Blackwell, 1977, which is not a work in which Wittgenstein subscribes to a sense-datum theory of perception.

the quoted passage is a certain view about the results to be attained by such an investigation: he used to think that they would be expressed in a unique way, the complete analysis of factual discourse which would hold up a mirror to the one and only phenomenal world,[36] but he now thinks that what is needed is a comparative study of different ways of speaking with the same function.

Is there a suggestion that he is also giving up the idea that the results of a philosophical investigation of factual language would be expressed in sense-datum language? If there is such a suggestion in this passage, it is faint and recessive, and the reason for this is clear: he still feels as he felt earlier when he wrote the *Tractatus*, that the precise categorization of the phenomena is not important. It is true that in another passage in *Philosophical Remarks*[37] he says that phenomenological language is about sense-data, but the crisis produced by all the problems of sense-data—their criteria of identity and their privacy—still lay in the future.[38]

This discussion of the first of the two extreme interpretations of Wittgenstein's logical atomism can be summarized briefly. The identification of the objects of the *Tractatus* with Russellian sense-data is a mistake, because at this time Wittgenstein kept open the possibility of identifying them with material points. There is really no reason to discount his later admission that he did not know what kinds of things objects would turn out to be. In any case, it is too blunt to ask whether they were or were not sense-data. What we need to do is to distinguish between two elements in the meaning of the word 'phenomenological'. A 'phenomenological language', in Wittgenstein's usage, is always a language for describing the world as we find it; or, to put the point in Kantian terms, it is a language for describing phenomena rather than things in themselves; or, in Schopenhauer-esque terminology, it is a language for describing the world as idea. The further implication, that a phenomenological language deals with private sense-data, remained in the background, to cause trouble

[36] See *TLP* 5.511, 6.13, and 6.124.

[37] *PR* § 57.

[38] Russell treats sense-data as private objects (see *The Philosophy of Logical Atomism*, pp. 195–6), in spite of sometimes equating them with physical events in the peripheral nervous system (see *The Relation of Sense-data to Physics*, § IV, in *Philosophical Essays*, Longmans, 1910); but he seems not to have found their privacy worrying, perhaps because his theory of communication was like the one later adopted by Carnap and Schlick (see Carnap: *The Unity of Science*, pp. 76ff, and Schlick: *Meaning and Verification*, § V. See above, Ch. 3 n. 21). Certainly, Russell did not think that their criteria of identity are problematical.

later. Wittgenstein's 1929 recantations of his earlier phenomenological project were not concerned with the special problems of private sense-data. What he was recanting in 1929 was the idea of a unique language, perfectly mirroring the essential nature of phenomena and providing the complete analysis of ordinary factual discourse. This recantation is an important step towards his later philosophy, but the crisis of sense-data did not occur until later. Before that point was reached, the precise categorization of the phenomena did not seem to him to be important. True, there was a move away from material points towards sense-data, a move which can be seen very clearly in the work that he did in 1929 and 1930, but there was no hint of the difficulties that lay ahead.

We must now cross the middle ground covered in the previous chapter and look at the interpretation which lies at the opposite extreme, according to which the objects of the *Tractatus* cannot be identified with any kind of independently specifiable thing. This suggestion maximizes the distance between Wittgenstein's logical atomism and Russell's, because it implies that Wittgenstein turned Russell's semantics upside down, and, instead of making elementary propositions depend on the objects named in them, made the objects named in them depend on the elementary propositions. H. Ishiguro and B. McGuinness,[39] who develop this interpretation, both base it on a cryptic remark in the *Tractatus*:

Only propositions have sense: only in the context of a proposition does a name have meaning.[40]

They both take this remark to mean that the object designated by a name depends on the propositions in which the name occurs.

[39] H. Ishiguro: 'The Use and Reference of Names', and B. McGuinness: 'The So-called Realism of Wittgenstein's *Tractatus*. See ch. 4 n. 8.

[40] *TLP* 3.3. 'Meaning' is the translation of 'Bedeutung'. See ch. 4 n. 43. The meaning of a name is its reference. The remark echoes Frege's dictum: 'Only in a proposition have the words really a meaning (reference)'. (*Foundations of Arithmetic* §§ 60 and 62.) Frege argues that numerals acquire their references from the propositional contexts in which their insertion makes sense, and not from any perceptual encounter with numbers. This opens up the possibility, exploited by Ishiguro and McGuinness, that Wittgenstein is making the same point about names of objects. But there are, of course, other possibilities. The second of the two suggestions distinguished below, that in the *Tractatus* the reference of a name depends on the propositional contexts in which its insertion yields a truth, is a long way from Frege's idea. The interpretation of Wittgenstein's remark proposed above, pp. 75-6, keeps it much closer to Frege's dictum and justifies the echo.

There are, in fact, two different ways in which the reference of a name might depend on the propositions in which it occurs. It might depend on which propositional contexts make sense when the name is inserted in them, or it might depend on which propositional contexts achieve truth when it is inserted in them. The first of these two suggestions fits 3.3 better than the second. Ishiguro, as will appear in a moment, adopts both of them. They are not incompatible with one another, but it would be astonishing if Wittgenstein combined them in a single short sentence. It is certainly necessary to disentangle them from one another and to hold them apart for separate assessment.

The first suggestion, that the reference of a name is determined by the propositional contexts in which it makes sense, is evidently the more basic of the two, and the discussion should begin with it. It is strikingly paradoxical, because it seems to go against the principle of representation. If the 'possibility of propositions is based on the principle that objects have signs as their representatives',[41] how can the identity of the objects represented by those signs depend on the senses of the propositions in which they occur? That is the question that has to be answered by those who make the first suggestion.

There is, however, an answer to it which, at least, reduces the sting in its implication that, on this interpretation, you could not establish the sense of a proposition before the references of its names or their references before its sense, and so language could never get off the ground. The answer is that, though the complete analysis of a factual sentence consists of names in immediate combination with one another,[42] the actual work of analysis is finished at the penultimate level, where there are no names but only quantifiers and variables. To put the point in another way, all the business of analysis is expressed in Quinese, and the final step, which translates the result into Russellian, is purely decorative.[43] Or, to put it in the terms used by Ishiguro and endorsed by McGuinness, the names of the *Tractatus* are dummy names, because they do not serve to distinguish one object from another, but only to designate objects which have already been distinguished from one another by the propositional contexts supplied by the penultimate level of analaysis in which their names can be inserted.[44] These propositional contexts contain predicative expres-

[41] Ibid,. 4.0312. See above, p. 73.

[42] See *TLP* 4.22.

[43] Quinese contains quantification and variables while Russellian contains names.

[44] Ishiguro, op. cit., pp. 45–7 and McGuinness, op. cit., p. 65. If these are sense-preserving insertions, this will only be the first step towards determining the references

sions which can be understood without acquaintance with particulars designated by Russellian proper names, and this makes it possible for language to get off the ground.

This answer raises a further question. How on this interpretation did Wittgenstein think that the predicative expressions constituting the propositional contexts got *their* meanings? But that question may be postponed for the moment, while we take a quick look at the second suggestion, that the references of names are fixed in a further way by the propositional contexts in which they produce truths. To this there is an obvious objection, that we cannot test for truth by placing a name in a propositional context unless the name already has a reference. However, Ishiguro has a ready answer: if the names that occur at the ultimate level of analysis envisaged in the *Tractatus* are all dummy names, there is no question of testing for truth until each name has had its reference fixed by the stipulation that in at least one specified propositional context its insertion produces a truth.[45] For example someone says, 'My next son will be Jonathan', and we do not wait to see whether this will turn out true, because we take him to be christening in advance.[46]

Before we go into any more details of this approach to the interpretation of Wittgenstein's early system, there are two general points that ought to be made in favour of it. First, the idea the *Tractatus* names are only dummy names seems to square very well with those passages in the *Notebooks* and the *Tractatus* in which Wittgenstein implies that 'signs signifying complexes' at the level of ordinary use will be analysed in Quinese at the next level down. The view taken of those passages in Chapter 4 was that Quinese would be used only by people who did not have enough knowledge to use Russellian, and this was illustrated by the case of the doctor who knew that measles was caused by a virus which he was not in a position to identify.[47] But the Ishiguro–McGuinness interpretation offers a simpler view of these

of names. It is obviously not sufficient by itself, because many different names with different references will make sense in the same propositional contexts.

[45] In support of this Ishiguro cites *TLP* 3.263 (op. cit. pp. 28–30 and 33). McGuinness dissociates himself from this part of her interpretation of the *Tractatus*, but it is not clear exactly what he puts in its place. Certainly, dummy names need to be tied down in some way that goes beyond finding out in what propositional contexts they make sense. See 'The So-called Realism of the *Tractatus*', p. 70.

[46] But this is not quite the kind of thing that Ishiguro means, because an advance christening could be followed by an ordinary christening in the priest's arms, but nothing like that can be done with a dummy name. See below, n. 91.

[47] See ch. 4 n. 52.

passages: Wittgenstein is just describing the ordinary course of logical analysis, because identification is always done by general specifications. These, then, are not cases of analysis handicapped by defective knowledge, but typical examples of completely successful analysis.

The second point in favour of this interpretation is that it takes seriously those passages in the *Tractatus* in which Wittgenstein seems to treat the use of names as primary and their meaning or reference as secondary. The most important one is, of course, 3.3 quoted on page 99. But there are others:

> In order to recognize a symbol by its sign we must observe how it is used with a sense.
>
> A sign does not determine a logical form unless it is taken together with its logico-syntactical employment.
>
> If a sign is *useless*, it is meaningless.[48] That is the point of Occam's maxim.
>
> (If everything behaves as if a sign has meaning, then it does have meaning.)[49]

The apparent implication, that use is primary and meaning or reference secondary, certainly seems to point forward to *Philosophical Investigations* and to distance the *Tractatus* from Russell's *Philosophy of Logical Atomism*.[50]

However, the message conveyed by these remarks may not be quite so extreme. It was pointed our earlier that there are really two interpretations of 3.3 which need to be considered before a conclusion is drawn.[51] They both start by rejecting Russell's view, that the attachment of names to objects is exactly like the tying of labels to luggage, an operation completed the moment that the knot is tied,[52] but they reject it in different ways. The first reaction against attributing this view to Wittgenstein is the Ishiguro–McGuinness interpretation, according to which the answer to the question 'To which object is this name attached?' depends on the propositions in which the name occurs.[53] But we need not go quite so far in our reaction against the Russellian interpretation, because there is a second possibility: a name may first be attached to an object in something like the way

---

[48] i.e. it lacks 'Bedeutung' or reference.
[49] *TLP* 3.326–3.328. Cf. 5.4733 and 6.53.
[50] See H. Ishiguro: 'Use and Reference of Names', pp. 20–1.
[51] See above, pp. 75–6.
[52] See Russell, *On the Nature of Acquaintance*, pp. 159–74.
[53] The natural interpretation of 3.3 on this view would be that it depends on the propositional contexts in which the name makes sense. See above, p. 100.

envisaged by Russell, but thereafter it will represent the object only so long as the possibilities presented by the propositions in which it occurs are real possibilities for that object. If 3.3 is taken in this way, it *qualifies* the direct attachment of names to objects but does not *replace* it with something completely different. The initial act of attachment is necessary for representation but not sufficient.

The emphasis put on the use of names in the *Tractatus* is enough to rule out the Russellian interpretation, leaving only its two rivals to be considered. Before we examine the evidence with a view to deciding between them, it is worth asking whether there are any general considerations that tell in favour of its second rival. It does, of course, take the middle road, but that does not count for much in the exegesis of a book like the *Tractatus*. But perhaps Wittgenstein's remarks about objects in the *Notebooks* and his later comments on the logical atomism of the *Tractatus* may be allowed to count in favour of the second alternative to the Russellian interpretation. Also, on a longer view of the development of his philosophy, the way in which his later ideas about meaning are presented in *Philosophical Investigations* may turn out to be another point in its favour. Let us see whether these things really are so.

It has already been observed that there are passages in the *Notebooks* in which Wittgenstein shows reluctance to push logical analysis to a point at which he is not yet able to identify the objects to which the ultimate names are attached.[54] But that never leads him to conclude that they are *in principle* identifiable only through the general specifications which it makes sense to say that they satisfy, or to conclude that they are *in principle* identifiable only through the general specifications that they actually satisfy. Temporary agnosticism is one thing[55] but unavailability for anything like a Russellian ceremony[56] of naming would be quite another thing. In any case, in the *Notebooks* he tries out the two main candidates for the post of objects, sense-data and material points,[57] and there is never any suggestion that they are in principle beyond the reach of the feelers with which names ought to be able to touch them.[58]

If we move on to the comments that he made in 1929 and 1930 on the logical atomism of the *Tractatus*, we find that he connects the theory more closely with the immediate deliverances of the senses, but

---

[54] See above, pp. 68–9.
[55] See *LWVC* pp. 182–4.
[56] Wittgenstein's word for it. See *PI* I § 258.
[57] See above, p. 89.
[58] See *TLP* 2.1515.

otherwise the impression given in the *Notebooks* is confirmed. The objects of the *Tractatus* belong to the world as we find it, and are, therefore, accessible in principle to philosophers who want to attach names to them. The only trouble is that he himself does not yet feel able to identify them. However, that is merely an uncertainty that happens to be his, and not an unavoidable uncertainty which he is attributing to everyone who has succeeded in reaching the penultimate stage in the analysis of factual discourse, but refuses to fix the references of names in any of the ways suggested by Ishiguro and McGuinness.

If we extend our view and take evidence from *Philosophical Investigations*, we find that the second interpretation of 3.3 gets corroboration of a different kind. The book contains Wittgenstein's later ideas about meaning and they are introduced after a lengthy criticism of the theory of language that he had published in the *Tractatus*. His new ideas are recommended as an alternative to the kind of Platonism that sees fixed rails already laid out ahead of anyone using a descriptive word. He evidently attaches importance to the rejection of this fantasy and the case for his new view of language rests quite heavily on the reductive argument which he uses against it.[59] Now if the objects of the *Tractatus* were the dominant partners in their associations with names, his early theory would be an example of the kind of Platonism that is under attack in his second book. For the question, what counts as the correct use of a descriptive word, would be settled entirely by reference to the nature of the object. So is he not implying that the *Tractatus* was, in that precise sense, basically realistic?

That does not necessarily follow. For it is not inconceivable that his sole target at this point was Russell. Similarly, it is not inconceivable that the logical atomism of the *Tractatus* was radically different from the logical atomism of the *Notebooks*, and that Wittgenstein's later comments were, through a lapse of memory, appropriate to the latter but not to the former. However, the evidence of the *Tractatus* that would be needed to establish either of these two theses would have to be strong. Is it, in fact, sufficiently strong?

But there is a prior question, 'Sufficiently strong for what?' For there are, as has already been pointed out, two different versions of the thesis that we find out the reference of a name by asking in which propositional contexts it can be substituted for the variable. According to one version, the result of the substitution has to be a singular

---

[59] See above, pp. 11–12 and 59–60.

sentence with a sense—that is with one of the two truth-values, true or false. This is certainly one of Ishiguro's theses, because she claims that, 'We settle the identity of the object referred to by coming to understand the sense, i.e. the truth conditions, of the proposition in which it occurs.'[60] McGuinness endorses her claim: 'The semantic role of the . . . name is that of being combined with other . . . names to produce a proposition having a truth-value.'[61] This squares very well with 3.3, which says nothing about the truth of any proposition in the context of which a name has reference.

However, both Ishiguro and McGuinness go further than this. Ishiguro, as already explained, adds that the reference of a name must be fixed by the stipulation that in at least one specified propositional context its insertion produces a truth. McGuinness does not subscribe to this further thesis. But there is a third point, not yet mentioned, on which they both agree. They both say that Wittgenstein uses a criterion of identity which makes any two objects in the *Tractatus* identical if they are indiscernible. Ishiguro says, 'Two names refer to the same object if the names are mutually substitutable in all propositions in which they occur without affecting the truth-value of the propositions:'[62] and McGuinness says, 'Any sign which in the same combinations will produce exactly the same truth-values is the same sign or has the same reference.'[63]

It is time to inquire what evidence there is in the *Tractatus* for ascribing these views to Wittgenstein. 3.3 and the other passages quoted above[64] are not decisive. So is there any further evidence that would settle the matter? We may start with the first view, because it is the more fundamental of the two: the reference of a name is fixed partly by the propositional contexts in which it makes sense. Ishiguro's main argument for this interpretation is eliminative. Its only serious rival is the middle interpretation which is being defended here, but, she claims, certain remarks in the *Tractatus* imply that objects cannot be identified in either of the two ways in which this rival interpretation assumes that they can be identified: they cannot be identified either by definite descriptions or by pointing.[65] It is not

---

[60] 'Use and Reference of Names', p. 34.
[61] 'The So-called Realism of the *Tractatus*', p. 65.
[62] Ishiguro, loc. cit.
[63] McGuinness, loc. cit.
[64] See p. 102 and n. 49.
[65] 'Use and Reference of Names' p. 28. Her argument is endorsed by B. McGuinness: 'The So-called Realism of the *Tractatus*', p. 66.

entirely clear which remarks she means. Near the beginning of her article[66] she reports Wittgenstein's view that an object in the *Tractatus* 'cannot be given by a definite description'. She may be relying on 3.221:

> Objects can only be *named*. Signs are their representatives. I can only speak *about* them: I cannot *put them into words*. Propositions can only say *how* things are, not *what* they are.

However, if she is relying on this remark to show that the objects of the *Tractatus* cannot be identified by definite descriptions, the argument is unconvincing. For what the remark means is that objects cannot be given by definite descriptions which analyse their names, because there are no such definite descriptions. To put the point in another way, the essential nature of an object cannot be spelled out in words.[67] It does not follow that it is impossible to give objects by definite descriptions which they happen to satisfy uniquely, nor did Wittgenstein believe this to be impossible:

> Either a thing has properties that nothing else has, in which case we can immediately use a description to distinguish it from the others and refer to it; or, on the other hand, there are several things that have the whole set of their properties in common, in which case it is quite impossible to indicate one of them.[68]

This clearly allows for the possibility of identifying an object by the definite descriptions that it happens to satisfy uniquely.

It seems likely that Ishiguro has another reason for thinking that the objects of the *Tractatus* cannot be given by definite descriptions, and in fact, she does put forward another reason, but very quickly *en passant*: '. . . if the objects cannot be identified by a definite description, nor be picked out by pointing, since they are "independent of what is the case" . . .'.[69] This shows that she is attributing the following line of thought to Wittgenstein: objects exist independently of what is the case, and therefore they must be identified independently of what is the case; but identification by definite description is not independent of what is the case; therefore objects cannot be identified by definite descriptions. She also credits Wittgenstein with the same view about pointing: the attachment of names to objects by pointing, in the

---

[66] p. 22.
[67] See *TLP* 3.26.
[68] *TLP* 2.02331.
[69] Ishiguro, op. cit., p. 28.

manner of Russell, is not independent of what is the case; therefore names cannot be attached to objects by pointing. McGuinness endorses her attribution of these two arguments to Wittgenstein: '. . . she points out quite correctly, that objects as spoken of in the *Tractatus* cannot be identified by a definite description or picked out by pointing, since their *Bestehen* (existence or subsistence) is supposed to be independent of what is the case'.[70]

If this is the argument, it is presumably based on the following remarks:

Things are independent in so far as they can occur in all *possible* situations, but this form of independence is a form of connection with states of affairs, a form of dependence. (It is impossible for words to appear in two different roles: by themselves, and in propositions.)[71]

Objects constitute the substance of the world. . . .[72]

It is obvious that an imagined world, however different it may be from the real one, must have *something*—a form—in common with it.

This unalterable form is constituted by objects.[73]

Substance is what subsists independently of what is the case.[74]

However, there is nothing in these remarks that rules out the possibility of using definite descriptions to identify objects in the way explained in 2.02331, and this is hardly surprising. The necessary existence of the number 5 does not stop us telling a child that it is the number of toes on one foot.

But what about pointing or ostension? The second claim made by Ishiguro and McGuinness is that in the *Tractatus* names cannot be attached to objects in the manner of Russell, because the existence of objects is independent of what is the case. Are they right about that? This questions takes us to the centre of their position.

Their second claim seems to be based on a misunderstanding of Wittgenstein's account of alternative possible worlds. It is true that in the ontological exordium of the *Tractatus* objects figure as the common core of all possible worlds. But even in that passage there are

---

[70] McGuinness, op. cit., p. 66.

[71] *TLP* 2.0122, a passage, incidentally, which could be used to support the second interpretation of 3.3. See above, pp. 102–3.

[72] *TLP* 2.021.

[73] Ibid., 2.022–2.023. The translation has been slightly changed in this quotation and in the previous one.

[74] Ibid., 2.024.

references to the possibility of our acquaintance with them,[75] and an alternative world to ours is called 'an imagined world'.[76] These hints suggest that the possible world in all of which objects exist are merely the results of varying the arrangement of the objects which underlie the world as we find it, and which thereby 'limit empirical reality'.[77]

It is, therefore, no surprise that these objects exist through this range of possible worlds. If we were operating at the level of complete analysis, we would not say to ourselves, 'Look, these objects just happen to exist, but what we want are objects that necessarily exist.' On the contrary, *these* objects would be intrinsic to the actual world as idea, and so a fixed part of the range of possible worlds constructed on that basis. It is not even accurate to say that the objects of the *Tractatus* necessarily exist. Wittgenstein's doctrine is more subtle: their existence cannot be questioned, asserted, or denied.[78]

This is a brief objection to the first claim made by Ishiguro and McGuinness, that in the *Tractatus* objects cannot be identified by the definite descriptions that they contingently satisfy. It will be expanded and strengthened in Chapter 7. Their second claim, that they cannot be identifed by pointing either, is based on the same line of reasoning. If objects were identified by definite descriptions in the *Tractatus*, that method of identification would be a hostage to the contingency of their possession of properties: similarly, if they were identified by pointing, that method of identification would be a hostage to the contingency of their existence.

These arguments fail to eliminate the second interpretation of 3.3, which is the most plausible rival of the Ishiguro–McGuinness suggestion, that in the *Tractatus* the reference of a name is fixed partly by the propositional contexts in which it makes sense. However, this suggestion may still have intrinsic merits which make it preferable. Let us see if that is so. The point was made earlier, that names of particulars can have their references fixed in the way proposed only if predicative expressions already have meanings. But how, on this interpretation, will they get them? Are we supposed to hold the references of proper names constant while we shuffle around the predicative expressions in order to find out in which propositional context *they* make sense? Again, it seems that language could never get

---

[75] Ibid., 2.0123–2.01231.
[76] 'Eine gedachte Welt' (ibid., 2.022).
[77] Ibid., 5.5561.
[78] See *TLP* 4.1211–4.1212 and 5.535.

off the ground. True, it is hard to be sure of Wittgenstein's views about the meaning of predicative expressions,[79] but directly or indirectly, objects must be involved. So the names of those objects will join the proper names in any proposition and present us with a dilemma: either one or more of them will have independent references, or else it will be impossible to fix the references of any of them by testing for sense in propositional contexts.

In any case, the theory of dummy names is irreconcilable with Wittgenstein's heavy emphasis on contact between name and object in the picture theory of sentences:

> One name stands for one thing, another for another thing, and they are combined with one another. In this way the whole group—like a tableau vivant—presents a state of affairs.[80]

How could this possibly be said by anyone who believed that the references of the names were fixed *after* this bit of language had been set up? Or, to take another of Wittgenstein's ways of describing the semantics of a factual sentence, how could he speak of 'the feelers' with which names 'touch reality', or of the 'graduating lines which actually *touch* the object to be measured',[81] if what he really meant was that the complete analysis of factual language would be in Quinese?

If the first and more fundamental of the two suggestions made by Ishiguro and McGuinness is mistaken, an alternative interpretation of 3.3 is needed:

> Only propositions have sense: only in the context of a proposition does a name have meaning.

So far, all that has been said about this remark is that it may be intended as a qualification, rather than as a replacement of the Russellian attachment of names to objects. For it may mean that, after that attachment, the name represents the object only so long as the possibilities presented by the propositions in which it occurs are real possibilities for that object. Is that what it means?

The context of the remark is important. In the 3.2s Wittgenstein has been expounding his theory of logical analysis. A proposition has one and only one complete analysis into elementary propositions consisting of names in immediate combination. A name means an object and

---

[79] His views on this matter will be discussed in Chapter 6.
[80] *TLP* 4.0311. Cf. *NB* 5 Nov. 1914: '. . . the proposition represents the situation as it were off its own bat.'
[81] *TLP* 2.151–2.1515.

the object is its meaning.[82] An object can only be named, because its essential nature cannot be spelled out in words. Behind all this we can feel the pressure of questions which cannot be postponed much longer. How does the relation between name and object explain the sense of a proposition in which the name occurs? The object which is the name's reference simply is what it is, inarticulate and lumpish. So how can it help the name to its miraculously articulate achievement in a proposition. How does this heavier than air machine ever get off the ground?

Now one move towards answering these questions would be to credit names with senses as well as references. However, there are two reasons why Wittgenstein will not make this move. First, even if he said that expressions designating complexes have senses, that would not really explain anything, because the inevitable question would be, 'What about the simple words in which the senses of these expressions are specified at the level of complete analysis?' Second, he could not answer that question by specifying the senses of the simple words, because at that level the use of definitions for 'further dissection' is ruled out.[83] So he rejects this move in the first sentence of 3.3: 'Only propositions have sense:' that is, referential expressions do not have sense.

What then is his alternative explanation of the miracle of propositional sense? The answer that Ishiguro and McGuinness give to this question is right in one way, but wrong in two ways. It is quite true that the reference of a name in the *Tractatus* depends partly on the propositional contexts in which its insertion makes sense. For that could be taken as another way of saying that after a name has been attached to an object, its occurrences in propositions must not violate the possibilities of combination inherent in that object. Another way of making this point would be to say that names in the *Tractatus* are not Russellian, extensional names, because each one picks out its objects *as* an object with certain possibilities of combination with others.

But there are two things wrong with the Ishiguro–McGuinness thesis, that the reference of a name in the *Tractatus* depends partly on the propositional contexts in which its insertion makes sense. First, the other thing on which the reference of a name depends is *not* the propositional contexts in which its insertion yields truths, but, rather, its direct linkage to its object. Second, their thesis misrepresents the

---

[82] In German 'bedeutet' and 'Bedeutung'. See above, n. 40.
[83] See *TLP* 3.26.

way in which Wittgenstein uses sense-preserving insertions in propositions contexts. They simply assume that the name in the proposition sets the standard of fit, and that its reference is whatever object meets that standard. But why should that be the direction of fit? Everything that Wittgenstein says when he is developing the picture theory of propositions implies that the direction of fit is the opposite one: the possibilities inherent in the object set the standard of fit, so that the name ceases to represent the object the moment that it occurs in a proposition which presents something which is not a possibility for it.

When Ishiguro and McGuinness assume that it is the name in the proposition that sets the standard of fit, they maximize the distance between Wittgenstein's logical atomism and Russell's version of the theory. The opposite interpretation was proposed in the previous chapter. When a name has beeen attached to an object, the object is the dominant partner in the relationship, and its inherent possibilities decide whether the name thereafter represents it: that is, the name will represent the object if and only if the propositions in which it occurs present real possibilities for it.[84] This interpretation still distances Wittgenstein from Russell, but not so far. It understands Wittgenstein's words, 'Only in the context of a proposition does a name have meaning', in the same *general* way as Ishiguro and McGuinness, but reverses the direction of fit, so that the *Tractatus* comes out as basically realistic.

There is strong evidence for this interpretation in the *Notebooks*, where Wittgenstein explains carefully and at considerable length that names represent objects not simply by being attached to them, but by thereafter respecting the possibilities inherent in them:

One name is representative of one thing, another of another thing, and they themselves are connected; in this way the whole images the situation—like a tableau vivant.

The logical connection must, of course, be one that is possible as between the things that the names are representatives of, and this will always be the case if the names really are representatives of the things. . . .[85]

This makes it clear that the things, with their inherent possibilities of combination, are the dominant partners in their relations with names. It also explains why the *Tractatus* begins with an account of objects

---

[84] See above, pp. 75–6.
[85] *NB* 4 Nov. 1914.

and does not introduce pictures until 2.1. The opening ontology is not something that we are supposed to discount because it is an attempt to say things that can only be shown.[86] On the contrary, here, as elsewhere in the *Tractatus*, the strict impossibility of formulating a thesis in factual language is, if anything, a sign of its importance. In this particular case, any doubts that we might feel about the seriousness of the ontology ought to be dispelled when we noticed the exact parallelism between 2.0122 and 3.3.[87] It is a mistake to read Wittgenstein's later criticisms of his basic realism back into the very texts in which he had formulated it.

Finally, something needs to be said about two further passages in the *Tractatus* which Ishiguro cites in direct support of the thesis that the business of analysis is completed at the penultimate level, and the names added at the ultimate level are merely dummies. Such a striking interpretation could hardly depend so heavily on inference, and it would be a weakness if 3.3 and the other remarks about use[88] were the only evidence for it in the text.

However, the two further passages cited by Ishiguro do not really give her interpretation any support. One occurs at 5.47.[89]

An elementary proposition really contains all logical operations in itself. For '*Fa*' says the same thing as

$$(\exists x) \cdot Fx \cdot x = a$$

Ishiguro notes that 'this would suggest that "*Fa*" could never be equivalent to an existential proposition since it is an existential proposition plus something more: namely the identity claim that $x = a$'. However, she goes on to argue that the references of names in the *Tractatus* 'are simple objects which "can only be named" and not given by descriptions. So in the proposition "$(\exists x) \cdot Fx \cdot x = a$" where "$a$" is a name [sc. in the *Tractatus*], a is merely identified as an object which is F.'[90] But the passage does not say this, and the most that she

---

[86] McGuinness seems to take a dismissive view of the ontology at the beginning of the *Tractatus* (op. cit., pp. 62–3).

[87] 2.0122 says, 'Things are independent in so far as they can occur in all *possible* situations, but this form of independence is a form of connection with states of affairs, a form of dependence. (It is impossible for words to appear in two different roles: by themselves, and in propositions.)'

[88] Quoted above, p. 102 and n. 49.

[89] *TLP* 5.47, second paragraph.

[90] Ishiguro, op. cit., p. 44. Her point is difficult to express. She does not mean that the reference of 'a' is fixed by the contingent properties of a, or even that it is fixed in the same way as the reference of 'Jonathan' in the example used above, p. 101. She means

is entitled to claim is that this is how it would have to be understood if her interpretation of Wittgenstein's logical atomism were correct. A more appropriate comment would be that, if her interpretation were correct, it would be very surprising that Wittgenstein allows himself to imply that the identity claim adds something contingent to the existential proposition.

The other passage cited by Ishiguro to show that the business of analysis is completed at the penultimate level is 5.526:

> We can describe the world completely by means of fully generalized propositions, i.e. without first correlating any name with a particular object.
> Then, in order to arrive at the customary mode of expression, we simply need to add, after an expression like, 'There is one and only one x such that . . .' the words, 'and that x is a'.

Here too there is no suggestion that the 'customary mode of expression' is logically equivalent to the fully generalized description. On the contrary, the implication is that the added words add to the sense and that the fully generalized description was an incomplete description.[91] Ishiguro opposes this natural interpretation of the passage on the following ground: the version in the *Notebooks* is 'And in order to arrive at ordinary language one would only need to introduce names etc. by saying, after an '$(\exists x)$', 'and this x is A' and so on'; on which her comment is that, since the name is *introduced* in this way it is impossible to 'envisage the A as not having the property F.'[92] This is not convincing. The choice of the word 'introduce' in the *Notebooks* can hardly carry so much weight. He may well be using the word merely because names do not appear in reports expressed in the other way. A more appropriate comment on the version in the *Tractatus* would be that he deliberately omitted the potentially misleading word 'introduce'.

In any case, there is an insuperable objection to the use that both Ishiguro and McGuinness make of the substitution of names in propositional contexts without change of truth-value. They both claim that when two names pass this test in all propositional contexts in which they make sense, they refer to the same object. But this is

that 'to identify a would be nothing more than to identify an F'. The sequel cannot contain an encounter with a or acquaintance with a. In fact, on her theory, a is not unlike the ego. See below, ch. 7.

[91] This is the view that Wittgenstein takes in *TLP* 5.156.
[92] Ishiguro, op. cit., p. 45.

directly contradicted by the passage in the *Tractatus* in which Wittgenstein rejects the identity of indescernibles:

Russell's definition of '=' is inadequate, because according to it we cannot say that two objects have all their properties in common. (Even if this proposition is never correct, it still has *sense*.)[93]

The proposition would not have sense if the introduction of names at the ultimate level of analysis added nothing to the version at the penultimate level.[94]

This discussion can be briefly summarized. There is no reason to deny, and there are many reasons to assert, that names in the *Tractatus* do make independent references and that the book is, in that sense, basically realistic.

[93] *TLP* 5.5302.

[94] It might be objected that Wittgenstein cannot have held that indiscernibles are not necessarily identical, because he counts specific temporal and spatial positions among properties. See below, p. 138. However, that does not prove, against the explicit evidence of this passage, that he cannot have held the view that indiscernibles are not necessarily identical. All that it shows is that on this point, as on many others, he had not worked out the details of the kind of complete analysis envisaged in the *Tractatus*.

6

Sentences as Pictures

THE theory that sentences are pictures has been mentioned several times in the exposition of Wittgenstein's logical atomism, and some of its more important aspects have been briefly sketched. It is a theory which uses the principle of representation to explain how sentences acquire and keep their senses.[1] Names are correlated with objects just as the flecks of paint in a pointillist picture are correlated with points in the scene that it depicts.[2] The theory has two striking features which are connected with one another, separatism and analytic depth. Each elementary sentence stands alone with a sense derived from its own bit of reality, and, if this isolated derivation of sense is not apparent at the level of everyday language, the analysis must be taken to a depth at which it will become apparent.[3] Sentences belong to systems, but their nature is not to be discovered by a lateral investigation of their connections with one another or their place in our lives: what we need to find out is how far their senses reach into the reality which they describe.[4] There is, however, a limit to this investigation, because the possibility of using sentences to say some things depends on the actuality of other things which cannot be said, but only shown.[5]

It would be possible to take this sketch of the picture theory and show how Wittgenstein's later account of language developed out of it, often by steps which look very short and easy in retrospect. Ask how sentences keep their senses, and immediately the weight of explanation will fall on use.[6] Treat sentences as ordinary instruments with a place and function in our lives, and immediately the lateral investigation of systems will take over from deep analysis.[7] This may not get rid of the mystery of the things that can only be shown, but it will at least diffuse it, so that it becomes the atmosphere of ordinary human activities rather than the elusive source of each sentence's sense.[8]

[1] See above, p. 73.   [2] See above, p. 74.
[3] See above, p. 79.   [4] See above, p. 82.
[5] See above, pp. 7 and 71.   [6] See above, pp. 102–3.
[7] See above, p. 87.   [8] See above, pp. 17–18.

However, what is needed now is a detailed account of the theory itself. It is a commonplace that there are certain similarities between sentences and pictures used to convey factual information, and if we are going to understand Wittgenstein's theory, we need to know which points of similarity he was exploiting. There is also something else that we need to know. He believed that what would be explained by his preferred points of similarity, whatever they are, was the way in which sentences acquire and keep their senses, but that is a very general way of identifying the problem, and something more specific is required. A theory is usually put forward against a background of assumptions: some things are taken to be perspicuous, while others look puzzling. So we need to know how Wittgenstein saw the situation when he was working out the picture theory. How much already seemed clear to him and how much remained problematical? To pose the question in another way, in 1913 he had put together a substantial account of the foundations of language and logic,[9] and we want to know what exactly was added in 1914 by the new idea that a sentence is like a picture.[10]

A short answer to this question would be that in August 1914, when the entries in the *Notebooks* began, he thought that he understood the relation between name and object: and, once sentences had acquired their senses, he thought that he could explain the development of logic by showing how they throw up tautologies at their outer limit;[11] but he did not see how to get from the naming of objects to the putting together of sentences, because the sudden appearance of sense seemed to him to be a new and unaccountable phenomenon. Russell had tried to account for it by making a further appeal to acquaintance and representation: according to him, we are acquainted not only with particulars and their properties, but also with the forms of their combination, and certain elements in factual sentences represent those forms in much the same way that names represent particulars and their properties.[12] But Wittgenstein would have none of this. His view was that a form is the possibility of a certain combination of objects, and he thought that these possibilities are taken up and expressed by language, not by acquaintance and naming but by the kind of osmosis that he describes in the picture theory.

[9] See *Notes on Logic* in *NB*, especially § 1.
[10] See *NB*, the entries on and immediately after 27 Sept. 1914.
[11] See above, pp. 23–4.
[12] See Russell: *Theory of Knowledge, 1913*, pp. 97–101.

So one way to understand the picture theory would be to measure the distance between it and the theory of language developed by Russell in 1913, as was done for the two philosophers' versions of logical atomism. However, the first priority is to see how the problem of sense presented itself to him in the *Notebooks*:

This is the difficulty: How can there be such a thing as the form of p if there is no situation of this form? And in that case, what does this form really consist in?[13]

When p is false, there does not seem to be anything in the world which would count as the objective possibility that it might have been true.[14] A few days earlier he had mentioned a solution to this problem which he no longer found convincing, although he had once accepted it:

I thought that the possibility of the truth of the proposition φa was tied up with the fact $(\exists x, \varphi) \cdot \varphi x$. But it is impossible to see why φa should be possible only if there is another proposition of the same form. φa surely does not need any precedent. (For suppose that there existed only the two elementary propositions 'φa' and 'ψa' and that 'φa' was false: Why should this proposition make sense only if 'ψa' is true?)[15]

In fact, six weeks earlier, near the beginning of this discussion in the *Notebooks*, he had rejected all solutions which make the sense of one proposition depend on the truth of another:

Then can we ask ourselves: Does the subject–predicate form exist? Does the relational form exist? Do any of the forms exist at all that Russell and I were always talking about? (Russell would say: 'Yes! That's self-evident.' *Well!*)

Then: if *everything* that needs to be shown is shown by the existence of subject–predicate SENTENCES, etc., the task of philosophy is different from what I originally supposed. But if that is not how it is, then what is lacking would have to be shown by means of some kind of experience, and that I regard as out of the question.[16]

It would not be an exaggeration to say that the principle, that the sense of one sentence can never depend on the truth of another, is just as important in the *Tractatus* as the principle of representation.[17]

[13] *NB* 29 Oct. 1914, paragraph 8.

[14] In *TLP* form is defined as 'the possibility of structure' (2.033).

[15] *NB* 21 Oct. 1914, last paragraph. Cf. *NB* 1 Nov. 1914: 'That precedent to which we should always like to appeal must lie in the sign itself'. Cf. *TLP* 5.525.

[16] *NB* 3 Sept. 1914, paragraphs 2 and 3. Cf. *TLP* 5.552, which is discussed below, pp. 124–5.

[17] See *TLP* 4.0312, discussed above, pp. 73–4.

Wittgenstein's logical atomism depends on one application of the principle of independent sense: the sense of a sentence can never depend on the truth of another sentence about one of its own constituents.[18] Here, in the argument for the picture theory, we find another application of the same principle: the sense of a sentence can never depend on the truth of another sentence of the same form.

In 1914 Wittgenstein believed that a sentence has a reference.[19] He had abandoned this idea by the time that he compiled the *Tractatus*, but even when he still held it, he never offered it as an explanation of a sentence's possession of sense. He saw very clearly that a sentence has to pick up its sense through the feelers which connect its names with objects,[20] whether or not those objects are actually combined as it says that they are:

The knowledge of the representing relation *must* be founded only on the knowledge of the component parts of the situation![21]

This knowledge puts a constraint on the use of the names in a sentence after they have been attached to objects:[22]

The logical connection [sc. between the names] must, of course, be one that is possible as between the things that the names are representatives of, and this will always be the case if the names really are representatives of the things. ...

In this way the proposition represents the situation—as it were off its own bat.[23]

But when I say: the connection of the propositional components must be possible for the represented things—does this not contain the whole problem? How can a non-existent connection between objects be possible?

'The connection must be possible' means: The proposition and the components of the situation must stand in a particular relation.

Then in order for a proposition to present a situation, it is only necessary for its component parts to represent those of the situation and for the former to stand in a connection which is possible for the latter.

---

[18] This application of the principle of sense and truth is formulated in *Notes Dictated to G. E. Moore in Norway*, NB p. 116 discussed above, pp. 66 and 71–3.

[19] See *NB* 22 Oct. 1914.

[20] See *TLP* 2.1515, discussed above, pp. 74 and 109 and *NB* 15 Oct. 1914, last paragraph.

[21] *NB* 3 Nov. 1914, paragraph 2. Cf. *NB* 20 Nov. 1914.

[22] See above, pp. 75–6.

[23] In German, 'auf eigene Faust': i.e. in conformity with the principle of independent sense.

The propositional sign guarantees the possibility of the fact which it presents (not that this fact is actually the case). . . .[24]

This explanation of sense is part of the early development of the picture theory in the *Notebooks*. So the next thing that we need to know is how the points made in these entries are connected with the idea that sentences are like pictures used to convey information.

The answer to this question suggested earlier was that the correlation of names with objects is like the correlation of flecks of paint on a canvas with points in the scene that is depicted. But that was only an approximate answer and it now needs to be made more precise. For if that is how the analogy is read, what is really happening is more complicated than it seems: each point on the canvas is correlated with a point in space and so it is like the name of a particular, and each colour on the painter's palette is correlated with the same colour in reality and so it is like the name of that colour. Then what corresponds to uttering a sentence is putting a spot of paint at a certain point on the canvas. This is a simple version of the analogy and it was used by Wittgenstein in his lectures in Cambridge in 1930–2 when he was explaining his earlier system.[25]

In the *Tractatus* he sometimes uses a slightly different, but equally simple version of the analogy. A sentence is like a model: the elements of the model stand for objects in reality, and so arranging the elements in a certain way is like using a sentence to say that the objects are actually arranged in that way.[26] Here the elements of the model are very like names of particulars and their spatial relations are correlated with the same spatial relations in reality, like the colours on the painter's palette in the other version of the analogy.

However, the version of the analogy which is preferred by Wittgenstein in the *Tractatus* is more sophisticated than either of these two. Names are like co-ordinates and what corresponds to uttering a sentence is giving the co-ordinates of a point in space; for example two co-ordinates are needed to fix a point on a map and giving them is like saying 'φa'. The idea is that a sentence claims that its particular point in reality is occupied, or, in other words, that the possibility which it indicates is realized:

A proposition determines a place in logical space. The existence of this logical place is guaranteed by the mere existence of the constituents—by the existence of the proposition with a sense.

---

[24] *NB* 4 Nov. 1914, last paragraph to 5 Nov. 1914, first 4 paragraphs and part of paragraph 5. See above, p. 111.   [25] *CLI* p. 10.   [26] *TLP* 3.1431.

The propositional sign with logical co-ordinates—that is the logical place.

In geometry and logic alike a place is a possibility: something can exist in it.[27]

This version does more justice to the fact that sentences belong to a system, but it still does not go far enough, because it does not allow for the systematic connections between properties like colours.[28]

Now we could ask at this point whether Wittgenstein's various ways of developing the analogy throw any light on his views about the nature of elementary propositions. Does the simple version in the *Tractatus* show that he believed that they would only contain names of particulars?[29] Or does the more sophisticated version, when it is read with his later criticism of it, show that there would also be names of properties at the level of complete analysis?[30] However, it is worth remembering the golden rule of interpretation: when Wittgenstein does not choose between two ways of developing his own theory, the choice is not necessary, because the matter is peripheral and the essence of the theory lies in what is common to the two alternatives.[31] This assessment is confirmed by his later admissions that when he wrote the *Tractatus* he did not know what kinds of things objects would turn out to be.[32] It is, therefore, a mistake to try to decide between the two ways of developing the analogy between sentences and pictures used to convey information, and the right way to achieve an understanding of the theory is to find out what they have in common, because that will be the essence of the matter.

What they have in common is something rather surprising. In both the versions, of the analogy that are used in the *Tractatus* once the system for producing pictures has been set up, there is no risk that a would-be picture might make an impossible claim. Any arrangement of elements in a simple spatial model will correspond to a possible

---

[27] *TLP* 3.4–3.411. Cf. *NB* 29 Oct. 1914, paragraphs 4 and 5 and 1 Nov. 1914, last 3 paragraphs.

[28] So Wittgenstein says later: 'In my old conception of an elementary proposition there was no determination of the value of a co-ordinate; although my remark that a coloured body is in a colour-space, etc., should have put me straight on to this.' (*PR* § 83, quoted and discussed above, p. 86.) He means that a colour is not an independent co-ordinate, but, rather, the result of determining the value of one or more continuously variable parameters.

[29] This interpretation is defended by G. E. M. Anscombe: *Introduction to Wittgenstein's* Tractatus, pp. 99–101.

[30] This interpretation is defended by E. B. Allaire: 'The *Tractatus*: Nominalistic or Realistic?' in *Essays on Wittgenstein's* Tractatus, ed. I. Copi and R. Beard, pp. 325 ff.

[31] See above, p. 89.   [32] See above, p. 64.

arrangement of the objects for which they stand, and any well-formed pair of six-figure co-ordinates, coupled with the name of a colour, will indicate the real possibility that the colour might be found at the corresponding point in space. The same is true of the simpler version of the analogy which was introduced first. All three versions offer systems which are foolproof to this extent: false claims are possible, but not nonsensical ones.[33] However, that is plainly not true of language, because it is not only possible but easy to produce nonsensical strings of words. Why then, does Wittgenstein say that the existence of the 'place in logical space' which is indicated by a proposition 'is guaranteed by the mere existence of the constituents— by the existence of the proposition with a sense'? How can this be the central point of the analogy, when it is precisely the point at which it breaks down?

There is evidently only one way of answering this objection and explaining what Wittgenstein was trying to do. His point cannot have been that words are *intrinsically* incapable of forming nonsensical groups. He must have meant that this is made impossible by the system that gives each word its meaning. So his idea was that the best way to understand the restrictions imposed on signs by the system that makes them the signs that they are is to start by looking at the kind of system that we use when we represent spatial facts spatially. But why is this the best way to see how sentences work? If we look at his simple version of the analogy, the straightforward spatial model, it seems positively misleading, and it is not much of a corrective to be reminded of pictures like Escher's. However, it is just worth adding that his sophisticated version of the analogy does allow for nonsensical concatenations of signs; for example, someone who is trying to give twelve-figure co-ordinates may use one digit too few. This shows very clearly that Wittgenstein was not interested in foolproof methods of representation. His interest lay in the restrictions imposed on signs by the systems to which they belong, and he started with spatial systems because that was where the working of the restrictions and their immediate effect seemed to him to be most perspicuous.[34]

Perhaps the best way to understand the strategy of his investigation of the senses of sentences is to reflect that anyone who fixes a point by

[33] See *TLP* 2.18.
[34] The idea that sentences can only be explained by their places in systems is commonly held to be peculiar to his later philosophy. In fact, it is one of the central points of the picture theory.

its co-ordinates is thinking about it laterally, because he will immediately see it in relation to other points. This is quite like the way in which anyone who understands the sense of a sentence, that is, the possibility that it presents, immediately sees it in relation to other possibilities. But how far can the analogy be taken? What will happen when this idea is added to Russell's straightforward account of the attachment of names to objects? It will at least qualify that account in the way explained in the previous chapter. Perhaps in the end it will destroy it, but, according to the interpretation that is being offered here, not immediately.

Anyway, neither Russell nor Wittgenstein believed that the mere attachment of names to objects is enough to explain the subsequent combinability of names in sentences with senses. Russell had started out with this belief, but he soon realized that it gave him a conception of sentences that was too static to account for the potentialities of names.[35] So he tried to correct this deficiency by adding a new idea: the objects named in a sentence are not the only things with which we have to be acquainted in order to grasp its sense; we also need acquaintance with 'logical objects'.[36] In May 1913 Wittgenstein read the manuscript in which Russell developed this idea and criticized it with some vehemence.[37] It seemed to him to be on the wrong track, because the deficiencies of the static name relation could hardly be cured by giving it a further function to perform.

Russell's *Theory of Knowledge, 1913*, was published in 1984[38] and it was immediately clear that Wittgenstein's picture theory of sentences had been developed in reaction against its incurably static conception of sense. Russell's earlier theory had been that, when a subject S judges that aRb, S must be acquainted with the three constituents a, R, and b, and all four must be related by *judging*.[39] This is hardly explanatory. It skates over the important fact that the subordinate relation R is judged to relate a and b[40] and must, therefore, be a kind of relation that is capable of relating them.[41] It also fails to explain the difference between an asymmetrical relation running from a to b and

[35] That is what is wrong with the theory of judgement which he produced in 1910. See Russell: *On the Nature of Truth and Falsehood*, in *Philosophical Essays*, Longmans, 1910.

[36] Russell: *Theory of Knowledge, 1913*, pp. 97–101.

[37] See R. W. Clark: *The Life of Bertrand Russell*, pp. 204–7.

[38] See above, ch. 2 n. 4.

[39] See Russell: *On the Nature of Truth and Falsehood*.

[40] Russell himself made this criticism later in *The Philosophy of Logical Atomism* p. 226.

[41] This was the central deficiency of the theory, and, according to Wittgenstein, it was not made good in the 1913 theory. See below, p. 125.

an asymmetrical relation running in the opposite direction, from *b* to *a*. Evidently, the trouble is that *S*'s acquaintance with *a*, *R*, and *b* is not enough to explain how he succeeds in understanding '*aRb*'. To put the point semantically, the mere attachment of the three names to the three constituents does not explain why '*aRb*' possesses a sense but '*RRb*' is nonsensical.

In *Theory of Knowledge, 1913* Russell tries to complete the explanation by making a further appeal to acquaintance. His new idea is that the extra thing that is needed by *S* is acquaintance with the pure forms of propositions. Now a pure form of a proposition is what he calls 'the utmost generalization' of it, because it is the result of replacing all the names by variables. So, in order to grasp the sense of *aRb*, *S* needs acquaintance with the pure form $x\xi y$. Russell calls this pure form a 'logical object', but he says that it is not a constituent of the proposition. For if it were a constituent, 'there would have to be a new way in which it and the two other constituents are put together, and if we take this way as again a constituent, we find ourselves embarked on an endless regress'.[42]

It is clear that Russell is trying to have it both ways. He wants to explain sense by invoking forms, and if this is going to work, forms must be potentialities and, therefore, must not be treated like objects. Yet his model for our knowledge of forms is static acquaintance, which is required to explain not only the internal structure of propositions, but also their logical relations with one another. He claims that 'besides the forms of atomic complexes, there are many other logical objects which are involved in the formation of non-atomic complexes. Such words as *or*, *not*, *all*, *some*, plainly involve logical notions; and since we can use such words intelligently, we must be acquainted with the logical objects involved.'[43] So 'there certainly is such a thing as "logical experience", by which I mean that kind of immediate knowledge other than judgement, which is what enables use to understand logical terms.'[44]

If this 'logical experience' is going to be explanatory, it evidently needs to be kept separate from judgement. For it is supposed to be experience of the potent nuclei from which the whole range of factual discourse can be seen to develop. To put the point in Wittgenstein's way:

[42] Russell: *Theory of Knowledge, 1913*, p. 98.
[43] Ibid., p. 99.
[44] Ibid., p. 97.

The 'experience' that we need in order to understand logic is not that something or other is the state of things, but that something *is*: that, however, is *not* an experience.

Logic is *prior* to every experience—that something *is so*. It is prior to the question 'How?', not prior to the question 'What?'[45]

However, Russell failed to keep his 'logical experience' separate from judgement. For he went on to equate the pure form $x\xi y$ with the fact that 'something has some relation to something'.[46] This equation had an unfortunate consequence. Understanding the sense of the sentence 'Something has some relation to something' was supposed to be explained by acquaintance with the pure form $x\xi y$. So, when that acquaintance was construed as acquaintance with the fact that something has some relation to something, this turned out to be a case in which understanding the sense of p could only be explained as apprehending the truth of p. Russell accepted this consequence.[47]

There is no need to examine the arguments that he used in his attempt to make it acceptable. His theory has been introduced here only because it is the background of Wittgenstein's picture theory of sentences. In May 1913 Russell showed Wittgenstein his manuscript and afterwards he describes his reaction in a letter to Ottoline Morrell:

> We were both cross from the heat. I showed him a crucial part of what I have been writing. He said it was all wrong, not realizing the difficulties—that he had tried my view and knew it wouldn't work. I couldn't understand his objection—in fact he was very inarticulate—but I feel in my bones that he must be right, & that he has seen something I have missed. If I could see it too I shouldn't mind, but as it is, it is worrying, & has rather destroyed the pleasure in my writing—I can only go on with what I see, & yet I feel it is probably all wrong, & that Wittgenstein will probably think me a dishonest scoundrel for going on with it. Well, well—it is the younger generation knocking at the door—I must make room for him when I can, or I shall become an incubus. But at the moment I was rather cross.[48]

It is interesting that Wittgenstein commented that he had tried Russell's view and knew that it would not work. In a letter written to

---

[45] *TLP* 5.552.

[46] Russell: *Theory of Knowledge, 1913*, pp. 113–14.

[47] He also accepted the corollary, that the truth of p was self-evident in such cases (see *Theory of Knowledge, 1913*, p. 141). But that could only be because p was necessarily true. So understanding the sense of φa involved knowledge of the truth of $(\exists x) \cdot \varphi x$, and that knowledge was construed as acquaintance with a pure form and, at the same time, knowledge of the corresponding necessary truth.

[48] Letter quoted by R. W. Clark: *The Life of Bertrand Russell*, pp. 204–5.

Russell in June 1913 he says something which throws light on this comment:

... I can now express my objection to your theory of judgement exactly: I believe it is obvious that, from the proposition '*A* judges that (say) *a* is in relation *R* to *b*', if correctly analysed, the propositions '*aRb* · v · ~*aRb*' must follow directly *without the use of any other premiss*. This condition is not fulfilled by your theory.[49]

This refers to the central fault in Russell's 1910 theory of judgement which remained uncorrected in his 1913 theory: nothing is said about the need for *R* to be a kind of relation that could relate *a* and *b*. Wittgenstein's implication is that he had expressed this objection before, but less precisely. So, given Russell's reference to his inability to understand Wittgenstein's inarticulate objection when they met and discussed *Theory of Knowledge*, it is a likely inference that the 'crucial part' which Russell showed him was the new version of his theory of judgement. It is then possible to fit another piece into the jigsaw with reasonable confidence: when Wittgenstein told Russell that he had tried his theory and knew that it would not work, he was probably referring to his own earlier suggestion, now abandoned, that 'the possibility of the truth of the proposition φa was tied up with the fact $(\exists x,\varphi) \cdot \varphi x$'.[50] This would explain the vehemence of his criticism, because his fundamental principle, which later found expression in the picture theory of sentences, was that the sense of one sentence can never depend on the truth of another sentence.

In any case, the wording of *TLP* 5.552 puts it beyond doubt that it is an implied criticism of Russell for making sense depend on truth: 'The "experience" that we need in order to understand logic ...'. This must be a reference to Russell's confident assertion: 'There certainly is such a thing as "logical experience". ...'[51] The context of the criticism is interesting. It is made in the course of the inquiry which

[49] *NB* p. 121. Cf. his next letter, dated 22 July 1913, which contains the following remark: 'I am very sorry to hear that my objection to your theory of judgement paralyses you. I think it can only be removed by a correct theory of judgement.' Cf. a remark in *Notes on Logic*, ibid., p. 96: 'Every right theory of judgement must make it impossible for me to judge that "this table penholders the book" (Russell's theory does not satisfy this requirement).'

[50] *NB* 21 Oct. 1914, paragraph 4, quoted above, p. 117. Russell's version of this unsuccessful theory was more complicated: the sense of φa was supposed to depend on the sense-which-involved-the-truth of $(\exists x,\varphi) \cdot \varphi x$. But the two versions are sufficiently close to one another to make Wittgenstein's reaction intelligible.

[51] Both quoted above, p. 123.

immediately precedes the discussion of solipsism in the *Tractatus*.[52] The question is, whether it is possible to lay down a priori specific limits to the possible forms of elementary propositions. Wittgenstein's answer is that this is not possible. The only thing that we know in advance about elementary propositions is that they must exhibit the general form of all factual discourse.[53] Further specific limitations cannot be laid down a priori. It is not even clear that we can ask the question to which no a priori answer can be given:

> It is supposed to be possible to answer a priori the question whether I can get into a position in which I need the sign for a 27-termed relation in order to signify something.
>
> But is it really legitimate even to ask such a question? Can we set up a form of sign without knowing whether anything can correspond to it?
>
> Does it make sense to ask what there must *be* in order that something can be the case?[54]

This is offered explicitly as a criticism of Russell's thesis,

> ... that there were simple relations between different numbers of things (individuals). But between what numbers? And how is this supposed to be decided?—By experience?[55]

Wittgenstein's answer is that it can neither be decided by experience nor be laid down a priori.

It is worth inspecting both horns of this dilemma, in order to see how Wittgenstein's picture theory of sentences grew out of his rejection of Russell's 1913 theory of judgement. The key to this development is Wittgenstein's distinction between what is said by a sentence and what cannot be said by it, because it is presupposed by its possession of sense and, therefore, can only be shown.[56] The best way to approach Wittgenstein's theory is to see how he draws the line through a sentence's total demand on the world separating what is said by it from what can only be shown, or, to put the point as it was put earlier, separating truth-conditions from sense-conditions.[57]

One horn of the dilemma is the infinite regress which threatens any theory that makes the sense of any sentence depend on the contingent truth of some other sentence. In the case of 'φa' the supporting truth is

---

[52] See above, p. 38.
[53] *TLP* 6.
[54] Ibid., 5.5541–2.
[55] Ibid., 5.553.
[56] Ibid., 4.12–4.1212.
[57] See above, pp. 70–1.

supposed to be '$(\exists x)(\varphi x)$', which presumably acquires sense before truth and, therefore, by parity of reasoning, needs the support of a further contingent truth, and so on *ad infinitum*. The central point in Wittgenstein's theory is that if 'φa' is elementary, it derives its sense from its own bit of reality through the feelers connecting its names with objects.[58] If this were not so, 'φa' would not be a sentence with a sense, and, given that it is so, we cannot even ask whether the two objects required for its sense exist. For if we know what we are asking, we can already see the answer in the question:

> A name means an object. The object is its meaning . . .[59]

Thus one proposition 'fa' shows that the object *a* occurs in its sense, two propositions 'fa' and 'ga' show that the same object is mentioned in both of them.[60]

Wittgenstein gave up the picture theory of sentences soon after he returned to philosophy in 1929, but he always retained the general idea on which it was based: he always believed that it is impossible to use language to question the conditions of its own sense; for example, we cannot ask whether the range of colours is really divided as we divide it.[61]

The other horn of the dilemma is equally interesting. Russell tried to stop the regress at the first step by treating fully generalized propositions, like $(\exists x,\varphi)(\varphi x)$ as necessary truths. Wittgenstein takes him to be making the a priori claim that there are *n* forms of elementary proposition, each associated with an a priori fully generalized propositions.[62] Against this he makes two objections. First, there is no way in which we can fix the value of *n* in advance. Now the claim that there are *n* forms of elementary proposition is a claim about the limits of language, because it means that there are *n* and no more than *n*. So Wittgenstein's point is that this would be a specific limitation of language and there is no a priori way of

---

[58] *TLP* 2.1515.
[59] Ibid., 3.203.
[60] Ibid., 4.1211.
[61] See above pp. 14–16. Cf. *PR* § 4.
[62] *TLP* 5.555–5.556. Cf. 6.124 and 3.342, discussed above, pp. 23–5. The development of this part of Wittgenstein's criticism of Russell confirms the interpretation of the *Tractatus* as basically realistic (see above, p. 8). The argument presupposes that a line can be drawn between features of language imposed by the general nature of reality and, therefore, identifiable a priori, and other features. It also suggests a further division of the other features: some of them will be freely chosen (see *TLP* 3.342), while others, like the coining of a word for a 27-termed relation, will meet a real need, but one which could not have been anticipated.

establishing it. The a priori is the province of logic and logic only reflects the general structure of reality. The general form of a proposition is dictated by reality, but the specific manifestations of the general form are invented by us independently of reality.[63] The only limit imposed on language a priori by reality is the general requirement that it must express the existence of objects:

> Empirical reality is limited by the totality of objects. The limit also makes itself manifest in the totality of elementary propositions.[64]

This leads into the discussion of solipsism. The solipsist thinks that he can do better: instead of adding a specific limitation to the general one, he tries to add a limitation derived from individual objects. But he forgets that the existence of objects is something that can only be shown in language and there is no way of closing the list.

> What the axiom of infinity is intended to say would express itself in language through the existence of infinitely many names with different meanings.[65]

> Logic pervades the world: the limits of the world are also its limits.

> So we cannot say in logic, 'The world has this in it, and this, but not that.'[66]

Nor can we restrict the list to things presented to this ego—but we are now encroaching on the topic of the next chapter, solipsism. The immediate point made by Wittgenstein against Russell is that he is mistaken if he expects logic to pronounce on the number of specific forms of elementary propositions.

Wittgenstein's second objection to Russell's theory of forms concerns their nature rather than their number. They are supposed to be simple objects and yet somehow to generate propositions spontaneously in the minds of those who are acquainted with them.[67] This double achievement is obviously one that Wittgenstein would find unacceptable and there may be an allusion to it in an ironical remark in *Notes on Logic*: 'Russell's "complexes" were to have the useful property of being compounded, and were to combine with this the agreeable property that they could be treated like "simples". But this alone makes them unserviceable as logical types (forms), since there would then have been significance in asserting of a simple that it

---

[63] Ibid., 5.555.
[64] Ibid., 5.5561.
[65] Ibid., 5.535.
[66] Ibid., 5.61.
[67] See Russell, *Theory of Knowledge, 1913*, pp. 98–9 and 114.

was complex.'[68] Russell's appeal to acquaintance must have made it easier for him to take the view that $(\exists x, \varphi)(\varphi x)$ is necessarily true, because it prepared the way for his introduction of self-evidence.[69] But even if Wittgenstein had allowed that such fully generalized propositions were necessarily true, he would not have passed Russell's explanation of their status:

Self-evidence, which Russell talked about so much, can become dispensable in logic, only because language itself prevents every logical mistake.— What makes logic a priori is the *impossibility* of illogical thought.[70]

In any case, these fully generalized propositions are not necessarily true:

The mark of a logical proposition is *not* general validity.
To be general means no more than to be accidentally valid for all things....[71]

It is well known that Wittgenstein substitutes tautological combinability for Russell's self-evidence as the mark of logical truth. What has not been so widely recognized is that he stands Russell's theory on its head, and that he achieves this inversion through the picture theory of sentences. Russell buries necessary truths in the foundations of factual discourse, while Wittgenstein place them at its outer limit. Russell has to show that they are apprehended first, before any factual sentences can be understood, and when he tries to explain this order of events, he deviates into mythology. The picture theory of sentences has it the other way round, because it represents logic as a development out of ordinary factual sentences. This puts Wittgenstein in a position to explain necessary truths in a way that at least connects them with our method of testing them.

If form cannot be explained in Russell's way, how can it be explained? This question sends us to the difficult passage in which Wittgenstein introduces the central concept of his theory, pictorial form:

The fact that the elements of a picture are related to one another in a determinate way represents that things are related to one another in the same way.

[68] *NB* p. 99.
[69] Russell: *Theory of Knowledge, 1913*, p. 141.
[70] *TLP* 5.4731. Cf. 5.1363 and 6.1271.
[71] Ibid., 6.1231.

Let us call this connection of its elements the structure of the picture, and let us call the possibility of this structure the pictorial form of the picture.[72]

According to 2.033, form is the possibility of structure.[73] So pictorial form is the possibility of the kind of structure that counts as a picture. That sounds simple enough, but there is a hidden complication. If a structure is going to count as a picture, it is not enough that it should realize a certain possibility—every structure does that: it must also be related in a certain way to what it depicts. It follows that pictorial form is partly derivative, and partly intrinsic. An example will make the two aspects of pictorial form clear, taking the intrinsic aspect first. A fleck of paint is put on a canvas at a certain point, and that realizes a possibility which, of course, existed before it was realized, namely the possibility that the point chosen on the canvas should be that colour. But if this possibility is going to count as a pictorial form, it must be linked to the possibility that in the scene depicted the point that is correlated with this bit of the canvas should be that colour too. That is the derivative aspect of pictorial form.

Put like this, Wittgenstein's theory of form seems to be true enough, but curiously difficult to appreciate. This is one of those cases that occur quite often in philosophy: we find it hard to hold two things in our minds at once, the solution and the original problem.

So it might not come amiss to restate the original problem and to review Wittgenstein's progress towards his solution, as it has been described so far in this chapter. That will, at least, fix the points of similarity between sentences and pictures used to convey factual information, so that we shall be able to appreciate how much is explained, instead of being reduced to exclaiming 'How true!' (or the opposite).

... How can there be such a thing as the form of p if there is no situation of this form? And in that case what does this form really consist in?[74]

The first step towards a solution was to reject Russell's suggestion that the form of p was a 'logical object' with which anyone who wanted to understand p must get acquainted. The only available acquaintance was with the objects named in p, and that was enough, because it somehow picked up their possibilities of combination. But how? That

---

[72] *TLP* 2.15 The German word which is translated 'represent' is 'vorstellen'.

[73] See above, n. 14.

[74] *NB* 29 Oct. 1914, paragraph 8, quoted above, p. 117. Cf. 25 Oct. 1914, paragraph 8 and *CLI* pp. 30–1.

was the question to which the analogy between sentences and pictures was expected to provide an answer. Wittgenstein's idea was not that it is physically impossible to combine names in ways that lacked sense, but only that it is logically impossible to do this while they are still functioning as names. This can now be put in a way that relates it to the two aspects of pictorial form: pictorial form is, intrinsically, the possibility that the names should be combined in a certain way, and, derivatively, the possibility that the objects named should be combined in the same way in reality.

But though this is true of pictures and sentences, why call it 'pictorial form' rather than 'sentential form'? Evidently, Wittgenstein found the way in which pictures convey information perspicuous and believed that it could be used to throw light on the parallel achievement of sentences. But why not the other way round? So far, very little attempt has been made to answer this question. It was suggested above that pictures and sentences both belong to systems and that in both cases the combinability of the elements can be explained by their place in a system.[75] It was also suggested that the systematic character of the representation of facts is more obvious and more perspicuous when it is pictorial than when it is linguistic.[76] It might now be useful to develop the suggestions a little further, before continuing the detailed interpretation of *Tractatus* 2.15–2.19.

The observation was made earlier, that anyone who fixes a point by its co-ordinates will think about it laterally, because he will immediately see it in relation to other points.[77] Now suppose that the point is the sense of the sentence 'φa', and that the two names 'φ' and 'a' are the co-ordinates that determine its position.[78] Then the sense of 'φa' will be seen in relation to the sense of other sentences. If we trace the co-ordinate 'φ', we shall find 'φb', 'φc', etc., and if we trace the other co-ordinate 'a', we shall find 'ψa', and 'χa', and so on.[79] The idea is that each sense is related to other senses in a system which, in Wittgenstein's later philosophy, would have been called the 'language-game' of ascribing qualities to particulars. This is a holistic idea and he presents it very clearly and persuasively when he compares this kind of linguistic system with the grid system of a map.

---

[75] See above, p. 121.
[76] See above, p. 121.
[77] See above, p. 122.
[78] See above, pp. 119–20.
[79] Cf. *PR* § 83.

That is one point of similarity between sentences and pictures: the constraints that govern the combinability of names are imposed by the system which makes them the names that they are. Here we have to remember that '*a*' stands for *a* not just because it has been attached to *a*, but because thereafter it faithfully represents *a*'s real possibilities of combination with other objects. If we concentrate on this aspect of the picture theory of sentences, we will emphasize the importance of use and we will be able to develop the connection between this part of his early system and his later insistence on the need to achieve a commanding view of our own linguistic practices.[80]

However, there must also be another side to the picture theory. For a map with its grid is like a group of sentences—a conjunction if we treat it as a message, or a system, if we treat it as a thesaurus of related sentences any of which could be used to convey a message; but Wittgenstein's fundamental idea is that each individual sentence is like a picture. This is the other side of the picture theory, its separatist aspect. What is the point of similarity between sentences and pictures on this side? And how is it related to the holistic aspect of the analogy?

There is evidently some tension between the two sides of the analogy. The holistic tendency points forward to Wittgenstein's later treatment of names:

. . . naming is something like attaching a label to a thing. One can say that this is preparatory to the use of a word. But *what* is it a preparation *for*?[81]

We may say: only someone who already knows how to do something with it can significantly ask a name.[82]

The separatist tendency points back to Russell's account of acquaint-ance and naming:

The reality that corresponds to the sense of the proposition can surely be nothing but its component parts, since we are surely *ignorant* of *everything* else.[83]

The knowledge of the representing relation *must* be founded only on the knowledge of the component parts of the situation![84]

---

[80] Cf. *PI* I § 5: 'It disperses the fog to study the phenomena of language in primitive kinds of application in which one can command a clear view of the aim and functioning of the words.'

[81] *PI* I § 26.

[82] Ibid., I § 31.

[83] *NB* 20 Nov. 1914.

[84] Ibid., 3 Nov. 1914.

The two tendencies are reconciled and held together by the thesis that all the possibilities of combination that belong to an object are inherent in it and so can be found in it:

> If I know an object I also know all its possible occurrences in states of affairs.
>
> (Every one of these possiblities must be part of the nature of the object.)
>
> A new possibility cannot be discovered later.[85]

This was a rather forced reconciliation and it produced an unstable equilibrium. Too much was extracted from the basic realism of the *Tractatus*, and too little weight was attached to our practices, especially in cases where we can exercise options.[86]

The best way to appreciate the instability of this equilibrium is to look at the sophisticated version of the analogy between sentences and pictures which Wittgenstein developed in the *Tractatus* but criticized in *Philosophical Remarks*:[87] names are like co-ordinates and they fix the sense of the sentence in which they occur in much the same way that a map reference fixes a point on the ground. Now this way of setting up the analogy works very well for sentences ascribing qualities to particulars, but it runs into complications with relations that take two or more terms.

This is easily seen. The language-game of ascribing qualities to particulars is a very restricted one and that is why it can be illustrated by the grid system of a map. But suppose that we remove the restriction by allowing the ascription of dyadic relations to pairs of particulars. Then the senses of the new propositions will be like points in a three-dimensional system fixed by Cartesian co-ordinates. However, there is no need to develop the analogy by extending it to relations with more than two terms, because it is obvious that no interesting difficulties lie in that direction.

But what we can and must do is to appreciate the more important, underlying difficulties that beset this version of the analogy and threaten the stability of the equilibrium between holism and separatism in the *Tractatus*. Never mind how many dimensions these co-ordinate systems have: the important point, which they all have in common, is that any intersection of co-ordinate lines will correspond to a sense.

---

[85] *TLP* 2.0123. The German word translated 'know' is 'kennen', which means 'to be acquainted with'.

[86] See above, pp. 10 and 24–5.

[87] See above, pp. 85–6.

However, this assumption breaks down if we include particulars and qualities of different types. It breaks down even for particulars and qualities of a single type, like visual or auditory particulars and qualities, the moment that we introduce dyadic relations and the three-dimensional grid system that they require. But the breakdown produced by different types is more striking and more important:

A spatial object must be situated in infinite space. (A spatial point is an argument-place.)
A speck in the visual field, though it need not be red, must have some colour: it is, so to speak, surrounded by colour-space. Notes must have *some* pitch, objects of the sense of touch *some* degree of hardness, and so on.[88]

All these type-differences must be respected if sense is to be preserved. So some of the intersections of the co-ordinate lines must be scrubbed out. To put it in the way that it was put above, there is tension between the intrinsic natures of objects and the uniform structure of the grid, and so there is a latent possibility of conflict between the separatism and the holism of the *Tractatus*.

There is also another place at which the assumption underlying this version of the analogy breaks down. Suppose that we claim not only that single propositions are true, one at a time, but also that conjunctions of propositions are true. In the analogue we would indicate not only that single intersections of co-ordinate lines were occupied, but also that sets of intersections were occupied. But what about conjunctions like the one discussed above, '*a* is red and *a* is green'? Evidently, we cannot fill in the grid in this particular way, but, if it were a map, we would expect to be able to fill in any arrangement of land and sea. So in 1929, when Wittgenstein criticized the system of the *Tractatus*, he said that he had failed to introduce something essential, namely 'determination of the value of a co-ordinate'.[89] He meant that he ought not to have represented the colour *red* by a line

---

[88] *TLP* 2.0131. In his pre-*Tractatus* writings Wittgenstein sometimes seems to imply that differences of type will not appear at the level of complete analysis: 'If "*A*" is used to mean a person, "*A* is sitting" is admissible, but not if "*A*" signifies this book.—But once a proposition is completely analysed, everything that depends on the understanding of its form must be unaffected by the meaning of its parts.'(*Prototractatus*, 3.201412.) If this implies that there are no differences of type at the level of complete analysis, it is significant that it is not included in the *Tractatus*. It uses a criterion of simplicity even more demanding than the criterion of *TLP* 4.211. It is interesting that in *NB*, when he discusses this question, he does not insist on this extreme criterion of simplicity. See *NB* 22 June 1915, paragraphs 8–11.

[89] See *PR* § 83, discussed above, pp. 85–6.

running across the grid: he ought to have used the line to represent *chromatic colour* and assigned the different colours to numbered points on it. So this is another place where we can see the tension between the intrinsic natures of objects and the uniform structure of the grid, with the consequent threat of conflict between separatism and holism.

In the *Tractatus*, when Wittgenstein introduces the idea that sentences are pictures, it is the separatist aspect of the analogy that is in the forefront.[90] This is because the first thing that needs to be explained is how an individual sentence is set up with a sense. The explanation is that a sentence is a fact with a certain multiplicity, which puts it in a position to depict any fact of the same multiplicity.[91] Now this multiplicity gives the sentence its own form—the possibility realized in its structure—but it is not yet pictorial form. It will become pictorial form when the words are linked with objects in whatever possible fact of the same multiplicity is chosen as its correlate in reality. So there are, as already explained,[92] two conditions to be met before the string of words achieves pictorial form: intrinsically, it must be composite, so that it will have a multiplicity of its own,[93] and extrinsically the individual words must be linked with objects in the possible fact that has been chosen—a linkage which is not achieved by one-off attachment, because the words must continue to be combined in ways that are real possibilities for the objects. When these two conditions are met, the sentence realizes its own form *as the form of the fact which it presents*.

But why is this called 'pictorial form'? Why not call it 'presentational form' and merely add in a footnote that spatial pictures too possess presentational form? This question was asked earlier[94] and so far it has been answered like this: pictures and sentences both belong to systems, and this is implicit from the beginning in the attachment of their elements to things out there in the world, but it is especially obvious and perspicuous in the case of pictures. But if we read on to *TLP* 2.18, we can add something to this answer. In the 2.16s and 2.17s Wittgenstein is concerned with homogeneous pictures like maps. He starts with them, because homogeneity produces linkages so natural that we accept them in an almost unexamined package deal. Because

[90] *TLP* 2.1ff.
[91] Ibid., 4.04.
[92] See above, p. 130.
[93] *TLP* 4.032.
[94] See above, p. 131.

this is his starting-point, presentational form is called 'pictorial form', and his account of it is then extended to sentences which are not homogeneous with their subject-matter, and so require artificial linkages set up piecemeal, word by word.[95] Nevertheless, they too realize their own forms as the forms of the facts which they present:

> What any picture, of whatever form, must have in common with reality, in order to be able to depict it—correctly or incorrectly—in any way at all, is logical form, i.e. the form of reality.
>
> A picture whose pictorial form is logical form is called a logical picture.
>
> Every picture is *at the same time* a logical one. (On the other hand, not every picture is, for example, a spatial one.)[96]

The move from homogeneous to heterogeneous representation is a move from the more perspicuous to the less perspicuous, but the two methods are essentially alike.

There is still something puzzling about this passage. If every picture is a logical picture why not call them all 'logical pictures'? The explanation of this piece of discrimination is that Wittgenstein is generalizing the concept of a picture. What any picture has in common with the fact that it depicts is a pictorial form which is logical. But some pictures are homogeneous, and in their case this logical pictorial form will satisfy another description: for example, in the case of spatial pictures it will be spatial pictorial form. So it is convenient to adopt the following convention: pictorial form is brought under the most specific description that it satisfies in a given case—'logical', if that is all that it is, but 'spatial' if it is not only logical but also spatial. We often stack up descriptions in this way, trumping the more general with the more specific.

The strategy adopted so far in this exegesis of the picture theory of sentences has been to focus on to the central point of the analogy and to avoid everything peripheral and inessential.[97] The central point has been located in the constraints imposed on the forms of pictures and sentences. In both cases the form has to be the same as the form of the depicted fact: in both cases the two facts, depicting and depicted, must be linked through their elements; and in both cases the linkage must be one-to-one attachment followed by faithful representation. But it is not easy to appreciate these constraints without being told something

---

[95] See *NB* 22 Oct. 1914.
[96] *TLP* 2.18–2.182.
[97] See above, p. 120.

about the criterion of identity of form in the depicting fact and the depicted fact. Now two facts have the same form only if each contains the same number of elements arranged in the same way. So, naturally, we want to know how to count the elements in the two structures.

However, given Wittgenstein's professed agnosticism about the nature of elementary propositions, we must be prepared to accept a rather disappointing result. It is possible that the *Tractatus* does not contain a definite answer to the question, whether all objects are particulars. It may be left open whether the fact that *aRb* contains two or three objects. Perhaps all that he felt certain about when he put the book together was that, whatever their number, there would be the same number of names in the corresponding sentence. If that was the situation, the principle of equal multiplicity of elements[98] was uncompromisable, but its application was uncertain. This is a real possibility, and so we must not assume that the *Tractatus* contains a definitive application of the picture theory of sentences worked out in full detail. It is better to extract the central point of the analogy from Wittgenstein's general pronouncements, and to show that it could have been developed in more than one way.

There are two sets of things to be counted and in each case the principle of counting is controversial. How many objects are there in the fact that *aRb*? And how many propositional elements are there in the corresponding sentence? It is notorious that Wittgenstein answered the first question in different ways in the period that ended with the publication of the *Tractatus*. In a letter to Russell, dated 16 January 1913, he writes:

. . . I have changed my views on 'atomic' complexes: I now think that qualities, relations (like love) etc. are all copulae! That means that I for instance analyse a subject–predicate proposition, say, 'Socrates is human' into 'Socrates' and 'something is human', (which I think is not complex). The reason for this is a very fundamental one: I think that there cannot be different types of things![99]

This view is maintained in *Notes on Logic*:

Indefinables are of two sorts: names and forms. Propositions cannot consist of names alone, they cannot be classes of names.[100]

However, two years later, in the *Notebooks*, he abandoned it:

Relations and properties, etc. are *objects* too.[101]

[98] See *TLP* 4.04.   [99] *NB* pp.120–1.
[100] Ibid., p. 98.   [101] Ibid., 16 June 1915.

He also abandoned the three associated theses, that 'something is human' is not complex,[102] that there are no differences of type between objects,[103] and that sentences can avoid being classes of names only if they also contain phrases signifying forms.[104] Evidently his new idea was that objects are essentially cohesive,[105] and that forms are not parts of facts but are exemplified by facts taken as wholes.[106]

These changes did not force him to maintain his new thesis, that 'relations and properties are *objects* too': they only made it possible for him to maintain it. There was nothing to prevent him from reverting to his 1913 view in the *Tractatus*. Did he in fact do so? It is not easy to get an answer to this question from the text, and it used to be debated at length by interpreters trying to unlock the secrets of the picture theory of sentences.[107] There are passages which suggest that objects are not all particulars,[108] but they seem to carry no more weight than two passages often cited in support of the opposite interpretation:

Space, time, and colour (being coloured) are forms of objects.[109]

Instead of, 'The complex sign "*aRb*" says that *a* stands to *b* in the relation *R*', we ought to put, '*That* "*a*" stands to "*b*" in a certain relation says *that aRb*'.[110]

However, neither of these two passages is decisive. In fact, it is a mistake to use the first one to support the view that the objects of the *Tractatus* are all particulars. For it does not say that determinate positions, times, and colours are forms of objects: it only says this about the determinables, *being coloured*, etc. So the doctrine is one that has already been encountered and explained:[111] visual objects must have some colour and may have any colour, and it is in this sense that *being coloured* is their form. This doctrine, which is extended to *occurring at a place* and *occurring at a time*, is evidently compatible with either of Wittgenstein's two views about the ontological status of determinate colours, positions, and times.

---

[102] See *NB* 25 Oct. 1914 and 31 Oct. 1914. Cf. *TLP* 4.0411.

[103] See *TLP* 2.0131, discussed above, pp. 86 and 134, and *TLP* 3.331–3.334.

[104] Ibid., 4.0311 and 3.142.

[105] Ibid., 2.03. Cf. 2.0121–2.0122.

[106] Ibid., 3.315. This view of forms is implicit in his criticism of Russell's view. See above, pp. 123–6.

[107] See D. Keyt: 'Wittgenstein's Picture Theory of Language', in *Essays on Wittgenstein's* Tractatus, ed. R. Beard and R. Copi, Routledge and Kegan Paul, 1966.

[108] e.g. *TLP* 4.123.

[109] Ibid., 2.0251.

[110] Ibid., 3.1432.

[111] See above, pp. 85–6.

But what about 3.1432? That is a remark which bears not only on the principle of individuation of elements in depicted facts but also on the principle of individuation of elements in depicting facts, and its interpretation may be postponed for a moment. Meanwhile, if we confine ourselves to asking how Wittgenstein counted elements in depicted facts, the answer is hard to find in the *Tractatus*. There are important sources of evidence not only in his preparatory work for the book, but also in his later comments on it, many of which imply that he had at least allowed for the possibility of counting relations and properties as objects.[112] But in the book itself he seems to be more non-committal than in his preparatory work for it, and, therefore, almost certainly deliberately non-committal. So we might well conclude that the key to the picture theory is not to be found in the resolution of this controversy. On the contrary, it lies in the more abstract features of form that have already been identified and explained. Wittgenstein was deliberately non-committal in the *Tractatus* because he did not think it necessary to take a definite stand on peripheral matters. Why should he jeopardize the central point of his theory by the unnecessary exposure of hostages to fortune?[113]

But what about 3.1432? At first sight it certainly seems to imply that the form shared by the two facts is *that x stands in a certain relation to y*, and that their elements are the values of *x* and *y*. So it looks as if there are only two elements in the depicting fact, the names '*a*' and '*b*', and, correspondingly, only two elements in the depicted fact, the objects *a* and *b*. However, this is one of those cases, not uncommon in Wittgenstein's work, where it is worth tracing a remark back to its first occurrence. His aphorisms often express complex insights and they are sometimes repeated at a later date with significant changes, and even when they remain unchanged, new contexts sometimes produce shifts of emphasis.

The remark first appears in *Notes on Logic*[114] in a form that is slightly but not significantly different from *Tractatus* 3.1432. The context is important. The preceding paragraph begins with these words:

[112] See above, pp. 137–8. Some of the later evidence supports a stronger conclusion. e.g. in 1930–1, D. Lee made the following note of Wittgenstein's answer to his request for an explanation of the first four remarks of the Tractatus: '2.01. "An atomic fact is a combination of objects (entities, things)." Objects etc. is here used for such things as a colour, a point in visual space etc.: cf. also above. A word has no sense except in a proposition. "Objects" also include relations; a proposition is not two things connected by a relation. "Thing" and "relation" are on the same level. The objects hang as it were in a chain.' (*CLI* p. 120.)

[113] See above, pp. 89 and 120. [114] *NB* p. 105.

A complex symbol must never be introduced as a single indefinable. Thus, for instance, no proposition is indefinable. . . .

The remark follows in the next paragraph, and then the comment:

Only facts can express sense, a class of names cannot. This is easily shown. In *aRb* it is not the complex that symbolizes but the fact that the symbol *a* stands in a certain relation to the symbol *b*. Thus facts are symbolized by facts, or more correctly: that a certain thing is the case in the symbol says that a certain thing is the case in the world.

When 3.1432 is read in this context, its main point is evidently that a sentence is an articulated fact. This is also the main point made by the remark in its context in the *Tractatus*:

What constitutes a propositional sign is that in it its elements (the words) stand in a determinate relation to one another.

A propositional sign is a fact.

A proposition is not a medley of words.—(Just as a theme in music is not a medley of notes.)

A proposition is articulated.

Only facts can express a sense, a set of names cannot.[115]

He then says that the factuality of sentences is obscured by the way they are written, which does not sufficiently mark the difference between them and names. The best way to bring out their factuality is to think of a propositional sign composed of spatial objects. Then 3.1432 follows. There is no attempt to establish the right way to apply the principle of equal multiplicity. All the emphasis is on the general point, that sentences are facts.

In both contexts, in *Notes on Logic* and in the *Tractatus*, this general point is presented as a corollary of the thesis that all complexes are really facts masquerading as objects.[116] This is important, because readers of the *Tractatus* who are familiar with the doctrine that sentences are facts are apt to take it in their stride and then to look in 3.1432 for some special point which may not be there. But Wittgenstein does not take the doctrine in his stride: he argues for it. All complexes must really be facts, but there is something special about sentential facts which emerges later. They are an extract from the complete product, spoken or written, and the way we make the extract

---

[115] *TLP* 3.14–3.142. The translation has been changed slightly.

[116] See above, pp. 27 and 79.

depends on linguistic conventions;[117] for example, the colour of the ink or the note hit by the speaker do not necessarily have any semantic function, and so would not necessarily be included in the specification of the depicting fact. A sentence may even contain a word which makes no contribution to its message, just as a map may sport a purely decorative mermaid in an empty corner of the ocean.[118] This too is important because it shows that things that look like propositional elements need not be propositional elements; from which it follows that, if we treat spatial relations in the world as objects, we are not forced to treat spatial relations between words on the page as propositional elements.[119] Of course, in this case the things that might be taken to be propositional elements, spatial relations between words, do contribute to the message, but not in the same way as names.

The next occurrence of the remark is in a different context in *Notes Dictated to G. E. Moore in Norway* (April 1914):

> ... in '*aRb*', '*R*' is *not* a symbol, but *that* '*R*' is between one name and another symbolizes. Here we have *not* said: this symbol is not of this type but of that, but only: *This* symbolizes and not that. This seems again to make the same mistake, because 'symbolizes' is 'typically ambiguous'. The true analysis is: '*R*' is no proper name, and, that '*R*' stands between '*a*' and '*b*' expresses a *relation*. Here are two propositions *of different type* connected by 'and'.[120]

Here Wittgenstein is not primarily concerned with the factuality of sentences. The question is, how differences of type can be conveyed, and he takes the factuality of sentences for granted and uses it in his answer. It is, however, interesting to be told that '*R*' is not a proper name, and so, by implication, that *R* is not an object, and yet to find that '*R*' plays an essential role in the depicting fact, because in this fact the relation between '*a*' and '*b*' is *standing on opposite sides of* '*R*'.

This is important, because it shows that if we supposed that all the objects of the *Tractatus* are particulars, we still would not be forced to

---

[117] A point well made by G. E. M. Anscombe: *Introduction to Wittgenstein's Tractatus*, p. 75.

[118] Cf. *TLP* 3.328: 'If a sign is *useless*, it is meaningless. That is the point of Occam's maxim.' Later he calls such a sign 'a wheel that can be turned though nothing else moves with it.' (*PI* I § 270–1.)

[119] The argument, that we would be forced to that conclusion, may be called 'the argument from the supernumerary', because it would show that the depicting fact always contains one more element than the depicted fact. e.g. it has been used to show that if the objects of the *Tractatus* included relations, the principle of equal multiplicity would be violated in this way. (See D. Keyt: 'Wittgenstein's Picture Theory of Language', pp. 380–1.) But the argument is invalid.

[120] *NB* pp. 108–9.

the conclusion that elementary propositions must consist of various spatial arrangements of their names on the page.[121] For we could take the relation between '*a*' and '*b*' mentioned in *TLP* 3.1432 to be *standing on opposite sides of* '*R*'. This interpretation would have a lot to recommend it.[122] For if we took the relation between '*a*' and '*b*' to be a spatial relation on the page, we would be creating an unnecessary peripheral problem: Wittgenstein would need as many ways of arranging the two names on the page as there are possible relations in the world between the two objects.[123] But if that were so, what would be its importance?

On the other hand, it must be admitted that it is one thing to allow words like '*R*' to occur in elementary propositions, but quite another thing to allow them to occur as names. In *TLP* 3.1432 it would be very odd to say that the depicting fact is the fact that '*a*' stands in a certain relation to '*b*', if what was meant was not only that the relation is *standing on opposite sides of* '*R*', but also that *R* is an object. But if Wittgenstein now includes relations among objects, it would still be a true thing to say, and, given the history of the remark, it is not impossible that he simply failed to adjust it to his new thesis.

However, it is really safer to accept his professions of agnosticism about the nature of the objects of the *Tractatus*, and to take the evidence to show no more than that he allowed for the possibility that they might include relations. The two most common reasons for trying to pin him down to a definite choice between the two alternative ontologies are both mistaken. It is wrongly assumed that this is the only way to locate the central point of analogy between sentences and pictures, and it is invalidly argued that either of the two choices will make it difficult for him to apply the principle of equal multiplicity. It then appears to be important to discover which choice he made.

One more thing is needed to complete this exegesis of the picture theory of sentences: the doctrine, that certain things cannot be said but only shown,[124] must be explained. There is a letter to Russell in which Wittgenstein says that it is a matter of cardinal importance,[125] but he never really tries to explain it in the *Tractatus*. He invokes it at various points in the text, but without much argument and without any

---

[121] That is G. E. M. Anscombe's conclusion. (See above, n. 29.)

[122] It is developed by E. Stenius in *Wittgenstein's* Tractatus, Blackwell, 1960.

[123] See D. Keyt, 'Wittgenstein's Picture Theory of Language', pp. 384–5.

[124] *TLP* 4.1212.

[125] Dated 19 Aug. 1919. See *NB* p. 130.

precise specification of its meaning. If we try to deduce the meaning of the doctrine and its justification from the things that he puts on the list of what can be shown but not said, we do not get much help. For the list includes such disparate items as the existence of a named object,[126] the identity of the world with my world,[127] and the value of anything that has value.[128] It is a baffling doctrine bafflingly presented.

Its presentation in this exegesis of the early system has been largely metaphorical so far. The point was put like this: the possibility of saying some things in factual discourse depends on the actuality of other things which cannot be said.[129] Then the analogy with pictures was used to illustrate the dependence of the sayable on the unsayable: a portrait relies on the projective geometry which links the canvas to the sitter, but it does not include a diagram of the linkage. However, that did not take the explanation very far, because in such a case it would certainly be possible to draw a diagram of the linkage, and the only thing wrong with that procedure would be that it could not be completed, because the last diagram would rely on a method of projection which was not analysed in a further diagram.[130] But is that a serious limitation?

Arguably it is, and the argument would be that a diagram of the method of projection used by the original portrait would have to pick out the same facts about the sitter and would have to use the same method of projection in order to pick them out. Here we do not have to suppose that the portrait is a good likeness, because there is a more radical form of the argument which applies to the artist's impressions, whether they are true or false: the possibility presented by the portrait can be presented in the diagram only if the same method of projection is used again. The argument, in this form, has a ready application to sentences: if someone wants to say that the sentence '*p*' is correlated with the possibility that *p*, he will have to use the same method of correlation in order to identify that possibility.[131] Of course, he may not actually use the same sentence, but, if he uses another one, it will have to be equivalent, just as the diagram might not use the colour of the original portrait, but would still have to reproduce its geometry. However, if the sentence '*p*' is elementary, it will not have an

[126] *TLP* 4.1211 and 5.535.
[127] Ibid., 5.62.
[128] Ibid., 6.4–6.421.
[129] See above, pp. 7, 71, and 115.
[130] See above, p. 7.
[131] See *CLI* pp. 12–13.

equivalent, and then he really will have to use the same sentence as well as the same method of correlation.

Now is this a serious limitation? There is certainly something here that we cannot do: we cannot give a complete account of the sense of any factual sentence. The reason why we cannot do this is that such an account would have to use language in order to identify the possibility presented by the sentence, and there is only one way for language to latch on to that possibility and that is to exploit the same method of correlation. We cannot avoid using this method of correlation, because a different method would give us a different possibility. There is only one way in which the ultimate grid of possibilities imposes its structure on all factual languages, and in this case it has been pre-empted by the original sentence. Now we might try to shrug off this limitation with the comment that it is an inevitable consequence of the way the task was set. It is, after all, accepted in formal semantics that either the sentence named on the left-hand side of an instance of Tarski's convention T or an equivalent sentence must be used on the right-hand side. ' "Snow is white" is true if and only if snow is white.' Evidently, the same limitation is in force when biconditionals of this kind figure in a theory of meaning rather than a theory of truth.[132]

However, a lot is going to depend on the next move. In Wittgenstein's case the next move was going to be all the more important because he treated language as the universal medium of all thought.[133] He says in a letter to Russell that he does not know what kind of thing the elements of an unspoken thought would be, but they must 'have the same sort of relation to reality as words'.[134] The picture theory of sentences is really a theory about any possible mode of symbolization:

> There is a general rule by means of which the musician can obtain the symphony from the score, and which makes it possible to derive the symphony from the groove on the gramophone record, and, using the first rule, to derive the score again. That is what constitutes the inner similarity between these things which seem to be constructed in such entirely different ways. And that rule is the law of projection which projects the symphony into the language of musical notation. It is the rule for translating this language into the language of gramophone records.

---

[132] See D. Davidson: 'Truth and Meaning', in *Inquiries into Truth and Interpretation*, Oxford 1981. The point made above is made very clearly by J. McDowell and G. Evans in their introduction to *Truth and Meaning*, Oxford, 1976, pp. vii–xi.

[133] See J. and M. Hintikka: *Investigating Wittgenstein*, ch. I.

[134] Dated 19 Aug. 1919. See *NB* p. 130. Cf. *CLI* pp. 38–9.

The possibility of all imagery, of all our pictorial modes of expression, is contained in the logic of depiction.[135]

This extension of the concept of language made his next move all the more important. A limited explanation of the phenomenon of sense might be achieved by pointing out similarities between one mode of symbolization and another, as the picture theory does, but what nobody will ever be able to do is to explain them all from some external standpoint.[136]

His next move was to formulate the doctrine of showing. This is a doctrine with two aspects, one superficial and the other deep. It is immediately clear why he believed that it is impossible to give in language a complete explanation of the phenomenon of sense. In the *Tractatus* all propositions are contingently true or false and anything that can be said at all can be said in propositions.[137] Now what we cannot do is to give a complete account of the sense of a factual sentence without exploiting that sentence's method of correlation with the possibility that it presents. But that means that the attempt to give such an account must end in tautology.[138] It will not come out with a contingently true sentence, and, therefore, what it tries to say will not be sayable. It can only be shown:

Thus one proposition '*fa*' shows that the object *a* occurs in its sense, two propositions, '*fa*' and '*ga*' show that the same object is mentioned in both of them.[139]

If we try to say that the object *a* occurs in the sense of '*fa*', we shall fail, because the only way to pick out the object that we mean is to use the method of correlation used by '*fa*' and then the result will be a tautology.[140]

This is the simplest possible illustration of the doctrine of showing, and so it is the best place to begin to interpret it. In fact, the doctrine originated at this point, and its numerous developments, some of which seem to be very loosely connected with its origin, came later.

---

[135] *TLP* 4.0141–4.015.
[136] Ibid., 2.173 and 4.12.
[137] Ibid., 4.1 ff.
[138] In the original sense of 'tautology', not in the technical sense of *TLP*.
[139] *TLP* 4.1211.
[140] There is an apt description of this result in *PI* I, § 433. Wittgenstein is describing a person who gives an order but finds that it is not understood. So he tries all sorts of ways of making his meaning clear, but without success: 'Here it looks as if the order were beginning to stammer.' Tautological reformulation is no use in practice.

What holds together the variety of things that can only be shown is their negative point of similarity: they are things that cannot be expressed in factual language. It is profitless to search for a positive theory of the mystical to unify the whole field of these rejects. The strategy must be to take them one by one and to ask why they are excluded from factual discourse. In a simple case, like this one, the reason is that the possibility of saying some things depends on the actuality of other things which cannot be non-tautologically said.

The doctrine of showing also has a deeper aspect. It may be obvious that we cannot give in language a complete non-tautologically true account of the sense of any factual sentence, but it is not at all obvious what our reaction to this limitation ought to be. Wittgenstein's reaction was to invoke a concept of showing with more negative than positive content. Its positive content, such as it was, was derived from the expectation that when language was put under the microscope of logical analysis, it would turn out to have a perspicuous structure.[141] It would be possible to see all the way to its ultimate edge where simple words make contact with simple things. This is evidently a development of Russell's idea, that factual language is founded on independent reference to separate things. If we could only penetrate the network of the analysis of a factual sentence we would see the ultimate constituents of its sense, the simple referents which it arranges in thought.[142] In Wittgenstein's later writings this vision is transferred to the surface: we need to achieve a commanding view of our own usage.

His confidence that logical analysis would achieve absolutely perspicuous results was not confined to the far-reaching senses of individual factual sentences. Already in the *Tractatus* there are intimations of systematic lateral connections between them, and these too would be immediately evident to a philosopher who achieved a commanding view of language.[143] The most conspicuous lateral connections were logical,[144] but there were other less familiar ones exploited by the picture theory of sentences.[145] The doctrine of showing must be read in the context of these expectations, because it is from them that it derives its positive content. When Wittgenstein made his selection from his copious exploratory notes and put the *Tractatus* together, his leading idea was that we can see further than we

---

[141] See *TLP* 4.112 and 4.116.
[142] See *TLP* Author's Preface, p. 3, 4.023, and *Protractatus*, 3.202111.
[143] See above, pp. 85–6 and 115.
[144] See above, p. 122.   [145] See above, pp. 131–4.

can say. We can see all the way to the edge of language, but the most distant things that we see cannot be expressed in sentences because they are the pre-conditions of saying anything.

What would have been the alternative to this vision? Perhaps it would have been possible to use one part of language to explain the structure of another part, as is done by logicians who construct calculi. However, that was a strategy which never appealed to him because he was concerned with the general explanation of all modes of symbolization and their connection with the world. Given that no factual theory could provide such an explanation, recourse to a more intuitive kind of understanding seemed to be the only possibility. Here, as so often, the framework of his philosophy was Kantian.

However, there was, in fact, another possibility, but it did not occur to him until later. He might have used one part of language to describe the application of another part rather than its structure.[146] Viewed from within, language presented an intricate network which seemed to be elucidatable only by an analysis which would find nothing more to say when it reached the edge, and so would be reduced to the characteristic stammering of semantics. Would it not be better to adopt the standpoint of a philosophical commentator on the whole human scene in which the various applications of language are set? This would not be a change of subject, because anyone who uses language knows how to adapt it to this setting and understands the point of what he is doing. We might expect, therefore, to learn more about meaning from this broader survey than from philosophical translations and retranslations, which are bound to produce mystification at the point where they peter out.

This is the origin of his later language-games, and it is interesting to find him hinting at the connection near the end of his life:

Am I not getting closer and closer to saying that in the end logic cannot be described? You must look at the practice of language and then you will see it.[147]

---

[146] See *PG* § 46: 'One is inclined to make a distinction between rules of grammar that set up "a connection between language and reality" and those that do not. A rule of the first kind is "This colour is called 'red'"—a rule of the second kind is "~~p = p". With regard to this distinction there is a common error; language is not something that is first given a structure and then fitted on to reality.'

[147] L. Wittgenstein: *On Certainty*, ed. G. E. M. Anscombe and G. H. von Wright tr. G. E. M. Anscombe and D. Paul, Blackwell 1969, § 501, quoted by A. Kenny, *Wittgenstein*, p. 218.

This is also the origin of his new ideas about the application of words to things.[148] In the *Tractatus* the reidentification of objects was never discussed,[149] and all that was said about the way in which their names remain attached to them was that their names must respect their inherent possibilities of combination with other objects. But what about us? How do we recognize an object when we encounter it again? These questions led straight into his later investigation of following a rule, an investigation which may be regarded as a demystification of the unsayable. Or perhaps the point should be put the other way round, as it was put earlier:[150] the mystery of the things that can only be shown is spread over the whole range of human life and consciousness. Whichever way we put it, the point is that we thinking creatures have certain insights into the attachment of our thoughts to the world, and these insights cannot be expressed in scientific language.

The doctrine of showing also has another dimension. If it is right, we cannot give a complete account of the sense of a factual sentence without reusing that sentence's method of correlation with the possibility presented by it. It follows that the best that we can hope for is a tautological account, and a tautological account will not be explanatory. Now there are two ways in which such an account would fail as an explanation. One deficiency, which has already been described,[151] is that a person who did not already know how the original factual sentence, or some equivalent version of it, was correlated with a possible state of affairs, would be no better off after he had heard an account of this kind. The specification that it gave him would be useless from this point of view. But suppose that we all know what the sentence means, and that what we want is an explanation of the fact that it has this meaning. Then the tautological account manifests another deficiency: it cannot explain a fact of this kind, because it has no way of getting past it and finding any further independently specifiable fact to support it.[152]

This aspect of the doctrine of showing is prominent in *Philosophical Remarks*, and in *Wittgenstein's Lectures, Cambridge, 1930—1932* it is the cardinal point in his explanation of the theory of meaning which he had published in the *Tractatus*. It is easy to miss the point, because,

---

[148] See above, pp. 10–11 and 59–60.

[149] See above, p. 9.

[150] See above, p. 17.

[151] See above, p. 145 for this deficiency and the relevant meaning of the word 'tautological'.

[152] See above, p. 16.

when we are told that we cannot explain the fact that an ordinary sentence, like 'That is green' has the particular meaning that it does have, we immediately think of ordinary ways in which we obviously can explain it. Children learn the meaning of the word 'green' from their parents and pass it on in their turn to their children. We might even be able to explain why the long line of imitators cut this particular band out of the spectrum and gave it a name. For different ways of setting up colour vocabularies might be related to the different needs of the people who use them.[153] But what Wittgenstein is denying is the possibility of explaining the fact that we have a certain colour vocabulary by saying things that can only be expressed in its terms:

> If I could describe the point of grammatical conventions by saying that they are made necessary by certain properties of the colours (say), then that would make the conventions superfluous, since in that case I would be able to say precisely that which the conventions exclude my saying. Conversely, if the conventions were necessary, i.e. if certain combinations of words had to be excluded as nonsensical, then for that very reason I cannot cite a property of colours that makes the conventions necessary, since it would then be conceivable that the colours should not have this property, and I could only express that by violating the conventions.[154]

It is, for example, necessary that a thing should not be both green and red, and it is a mistake to say that it might not have been necessary but is, in fact, necessary because there is something about the two colours which makes it necessary, but which might have been otherwise.

The point can be put more succinctly:

> ... if anything is to count as nonsense in the grammar which is to be justified, then it cannot at the same time pass for sense in the grammar of the propositions that justify it (etc.).[155]

Or more grandiloquently:

> ... the essence of language is a picture of the essence of the world; and philosophy as custodian of grammar can in fact grasp the essence of the world, only not in the propositions of language, but in rules for this language which exclude nonsensical combinations of signs.[156]

This is the cardinal point of the picture theory of the *Tractatus*, but in that context it does not seem so paradoxical as it does in the work that

---

[153] Cf. *PI* II § xii.
[154] *PR* § 4. Cf. *CLI* pp. 47 and 95.
[155] *PR* § 7.
[156] Ibid., § 54.

Wittgenstein produced immediately after his return to philosophy in 1929. The reason why the same doctrine can strike us in two different ways is interesting. In the *Tractatus* all necessity is logical necessity and so it can always be dug up and exhibited in tautological combinations of sentences.[157] There are no specific necessities which have to be left embedded in the natures of things: they can all be exhibited in the completely analysed structure of factual language. At this stage the only mysterious necessity is the necessity that the world have the general structure which makes this exhibition possible.[158] This is something so remote and abstract that we do not find it paradoxical that it can only be exhibited in tautological combinations of sentences. 'That's just logic', we say to ourselves with complacent tolerance. But when Wittgenstein changed his mind about elementary propositions and allowed the specific necessities of the colour circle to remain buried in the natures of the colours,[159] the same doctrine produces a different reaction. 'Surely we can say what it is about the colours that generates these necessasry connections between their names.' But can we? If Wittgenstein is right, we cannot, and our best efforts inevitably founder in the other kind of tautology, the tautology of the semantic stammer.

The connection with the picture theory of sentences is made very perspicuously in *Wittgenstein's Lectures, Cambridge 1930—1932*:

... in order that propositions may be able to represent at all something further is needed which is the same both in language and reality. For example, a picture can represent a scene rightly or wrongly; but both in picture and scene pictured there will be colour and light and shade.[160]

He is starting with homogeneous pictures, just as he did in the *Tractatus*,[161] because they immediately make the theory acceptable to intuition. But the generalization follows immediately:

Thought must have the logical form of reality if it is to be thought at all.
Grammar is not the expression of what is the case but of what is possible. There is a sense therefore in which possibility is logical form.[162]

---

[157] In the technical sense of 'tautology'. See above, pp. 22–3.
[158] See *TLP* 6.124, discussed above, pp. 23–5.
[159] See above, pp. 82–7.
[160] *CLI* p. 10.
[161] *TLP* 2.17–2.171.
[162] *CLI* p. 10. This should be read as a comment on *TLP* 2.033 and 2.18. See above, pp. 116 and 129–31.

Several lectures later there is a particularly clear explanation of this doctrine:

What is 'in common' between thought and reality must already be expressed in the expression of the thought. You cannot express it in a further proposition, and it is misleading to try. The 'harmony' between thought and reality which philosophers speak of as 'fundamental' is something we can't talk about, and so is not in the ordinary sense a harmony at all, since we cannot describe it. What makes it possible for us to judge rightly about the world also makes it possible for us to judge wrongly.[163]

But how can anything so essential be latent in ordinary language and not elicitable in philosophical language? This is the natural protest of those who find the doctrine acceptable in the context of the *Tractatus*, where what must be left unsaid is so abstract and rarefied, but unacceptable in its later context, where the rule of silence excludes explanations that look more substantial and, therefore, more tempting. Wittgenstein's response to this protest was to develop a new philosophical method designed to elicit from ordinary language everything that it showed but could not say, but, of course, not to try to express it in philosophical language. However, that lay in the future, and in these lectures he simply says this:

You cannot justify grammar. For such a justification would have to be in the form of a description of the world and such a description might be otherwise, and the propositions expressing this different description would have to be false. But grammar requires them to be senseless. Grammar allows us to talk of a higher degree of sweetness, but not of a higher degree of identity; it allows the one combination but not the other, nor does it allow us to use 'sweet' instead of 'great' or 'small'[164] Is grammar arbitrary? Yes, in the sense just mentioned, that it cannot be justified. But it is not arbitrary in so far as it is not arbitrary what rules of grammar I can make use of. Grammar described by itself is arbitrary; what makes it not arbitrary is its use.[165]

It would, of course, be highly paradoxical to suggest that grammar is arbitrary whichever way we look at it. The paradox is reduced if grammar is arbitrary only when it is abstracted from its use. However, we might still find it paradoxical that we cannot say what it is about its use that makes it non-arbitrary. But this paradox too is at least reduced when it becomes clear that Wittgenstein is not saying that

[163] *CLI* p. 37.
[164] Something seems to have gone wrong with the note-taking at this point.
[165] *CLI* p. 49.

there is nothing about its use that makes it non-arbitrary, but only that we cannot get it out into propositions:

'The only correlate in language to an intrinsic necessity is an arbitrary rule. It is the only thing which one can milk out of this intrinsic necessity into a proposition.'[166]

That only shows that what is left behind to be revealed by a comparative study of language-games is the true essence of whatever world is ours.

---

[166] *PG* § 133. He is probably quoting himself. Cf. *CLI* p. 57.

7
Solipsism

SOLIPSISM stands at the intersection of several different lines of thought in Wittgenstein's mind. He introduces it in the *Tractatus* as a failed attempt to impose a personal limit on language. It is true that language is limited, but only in a general, impersonal way: anything that we can say is a truth-function of elementary sentences mirroring arrangements of objects. If we try to impose a further, specific restriction on what can be said, by setting up a list of canonical types of object, each linked to its own form of elementary sentence, we run into all the difficulties rehearsed in the 5.55s. These forms are possibilities and we cannot get outside language in order to treat their existence as a fact, and, when we work from inside language, we have no way of establishing it as a necessity, because there is absolutely no a priori reason why these and only these possibilities should exist. Then, in 5.6, he moves on to the treatment of solipsism as another failed attempt to impose an unjustifiably narrow limit on language—not an impersonal limit this time, but an egocentric one.[1]

Anyone can see that this way of introducing solipsism makes prominent certain features of the doctrine which are recessive in the usual presentations of it. It is an approach which keeps a crucial question clearly in view right from the start: 'Who is this subject who claims to be the fixed point from which all the objects underpinning factual language have to be identified?' Wittgenstein assumes that anything that can be said must be linked to underlying objects, and then, faced with the question, 'What objects?', argues that they cannot be identified by their connection with any privileged subject. The solipsist supposes that this subject deals out existence and non-existence to everything *ex cathedra*, but that is really a fantasy. For if the subject is part of the world, the doctrine is self-refuting, and if he is not part of the world, the doctrine is empty.[2]

Although it is easy to see that this concentration on the question of

---

[1] See above, pp. 38–9.
[2] This dilemma is equally effective against a Humean solipsist who does not believe in a separate ego. See above, p 36.

the privileged subject's identity is the distinctive feature of Wittgenstein's treatment of solipsism, it is not at all easy to hold on to the point. The trouble is that, for all the practical purposes of life, I know very well who I am, and so when I contemplate the solipsistic project of dealing out existence and non-existence from nowhere, it is natural for me to assume that I shall still sufficiently know who I am. This assumption lies behind the traditional treatments of solipsism, which, with few exceptions, find no problem in the identity of the subject, but are obsessed by the veil of sense-data which they see hanging between the subject and the world in which he supposedly lives.

This tends to push us into a misunderstanding of what Wittgenstein says about solipsism in the *Tractatus*. Surely he could take his own identity for granted in the customary way, and so it must have been those inpenetrable sense-data that were bothering him. If he did not actually identify objects with sense-data, that was only because it went without saying that that is what they were. Some headway has already been made against this interpretation in earlier chapters, and an alternative to it has been sketched. It seems that, though he was concerned with the illusory detachment of the phenomenal bubble from the physical world, the point of severance that interested him was the subject of awareness rather than its objects, the eye behind the visual field rather than its contents. So the status of phenomena, 'the world as I found it', was left unexamined and all his attention was directed on to the ego.

This alternative interpretation still needs to be supported by an examination of the two texts, *Notebooks 1914—16* and the *Tractatus*. However, before the evidence is collected and sifted, something more needs to be said about the relation between the solipsist's world and the visual field.

The solipsist's world is 'the world as I found it', the phenomena encountered by him in his lifetime. It includes his visual field, but, of course, it also includes the fields of his other senses. When he writes his report on it he has to mention his body,[3] and so it is not a world of mental sense-data. In fact, nothing is going to turn on the precise categorization of the objects in his world. That will be a problem later, but in the *Tractatus* his world is presented naïvely as what he has experienced.

So far, we could say that the visual field merely stands in as the representative of the total field of all the solipsist's senses. The sense

[3] *TLP* 5.631.

of sight is so clear and vivid that it has taken the centre of the philosophical stage, as it often does. But the next step is more unusual. Wittgenstein is concerned with the limits of the solipsist's world. Consequently, his interest in the visual field is also an interest in the peculiar way in which it is limited. It is not just that the sense of sight is one of my ways of apprehending phenomena, perhaps my main way: it also provides me with a very apt analogue of the structure and limits of my world.

In fact, there may be two points of analogy. First, there is nothing in my world that I can use as a reference-point or point of origin for plotting its boundary. Second, there is nothing like my world outside its limits, and so I must not think of its boundary as a line dividing one set of things from another, like a hedge running between two fields. He certainly exploited the fact that the first of these two features of the limits of my world is reproduced by the limits of my visual field, and he must have realized that the same is true of the second feature too.

This is a mind-spinning multiple use of the visual field, the kind of thing that one might expect to find in the writings of Plato rather than in the writings of a philosopher like Wittgenstein. But it is better to avoid all preconceptions about the working of Wittgenstein's mind and to analyse what he actually says in the *Tractatus*, however involuted it may turn out to be. There is no reason to suppose that his use of the visual field must have been simple, and he may really have introduced it both in its own right and, at the same time, to serve as an analogue. It is worth remembering that his treatment of solipsism stands at the intersection of many lines of thought, some already laid down by Schopenhauer, some derived from Russell, and some original. Drawing all these threads together in a couple of pages may well have bent the plane surface on which we delude ourselves that clear thinking should always be set out. Certainly, it would be a counsel of depair to cut out the complications by assuming that the importance of the visual field is simply that it is filled with impenetrable sense-data.

Perhaps the best point at which to start unravelling these ideas is the concept of *the limits of my world*. First, there is evidently no need for me to worry about the tiresome fact that my language has not yet been analysed into elementary sentences. Wittgenstein's treatment of solipsism is not concerned with the dimension of depth. We may, therefore, pretend that the analysis of factual sentences has been carried all the way down to simple objects with which I am directly confronted. This is merely an expository device and it does not revoke anything in the account given in Chapter 4 of the differences between Wittgenstein's logical atomism and Russell's.[4] It allows us to concentrate on the limits of the range of alternative possible worlds with which Wittgenstein's treatment of solipsism is concerned,[5] and it serves as a device for focusing our attention on to the lateral extensions of an acquired language without worrying about its deep analysis.

The way in which Wittgenstein invites us to do this can cause confusion. If 'the world is the totality of facts',[6] we might expect 'the limits of my world' to be the beginning and the end of the list of facts established by me in my lifetime. However in the 5.6s he is evidently using the phrase in a different way, to mean the limits of the range of alternative possible worlds that I can construct in imagination on the basis of the world as I find it. These are the limits of the space of possibilities in which my world of facts floats. The point is that, given our expository fiction, this range will be a function of the objects that I have encountered in my lifetime.[7]

My range of possible worlds is, of course, the material counterpart of the range of descriptions of the world which my experience allows me to construct in my language. To put it more concisely,

The limits of my language mean the limits of my world.[8]

The point has already been made, that this was a development of a thesis put forward by Russell.[9] Now it is easy enough to appreciate why the visual field is introduced here in its own right. It stands in for the fields of all the senses, and, given our expository fiction, the limits of my language will be a function of the simple objects with which I have achieved acquaintance through all five of them. What is not so easy to see is how the superimposed analogy is supposed to work.

One point of similarity is that no ego appears in the field of consciousness just as no eye appears in the visual field. This is a point taken from Schopenhauer,[10] and it is one side of the dilemma offered

[4] See above, pp. 63–4.
[5] See above, pp. 107–8.
[6] *TLP* 1.1.
[7] Ibid., 2.022–2.023 and 5.5561.
[8] Ibid., 5.6
[9] See above, p. 34.
[10] Schopenhauer: *The World as Will and Idea*, Vol. 3, p. 285. See above, ch. 3 n. 9.

by Wittgenstein to the solipsist: if his thesis is not self-refuting it is empty. It is self-refuting if his ego is identified by attachment to a body some of which will necessarily lie outside the field of his consciousness. If he does not identify it in that way, he can only postulate it as the focal point behind the field of his consciousness, like what he later called 'the geometrical eye'.[11] However, this a priori procedure will make his thesis empty, because an ego postulated to account for his awareness of a range of objects cannot possibly be used to impose a real limit on that range of objects, and so cannot possibly be used to impose a real limit on his language. The 'geometrical' ego is not discoverable by introspection or in any other way and it cannot serve as an identifiable reference-point.[12] Wittgenstein makes good use of this idea of Schopenhauer's, and the details will be set out below.

The suggestion, that he also exploited a second point of analogy between the solipsist's world and his visual field, is more speculative. When he drew the outline of the visual field in the *Tractatus*,[13] he might have said that there is nothing outside it, just as there is nothing identifiable that fails to be a possibility outside the limits of my world. If he had said this, he would have established a clear connection between his treatment of the outer limit of the solipsist's world and the main point of the doctrine of showing which is that we cannot go behind the possibilities or consider other identifiable alternatives and ask why they are not possibilities.[14] However, in the *Tractatus* he does not make this comment on the outline of the visual field. He only implies that there is no reference-point within it from which its outline could be plotted. This is understandable. For someone who emphasizes and exploits the fact that there is nothing like my visual field outside it, or, as he put it later, that 'my visual field has no neighbour',[15] must be treating its contents as sense-data rather than objects in the physical world. It is, therefore, not surprising that this thought is not expressed in the *Tractatus*, but makes its first appearance later, when the investigation has shifted from the subject of awareness to its objects. This aspect of the analogy can certainly be discerned in the *Tractatus* but only below the surface of the thoughts that are actually developed in the text.

[11] See Wittgenstein: *Blue Book*, pp. 63–5 and *NLPESD* p. 297, quoted below, pp. 175–6. See above, p. 59.

[12] The argument can be generalized to deal with a Humean solipsist. See above, n. 2 and p. 36.   [13] *TLP* 5.6331.

[14] See above, pp. 149–51.

[15] Cf. *Blue Book*, pp. 71–2 and *NLPESD* pp. 283 and 297.

In general, it is not easy to give a firm description of Wittgenstein's early treatment of solipsism. Perhaps it would be best to say that he picks a certain path through its problems without looking too closely at the topics that he skirts. Certainly, he does not use the concept of *phenomena* in a way that actually precludes their identification with mental sense-data. The situation is more delicate than that. He concentrates on the problem of the owner of experiences and leaves their categorization and all the problems that stem from their categorization in limbo. It would not be wrong to read these later thoughts between the lines of the *Tractatus*, but what we must realize is that they are not the actual topics of discussion.[16]

There are two more general points that need to be made before the texts are examined. The first one was made before,[17] but it is something that bears repetition. Among the many lines of thought combined by Wittgenstein in his discussion of solipsism there are two that especially need to be singled out and distinguished from one another. One is the investigation of the way in which I ascribe an experience to myself, and the other is the dilemma offered to the solipsist, self-refutation or emptiness. These two lines of thought are closely connected with one another, because the self-ascription of an experience presupposes the embodiment of my mind,[18] and this embodiment, which destroys solipsism, seems to be the only way in which it can avoid emptiness. The importance of the illusion of a discoverable ego is only that it makes embodiment look unnecessary, because it is a sort of surrogate internalized body.[19] Even if we never suffered from this illusion, Wittgenstein's dilemma could still be put to the solipsist in exactly the same way.

The other point that needs to be made in this introduction to Wittgenstein's treatment of solipsism concerns the illusion that the ego can be used as a surrogate internalized body. He evidently endorses Hume's thesis that the ego cannot be discovered by introspection. But that thesis is only a kind of skirmisher, behind which there stands another, much more powerful argument. This is quite clear in the text in the *Treatise*,[20] where we find first of all Hume's report that he cannot discover an impression of the self, then his

---

[16] See above, p. 98.

[17] See above, pp. 39–40.

[18] See *Wittgenstein's Lectures, Cambridge 1932–1935*, ed. A. Ambrose, Blackwell, 1979, p. 62, and *NLPESD* p. 297.

[19] See *NLPESD* p. 282: 'The idea of the ego inhabiting a body to be abolished.'

[20] Hume: *Treatise of Human Nature*, I. iv. 6.

ironical aside that others may be luckier, which is not an admission of weakness, because it is immediately followed by the really crushing criticism, that those who say that there is an impression of the self are guilty of a 'manifest contradiction and absurdity'. This criticism is the one that needs to be analysed before Wittgenstein's remarks about the ego can be understood. For when he says that 'the subject does not belong to the world',[21] he evidently does not intend this to be taken as a contingent statement, like 'Wheels are not part of the physiology of any animal'.

So why would it have been absurd or contradictory if one of Hume's adversaries had claimed that he, at least, had an impression of his ego? Suppose that he made this claim because he noticed that, whereas most of his impressions vanished very quickly, there was one which never vanished so long as there were others for it to accompany. This constant impression would be among the last to depart when he fell asleep and among the first to arrive when he awoke, and he could never get rid of it without getting rid of all the others as well. Perhaps this claim would be hard to believe, but why would it be absurd or contradictory?

One reason that is sometimes suggested is that the ego has to function as the subject of awareness and cannot simultaneously occupy the position of object. But that is hardly self-evident because the eye which sees the world can also see itself in a mirror. Indeed, if the eye were concave instead of convex, it might not even need a mirror and Mach, who included the tip of his nose in his sketch of his field of vision, could have included at least the outer circle of the pupil. So it is certainly not from the physical world that we get the idea of a subject that is never an object.

If the claim made by Hume's adversary is absurd or contradictory, it must be so for a deeper reason. Hume hints at such a reason and Wittgenstein develops it. But unfortunately, the development in the early texts *Notebooks* and *Tractatus* is a very incomplete sketch, and it will help the exposition if we bring in a concept which he did not introduce explicitly until later. In the *Blue Book* he defines 'the geometrical eye' as 'whatever sees all this',[22] meaning by 'all this' the world as I see it. Now let us assume that I already know that the 'geometrical eye' will turn out to be identifiable with some part of my body and that I can already pick out my body on any identity parade.

---

[21] *TLP* 5.632.
[22] *Blue Book*, pp. 63–5.

Evidently, I shall be able to discover by experiment which part of my body does the seeing. Similarly, if I start the inquiry even further back, I shall be able to discover by experiment which body is mine. My discovery of the physical subject of all this seeing will be achieved by elimination: it is not my finger-nails or even my forehead, but my physical eyes. The same is true of my discovery of my own body: it is the one that moves when I decide to move, etc. Now what happens if I am asked to internalize the inquiry and discover the inner subject of all this awareness—that is, the subject which takes in the contents of my mind in so far as I am conscious of them? If there is any absurdity or contradiction, this is where it ought to begin to appear.

The plain fact, that I do not have an impression of my ego, would be very surprising if I had an ego, but that is not enough to make it absurd to suggest that I might have had one. But perhaps the trouble is not just that there is nothing that would count as such an impression. Maybe I do not even understand the conditions that any candidate would be required to meet. First of all, it would presumably have to be an impression of something within my mind capable of acting as the subject of all my awareness. But is that really an intelligible require-ment? Also it would not be the only impression of anything internal, and so elimination would be needed to establish its claim to be the impression of my ego. That would require experiment, and another trouble is that there seems to be no medium in which the experiment could be carried out and no method for it to use. Things are even worse if I start the inquiry further back and set out to discover by experiment which subject, or which mind is mine. For that would be an even more obviously unintelligible enterprise. In short, if the subject is internalized, it is absurd to treat its identity as a matter for scientific inquiry, and to that extent Hume was right. However, it does not follow that there is no sense 'in which philosophy can talk about the self in a non-psychological way. What brings the self into philo-sophy is the fact that "the world is my world".'[23]

Let us leave this mysterious remark unanalysed for the moment, and take a look at Russell's views about the self. Wittgenstein's treatment of solipsism is the most difficult section of the *Tractatus*, and, as usual, Russell's writings on the topic provide the necessary background. There is nothing surprising about this. Wittgenstein read Russell's latest account of self-knowledge and solipsism in 1913, and

[23] *TLP* 5.641.

he reacted against it in the entries that he made on these topics in the *Notebooks* in the next three years.

Russell's 1913 theory was that the ego is known only by description and never by acquaintance. He developed it in *Theory of Knowledge, 1913*, which he showed to Wittgenstein in May of that year.[24] It can be found in the section which was published as a separate paper, *On the Nature of Acquaintance*, in 1956.[25] We have already seen Wittgenstein developing another idea that Russell put into that paper, the idea that solipsism tries to limit what I can understand rather than what I know,[26] and we have noted his rejection of Russell's attempt to argue against solipsism inductively.[27] So he might also be expected to comment on Russell's theory that the ego is known only by description.

This theory about the ego was the result of a complete change of mind. In 1912 Russell had published the opposite view, that the ego is known by acquaintance.[28] He was familiar with Hume's contention that such ego-awareness never in fact occurs, but he attached more weight to the argument that, if it did not occur, nobody could establish the truth of any sentence containing the word 'I' or even understand its meaning, but these are not impossible achievements. To be fair, his adoption of the theory that the ego is known by acquaintance was only tentative, and he very soon abandoned it in favour of the theory that it can only be known by description.

His first statement of this theory too is tentative,[29] and the reason for his hesitation is worth exploring, because it will throw light on a puzzling feature of Wittgenstein's argument in the *Tractatus*. Russell points out a difficulty in his new view: the word 'I' is defined as 'the subject-term in awareness of which I am aware', but that is a circular definition.[30] Later, in *On the Nature of Acquaintance*, he suggests a way of getting round this difficulty: the description under which I know my own ego is 'the subject attending to "this", where "this" is treated as a logically proper name of a sense-datum'.[31]

[24] See R. W. Clark: *The Life of Bertrand Russell*, pp. 204–7.
[25] Russell: *On the Nature of Acquaintance* in *Logic and Knowledge, Essays 1901–1950* pp. 125–74. *Theory of Knowledge, 1913* is now published as Vol. 7 of *The Collected Papers of Bertrand Russell*, ed. E. Eames and K. Blackwell, Allen and Unwin, 1984.
[26] See above, p. 34.
[27] See above, p. 36.
[28] In *The Problems of Philosophy*, Home University Library, 1912, ch. 5.
[29] In *Knowledge by Acquaintance, Knowledge by Description*, (in *Mysticism and Logic*, Longmans, 1918).
[30] Ibid., p. 212.   [31] *Logic and Knowledge, Essays 1901–1950* p. 168.

Russell's views about the self underwent a further transformation in 1918, too late to affect the *Notebooks* or the *Tractatus*. The influence of Schopenhauer still remains to be described, but that can be brought in where it is relevant to a particular text. We have filled in enough of the background for the detailed exegesis to begin.

In the *Tractatus* the discussion of solipsism is part of an investigation of the way in which empirical reality is limited:

> Empirical reality is limited by the totality of objects. The limit also makes itself manifest in the totality of elementary propositions.[32]

This comes from the first part of the investigation, which rejects the idea that specific restrictions can be imposed on the types of objects and so on the forms of elementary propositions. As already explained, the limit of empirical reality is not a line drawn around the totality of facts, but a line drawn around the totality of possibilities. To put the point in the way in which it was put earlier, the limit of the world is the limit of the range of alternative possible worlds which can be constructed in imagination on the basis of the actual world.[33] These constructions will all be expressible as truth-functions of elementary propositions linked to actual objects.

So, though the next section opens with a startling remark, the way has already been prepared for it:

> *The limits of my language* mean the limits of my world.[34]

As before, the line drawn around world-possibilities is correlated with the line drawn around discourse-possibilities. The new step is that the world is now my world and the language my language. This is because the new section, which opens with this remark, is concerned with the suggestion that another specific restriction might be imposed on language, over and above its general limitation to truth-functions of elementary propositions. This time the suggested further restriction is not based on the specification of types of objects, but on the specification of the person who has encountered[35] them, namely myself.

It is worth remarking that the topic of this section is clearly and unequivocally introduced right at the start. The topic is a proposed

---

[32] *TLP* 5.5561.

[33] See above, pp. 107–8.

[34] *TLP* 5.6.

[35] It is, of course, an over-simplification to put it like this, but an innocuous one. See above, pp. 155–6.

further way of restricting language through the explicit specification of a particular person and not through the implicit specification of the types of object that he, or anyone else, encounters. If the topic had been a further restriction based on the implicit assumption that those objects would be mental sense-data, Wittgenstein would surely have made it clear from the start that this section, like the preceding one, was concerned with a restriction based on types of object. In any case, this interpretation is ruled out by 5.631.[36]

The first supplement to 5.6 is a very important one, because it explains a peculiarity of the limit of language. It is not like a boundary between two fields on a farm, because its position cannot be related to what lies on the other side of it

> Logic pervades the world: the limits of the world are also its limits.
> So we cannot say in logic, 'The world has this in it, and this, but not that.'[37]

The second of these two remarks echoes an observation of Russell's,[38] but the continuation of 5.61 immediately extends the point to possibilities, because they are a function of objects. What Wittgenstein says is that we are not excluding identifiable possibilities on the far side of the limit. This is connected with his doctrine of showing in a way that has already been explained. Science can exclude a fact from the actual world by identifying the possibility and saying that it is not realized, but there is no comparable way in which philosophy can exclude a possibility.[39]

The next supplement 5.62 mentions solipsism for the first time. It opens with these words:

> This remark provides the key to the problem, how much truth there is in solipsism.

Wittgenstein's system of numbering indicates that this is not a comment on 5.61, which immediately precedes it, but on 5.6. He continues:

---

[36] See above, p. 154.

[37] *TLP* 5.61, first two paragraphs.

[38] See *On the Nature of Acquaintance*, p. 134: 'Every word that we now understand must have a meaning which falls within our present experience: we can never point to an object and say: "This lies outside my present experience".' But Wittgenstein, unlike Russell, includes remembered experience. See *TLP* 5.631.

[39] See above, pp. 146–52 for the full explanation of this doctrine, which is also stated slightly less perspicuously in the third and fourth paragraphs of the Preface to the *Tractatus*.

For what solipsism *means* is quite correct; only it cannot be *said*, but makes itself manifest.

The world is *my* world: this is manifest in the fact that the limits of *language* (of that language which alone I understand) mean the limits of *my* world.

This is one of the most difficult texts in the *Tractatus* and there is very little agreement between commentators about its meaning.

We can start by making two points that are incontrovertible and must serve as the foundation of any interpretation. First, Wittgenstein criticizes the solipsist's claim the 'The world is *my* world' on the ground that it cannot be made in factual language. It is, of course, characteristic of metaphysics to present its claims inappropriately, as if they were scientific hypotheses, and Russell had recently provided a very clear example of this inappropriate procedure when he set up solipsism as a thesis against which he could only argue inductively.[40]

The second incontrovertible point is that Wittgenstein immediately goes on to concede that there is something right about the solipsist's claim. It is not a factual truth but something deeper, which underlies all factual truths about the world and manifests itself in a certain feature of the language in which I describe the world. The general idea is clear enough: when Wittgenstein excludes the solipsist's claim from factual discourse, he implies that it literally lacks sense, but he does not imply that it is rubbish. On the contrary, he allows that among the theses of metaphysics, all of which are literally senseless, there are some that are acceptable for a deeper and more interesting reason than that they make successful claims to factual truth.[41]

So far, so good. Uncertainty begins when we ask why the solipsist claims that the world is his world. Is it because he is confronted by an impenetrable veil of mental sense-data? Or is it because the limits of the world as he finds it are fixed from the inside by their relation to his ego? The interpretation adopted here has been built up around the second of these alternatives, but, though arguments have been given for this choice, its appropriateness to the 5.6s has yet to be demonstrated.

There is also uncertainty about the reason why Wittgenstein excludes the solipsist's claim from factual discourse. The reason that has been suggested here is that his claim would be factual only if his ego could be identified independently of its experiences. Some evidence has been given for this interpretation, but it too remains to be

[40] See Russell: *On the Nature of Acquaintance*, pp. 134–8.
[41] See G. E. M. Anscombe: *An Introduction to Wittgenstein's* Tractatus, p. 162.

squared with the 5.6s. It is, of course, an integral part of this interpretation, that the only way for the solipsist to make his ego independently identifiable is to attach it to his body, but then his claim immediately falsifies itself, because his body necessarily lies partly outside his field of consciousness. That is why this stage of Wittgenstein's argument has been presented as a dilemma: if the solipsist's claim is meant as a factual claim, it is either empty or self-refuting. If this interpretation of his argument is correct, it too ought to find supporting evidence in the 5.6s.

Finally, there is uncertainty about the precise way in which the solipsist's valid insight manifests itself in factual discourse. If I start to describe the world what is it about language that shows that, in some deep sense, it is *my* world? In Chapter 3 the solipsist's insight was said to be that the 'phenomenal bubble' of his life as he lives it 'has a subject, but does not contain it, and so, though it is attached to the common world through its subject, it does not contain within itself any aspect of that attachment'.[42] Another way of putting this would be to say that any experience is had from a point of view which is not represented in that experience.

But that is only the beginning of the solipsist's insight. In order to give his thesis its full scope, we have to add the two points that transform it into linguistic solipsism.[43] 'The world' is the range of possible worlds alternative to 'the world as I found it', and the objects in 'the world as I found it' underpin the language covering that range of possible worlds. So the solipsist's further insight is that any language has to be understood from a point of view which cannot be captured in that language.

It is an integral part of this interpretation that the privileged position of the inner subject, as a sort of power behind the scenes or *éminence grise*, leads the solipsist to make one of two complementary mistakes: either he says that he, like anyone else, can get along without any identificatory representation of his ego,[44] or else he claims that there must be a way of identifying it by introspection, and maintains this claim in the teeth of all the absurdities of the search for a purely mental analogue of getting the tip of his nose into his visual field. This interpretation too will have to be confirmed by the evidence of the 5.6s.

[42] See above, p. 38.
[43] See above, pp. 34 and 156.
[44] See above, pp. 35 and 154.

There are, then, three major uncertainties, which, we may hope, will be resolved by an examination of this part of the text of the *Tractatus*. We can also appeal to the *Notebooks*, where some of the same ideas are developed experimentally, so that it is easier to see the connections between them. We also have another resource: many of the entries in the *Notebooks* are part of a literary dialogue with two other philosophers, Schopenhauer and Russell. Wittgenstein's attitude to Schopenhauer is positive, and he often takes over his ideas unaltered, while his attitude to Russell is more critical, and some of his negative reactions to his ideas have already been noted. If his remarks in both texts *Notebooks* and *Tractatus* are often contributions to these dialogues, made, as it were, on the staircase, they are likely to be most revealing when they are read in that context.

Let us begin with the evidence for the answer to the third question about the interpretation of Wittgenstein's treatment of solipsism. What is it about language that shows that, in some deep sense, the world is *my* world? In 5.62 he gives an explicit answer to this question: 'This is manifest in the fact that the limits of *language* (of that language which alone I understand) mean the limits of *my* world.' One possible reason has just been suggested for saying that this fact shows that the world is *my* world: any language has to be understood from a point of view which cannot be identified in that language. If this is the right interpretation, he is still talking about a restriction imposed on the range of possible topics for a language, and not about a restriction imposed on the range of possible decoders of a language. He is not saying that my language is identifiable as the language that is intelligible to me alone, but, rather, that it is identifiable as the language that expresses only what is intelligible to me. The source of this limitation of my language is my point of view and yet my point of view cannot be identified or mentioned in my language. The ego is the self-effacing centre of my understanding, or, to put it in another way, there is a sense of 'I/me' in which my language cannot talk about me.

The first of these two issues is a familiar one: if the objects underpinning my language are my sense-data, then arguably nobody else will be able to understand it. There is no doubt that Wittgenstein tackled this problem after 1929.[45] The question is only whether he is tackling it in the 5.6s of the *Tractatus*. Some general reasons have already been given for returning a negative answer to this question,[46]

---

[45] See above, pp. 43–60.
[46] See above, pp. 89–99.

but two more things are now needed. One is an interpretation of the text which will determine whether it means 'the only language that I understand' or 'the language that I alone understand'. The other is an explanation of the thesis that there is a sense of 'I/me' which is such that my language cannot mention me. If the latter is the issue in the 5.6s, it must be admitted that it is more difficult to grasp than the question whether anyone else can understand my sense-datum language.

It is, however, easy to identify the source of the difficulty and so this is a good place to start. Wittgenstein's idea would be that one of the things that cannot be mentioned in any language is the ego which serves as the point of view from which that language can be understood. This idea has two peculiarities. First, the ego will not be in the same position as an object that I have not yet encountered.[47] This is something that has already been expressed in Humean terms: it is not just that I am not acquainted with my ego, but, rather, that I could not be acquainted with it. When the treatment of solipsism takes a linguistic turn, this thesis goes with it: no language can possibly mention the point of view from which it can be understood. It is in this sense that the ego or subject is a limit of the world.[48] It is, therefore, not in the same position as a nameable object, which, once it is named, is inside the limit of language although its existence cannot be asserted.[49]

The point deserves scrutiny. It is true that unencountered objects cannot be named, but Wittgenstein's point is that the ego is unencounterable. So it is not in the same position as objects which cannot be named merely because they have not been encountered. The special remoteness of the ego could be described in the following way. We cannot say that a particular object exists or that another object does not exist, and so we cannot say that a particular object generates certain possibilities against the background of identifiable impossibilities, and, more generally, we cannot explain anything that underpins language, but we can, at least, name objects when we encounter them. The ego is more remote, because it can never be named. Nevertheless, it too is part of the transcendental underpinning of language.

The other peculiarity of Wittgenstein's treatment of the ego is that he does not individuate it personally. This is a stumbling-block for

---

[47] The expository device introduced above on pp. 155–6 is still in force.
[48] See *TLP* 5.632, discussed below, p. 179.   [49] Ibid., 3.203 and 5.535.

commentators who take it for granted that my ego is distinct from yours. Why else, they ask, would I seek it through introspection? This is the first step towards the interpretation which takes Wittgenstein to be concerned with a solipsism based on the theory that each person's acquaintance is restricted to the contents of his own mind.

However, if we look at the entries in the *Notebooks* where his ideas about solipsism make their first appearance, we find something entirely different:

The limits of my language mean the limits of the world.
There really is only one world-soul, which I preferentially call *my* soul and as which alone I conceive what I call the souls of others.
The above remark provides the key to the problem, how much truth there is in solipsism.[50]

Now in this passage he writes 'soul' rather than 'ego' and there is a later entry in which the two are explicitly distinguished from one another:

The philosophical I is not the human being, not the human body or the human soul with the psychological properties, but the metaphysical subject, the boundary (not a part) of the world.[51]

However, he immediately goes on to make a point which must be connected with his earlier remark about the unique world-soul:

The human body, however, my body in particular, is a part of the world among others, among animals, plants, stones, etc., etc.
Whoever realizes this will not want to procure a preferential place for his own body or for the human body.
He will regard human and animals quite naïvely as objects which are similar and belong together.[52]

But what exactly is the connection between these entries and his earlier remark about the 'world-soul'?

It would be too much to hope for certainty in the interpretation of these very experimental remarks, but here is a plausible suggestion: a philosopher who wants to procure a preferential place for his own body wishes it to be the seat of the universal ego; but the ego is not

[50] *NB* 23 May 1915 (slightly altered translation). When Wittgenstein writes 'the above remark', he probably does not mean the second of the three remarks, which he would have called 'This remark', but the first one. If this is the right interpretation, the cross-referencing is the same as in *TLP*.
[51] *NB* 2 Sept. 1916.
[52] Ibid. (slightly altered translation).

individuated personally until he explicitly defines it as the ego attached to his own body, at which point it immediately loses its universality and any solipsistic claim that he makes becomes self-refuting. This suggestion fits very neatly into the dilemma which, according to the interpretation that is being developed here,[53] is being used by Wittgenstein against solipsism. For if this philosopher refuses to attach the ego to his own body, any solipsistic claim that he makes is empty.

Against this suggestion there stands the point made above: *die Seele* ('the soul') is an entity with ordinary psychological properties, which Wittgenstein, therefore, distinguishes from the ego. How, then, can he connect the depersonalization of the soul with the depersonalization of the ego? But there is an answer to this. According to him, it is a mistake to treat the ego as an introspectible entity, but it is a natural mistake which is frequently made, and anyone who makes it is likely to make the further mistake of failing to distinguish the (empirical) soul from the (transcendental) ego. Given these two mistakes, it is easy to make a third one: when the ego eludes discovery, both it and the soul may be allowed to float free of any personal connections. It is therefore understandable that when he is discussing the vicissitudes of the ego, he should explain the depersonalized 'world-soul' by appealing to the tendency to depersonalize the ego.[54]

In fact, there is an entry in the *Notebooks* made about a month later in which he explicitly offers this explanation of the idea of a 'world-soul' or 'world-spirit'. He has been discussing psycho-physical parallelism and he asks,

Is this the solution of the puzzle why men have always believed that there was *one* spirit common to the whole world?
And in that case it would, of course, also be common to inanimate things.

---

[53] See above, pp. 38 and 156–7.

[54] There is a good description of the latter tendency in *NLPESD* (p. 281): 'It seems as though I wished to say that to me, L. W., something applied which does not apply to other people. That is, there seems to be an asymmetry. I *express* things asymmetrically, and could express them symmetrically; only then would one see what facts prompt us to the asymmetrical expression. I do this [sc. express them symmetrically] by spreading the use of the word "I" over all human bodies as opposed to L. W. alone." I.e. no body is given the preferential treatment mentioned in the two passages quoted above from *NB*. On p. 282 he goes on to put the point in a way that makes the reference to his earlier work even clearer: 'The idea of an ego inhabiting a body to be abolished. If whatever consciousness [there is] spreads over all human bodies, then there won't be any temptation to use the word "ego".'

This is the way I have travelled. Idealism singles human beings out from the world as if they were unique, solipsism singles me alone out, and at last I see that I too belong with the rest of the world, and so on the one side *nothing* is left over, and on the other side there remains something really unique, *the world*. Thus idealism leads to realism if it is strictly thought out.[55]

This can only be an attempt to explain the depersonalization of the soul or spirit by tracing the vicissitudes of the ego through various philosophical theories. The uniqueness attributed to all human beings by idealism, and to me alone by solipsism, is the privilege of serving as the seat of the ego. These two theories give this preferential treatment to different candidates, but the explanation of their favouritism is the same in both cases.

The explanation starts from the fact that the word 'ego', as used by philosophers, is a count-noun, and egos are individuated through their attachment to bodies. But unfortunately, this criterion of individuation is forgotten by Cartesian thinkers, who are over-impressed by their immediate knowledge of their own identities, which seems to them to be in no way dependent on their bodies. So they confine the criterion of ego-individuation to the world within the mind, and then rather surprisingly they are not bothered by the complete absense of any empirical data that could possibly service such a criterion (Hume's first point). The reason why this does not worry them is that they find they can get along without using any criterion—they already know who they are. What they fail to see is that there is no conceivable criterion of ego-individuation within the mind (Hume's second point), and so their theory, instead of exploiting the fact that they do not really need to use any such criterion, is destroyed by the fact that it is inconceivable.

The remedy proposed in this passage in the *Notebooks* is to let the ego float freely, but then to make it take the consequences of floating freely. This is, of course, one of the two options offered to the solipsist in the *Tractatus*: his theory is empty. Here in the *Notebooks* we are shown just how empty it is. The most important consequence of this letting go is that the word 'ego' ceases to be a count-noun. This comes out very clearly in the transition from solipsism through idealism to panpsychism. If there is no empirical criterion for its individuation, the ego will be spread over everything. But that means that it will

[55] *NB* 15 Oct. 1916, (slightly altered translation). Cf. *TLP* 5.64, discussed below, pp. 184–5.

extend to inanimate things. Of course, Wittgenstein's point is not that we would still associate the ego with consciousness and *believe in* panpsychism: his argument is, as so often, reductive, and the implication is that the content of the word 'ego' would drain away too, leaving us with a completely empty panpsychism.[56]

There is something else in this passage in the *Notebooks* which requires comment, namely its use of the concept of uniqueness. Idealism treats the human species as the unique seat of the ego and so exalts the world as we, collectively, find it. Solipsism treats me as the unique seat of the ego with the same happy consequence for the world as I find it.[57] Both theories are mistaken, because there is no background against which any *world* can be set in relief.[58] Uniqueness belongs only to the whole phenomenal world, and if a philosopher chauvinistically picks something out of that world, defines a miniature world by its attachment to that thing, and then attributes uniqueness to this miniature world, he will necessarily be mistaken. For his theory will necessarily be self-refuting or empty. We have seen how this dilemma destroys solipsism. It destroys idealism and any other similarly chauvinistic theory in the same way.

It is a good idea to place this dilemma in the wider context of Wittgenstein's early system of thought, because it is apt to look shallow when it is taken in isolation. We are apt to protest that the solipsist is unlikely to make the mistake of the lady who wrote to Russell telling him that she was a solipsist and that she was surprised that there were not more of them. But what we need to appreciate is that Wittgenstein's dilemma is founded on an insight that goes very deep. The phenomenal world cannot be set in relief against the background of a noumenal world. That would be an obviously impossible advance beyond the limits of the one and only world. On the other hand, if we retreat, more cautiously, into the miniature world of the solipsist,[59] we run into another form of the same difficulty: we

[56] Cf. *PI* I. § 284: 'Look at a stone and imagine it having sensations.—One says to oneself: How could one so much as get the idea of ascribing a *sensation* to a *thing*? One might as well ascribe it to a number!—And now look at a wriggling fly and at once these difficulties vanish....'

[57] See the discussion of this 'world' apropos of *TLP* 5.631 below, pp. 178–9.

[58] This point is made most perspicuously in *PR* § 47, quoted and discussed above, p. 95. Its full development belongs to Wittgenstein's later philosophy, which will be examined in Vol. II. His 1929 account of the two languages, primary and secondary, is really a mistaken attempt to set one world in relief against the background of another. See *PR*, § 58 and *LWVC*, pp. 49–50, both of which will be analysed in Vol. II.

[59] His microcosm. See *TLP* 5.63 discussed below, pp. 177 ff.

cannot place this miniature world in the larger world without crossing the very boundary that our theory claims to be uncrossable.

Both these insights were Schopenhauer's, and, when Wittgenstein accepts them, he gives them a linguistic turn. The first veto then becomes the prohibition of any attempt to take things that really are possibilities expressible in language, for example that grass is white and snow is green, and to set them in relief against the background of a further world of *candidates* for possibility. The second veto undergoes a more elaborate transformation. What it now prohibits is any attempt to use existing language to set up a more restricted language, as it were, within it. For any theory that tries to do this will have to cross the limits of the inner language in order to put them in their place.

Perhaps enough has now been said to introduce the thesis, that there is a sense of 'I/me' in which my language cannot talk about me. This thesis, according to the interpretation that is being developed here, is the central insight of the solipsist, which is conceded validity in 5.62. If the elucidation of it that has been given above is correct, Wittgenstein's concession is a very guarded one. For his main contention is that the solipsist is entangled in absurdities the moment that he tries to express his insight as a theory to be checked for truth or falsehood.

We may now return to the text of 5.62 and inquire whether Wittgenstein meant 'the only language that I understand' or 'the language that I alone understand'. This is a much easier question to settle. If he meant 'the language that I alone understand', he would need a reason for restricting the intelligibility of this language to me alone, and some commentators supply what strikes them as the obvious reason: it is the language in which I report my own sense-data, which are accessible only to me. The situation would be different if he meant 'the only language that I understand', because in that case his point would be that my understanding cannot reach beyond the limits of this language. According to the first interpretation a restriction is imposed on the decoders of my language, while according to the second one, a restriction is imposed on my understanding of language. Either way, the language is identified through the restriction that is imposed on it. It is my language, because language is, from my point of view, my language. It is what I can understand, and yet the 'I' that is the subject at the centre of my circle cannot figure in it as an object.

It would be a mistake to pin too much on the translation of a single German sentence. Solipsism is not a side-issue in Wittgenstein's early system and his line of thought about it ought to be recognizable elsewhere in the *Tractatus*, and also in the *Notebooks*. In particular, in the 5.63s he offers arguments for his curiously split verdict on solipsism, and his arguments really ought to make it clear whether the theory on trial is based on sense-data or on the ego.

However, for what it is worth, the German word 'allein' usually qualifies what precedes it, but does sometimes qualify what comes after it. Now the phrase 'die allein', a relative pronoun followed by the word for 'alone', is a standard linguistic unit and so the pressure of the normal convention, that 'allein' qualifies what precedes it, is greatly reinforced in this case. The objection, that it *could* still be taken with the word that comes after it, as in 'Alone I did it', is answerable. The intellectual effort required to focus the word 'allein' on to what comes after it would be too great, and German has other devices which would achieve this effect easily and unequivocally.[60] So Wittgenstein's use of the word 'allein' instead of one of the other available devices shows that he meant 'the only language that I understand'. If it were needed, we have confirmation of this interpretation in Wittgenstein's own comment on Ogden's translation of 5.62.[61]

In any case, it would be inappropriate at this point for Wittgenstein's solipsist to mention the exclusion of other people from understanding his language. For the question under discussion in the 5.5s and 5.6s is whether language, which has already been restricted to truth-functions of elementary propositions, needs to have some further restriction imposed on it. It is at this point that the solipsist proposes a retreat into his microcosm, limited by the possible reach of his language. Attention is, therefore, focused on to what this move excludes, and what it excludes is the macrocosm, limited by the possible reach of 'language' unqualified by any possessive pronoun. What Wittgenstein is arguing is that the solipsist cannot set his world in relief against the background of 'the world', and other people are irrelevant to his argument.

After 5.62 the remaining remarks about solipsism are put together in

---

[60] See J. Hintikka: 'On Wittgenstein's Solipsism', *Mind*, Vol. 67, Jan. 1958: reprinted in *Essays on Wittgenstein's* Tractatus, ed. R. Beard and I. Copi, pp. 157ff.

[61] See C. Lewy: 'A Note on the Text of the *Tractatus*', *Mind*, Vol. 76, 1967. Ogden's original version of the parenthesis had been '(the language which only I understand)'. On Ramsey's copy of the first edition Wittgenstein corrected this to '(the only language which I understand)'. In the 1933 reprint it is translated '(*the* language which I understand)', which emphasizes the uniqueness of the language, as Wittgenstein's argument requires, but does so a little grudgingly.

a way that is clearly indicated by their numbering. The 5.63s develop a continuous line of thought, which is, in fact, Wittgenstein's argument for his assessment of solipsism, and the 5.64s sum up the case. But first comes 5.621, a brief and enigmatic comment on 5.62:

> The world and life are one.

This is intended as an explanation of his use of the word 'world' in 5.62. The point was made earlier that in this part of the *Tractatus* 'the world' does not mean 'all the facts',[62] but 'all the possibilities'. Some of these possibilities are realized as facts and others are not, but I can always explore them in imagination.[63] So 'the world' is 'the world as I find it' and as I construct it in imagination.[64] It is the world of phenomena or, in Schopenhauer's terminology, the world as idea. If it seems strange that Wittgenstein should identify this world with life, it is worth remembering that perceiving and imagining are things that we do. However, his point goes deeper than that. He does not mean that we do these things against the background of an independent world: he means that they *constitute* the world.[65] So in the *Notebooks*, after saying that 'the world and life are one', he goes on to explain that

> Physiological life is, of course, not 'life' and neither is psychological life. Life is the world.[66]

If this is still not clear, there are several other texts to which we can have recourse.

First, there is 5.631, to be discussed below, which shows that the 'world as I find it' is not the world of my mental sense-data.[67] This is confirmed by an interesting passage in the *Notebooks*, where he expresses his own tendency to solipsism by asking,

> What has history to do with me? Mine is the first and only world!
> I want to report how *I* found the world.

---

[62] As it does in *TLP* 1.1.   [63] See above, pp. 107–8.

[64] 'With the help of a logical scaffolding', as he puts it in *TLP* 4.023.

[65] Derek Bolton ('Life-form and Idealism', in *Idealism, Past and Present*, ed. G. Vesey, Cambridge, 1982, pp. 269–82) shows how human activity constitutes 'the world' of Wittgenstein's later system. He calls this philosophy 'life-philosophy' and distinguishes it, surely correctly, both from idealism and realism. See above, pp. 170–2 and below 188–90. Bolton also places Wittgenstein's later sketches of language games and 'Forms of life' in the context of this 'life-philosophy'. A further point could be added to his penetrating analysis of Wittgenstein's thought: *TLP* 5.621 shows that these ideas originated in his early work, even if they were not properly developed until much later.

[66] *NB* 24 July 1916.

[67] Because it includes part of my body. See above pp. 35 and 154.

What others in the world have told me about the world is a very small and incidental part of my experience of the world.

I have to judge the world, to measure things.[68]

He does not ask 'What has the physical world behind the veil of my sense-data to do with me?' The limitation, such as it is, is imposed by the subject and not by the nature of the objects presented to the subject.

Second, there is the passage in *Philosophical Remarks*[69] in which he inveighs against the attempt to set the phenomenal world in relief against the background of a world of things-in-themselves. It was quoted and discussed above,[70] but perhaps the repetition of three of its sentences will not come amiss:

What I wanted to say is it's strange that those who ascribe reality only to things and not to our ideas move about so unquestioningly in the world as idea and never long to escape from it. . . .

This, which we take as a matter of course, *life*, is supposed to be something accidental, subordinate; while something that normally never comes into my head, reality! . . .

Time and again the attempt is made to use language to limit the world and set it in relief—but it can't be done.

Here life is implicitly identified with the world as idea.

There is one more resource available to us. We can go to the most profound discussion of solipsism in Wittgenstein's writings, a passage in his 'Notes for Lectures on "Private Experience" and "Sense-data"',[71] in which he develops a version of the 'private language argument' of *Philosophical Investigations*,[72] and imagines someone making the usual objection to it,

'But aren't you neglecting something—the experience or whatever you might call it—? Almost *the world* behind the mere words?'

But here solipsism teaches us a lesson: it is that thought which is *on the way* to destroy this error. For if the *world* is idea it isn't any person's idea. (Solipsism stops short of saying this and says that it is my idea.) But then how could I say what the world is if the realm of ideas has no neighbour? What I do comes to defining the word 'world'.[73]

---

[68] *NB* 2 Sept. 1916.
[69] *PR* § 47.
[70] See above, p. 95. [71] *NLPESD* pp. 296–7.
[72] i.e. the argument beginning at *PI* I § 243. See above, pp. 52–8.
[73] A clear allusion to the dilemma underlying the treatment of solipsism in *TLP*. If the solipsist takes this line, wherever he stops on it, his thesis is empty.

'I neglect that which goes without saying.'

'What is seen *I* see' (pointing to my body). I point at my geometrical eye, saying this. Or I point with closed eyes and touch my breast and feel it. In no case do I make a connection between what is see and a person.

Back to 'neglecting'! It seems that I neglect life. But not life physiologically understood but life as consciousness. And consciousness not physiologically understood or understood from the outside, but consciousness as the very essence of experience, the appearance of the world, the world.

The full explanation of this important text is not needed here,[74] because it makes the transition from the treatment of the detached subject to the treatment of its detached objects, sensations and their properties as seen by introspectionism.[75] But even when it is left without comment, it throws a lot of light on the identification of the world of ideas with life.

The 5.63s develop a line of thought which can be read both as a criticism of Russell's theories about the ego as subject and as an argument for Wittgenstein's own assessment of solipsism in the 5.62s. As already explained,[76] the argument introduces the visual field and uses it in more than one way. First, it is brought in as the representative of the fields of all five senses, because the objects underpinning factual language are, in some remote way,[77] given empirically. Second, it serves as the analogue of the world as idea. For when my mind ranges over the phenomena and the alternative possibilities constructed on the basis of the phenomena, it cannot encounter the focal point behind all these sequences, and that is really quite like the elusiveness of the eye, which does not figure in the visual field.[78] There is also another possible point of analogy which was mentioned earlier:[79] Wittgenstein was impressed by the fact that the boundary of the visual field is not like a hedge with another field on the far side of it, and this makes the visual field a perfect analogue for the world,

---

[74] It will be given in Vol. II.

[75] See above, pp. 43–5.

[76] See above, pp. 154–5.

[77] See above, pp. 155–6, for the need for this qualification.

[78] The analogy is Schopenhauer's: 'But the "I" is the dark point in consciousness, as on the retina the exact point at which the nerve of sight enters is blind, as the brain itself is entirely without sensation, the body of the sun is dark, and the eye sees all except itself', (*The World as Will and Idea*, Vol. 3 p. 285). It is, of course, a necessarily imperfect analogy, because, like any other, it is physical, and anything in the physical world could have been otherwise, but the 'I' could not conceivably encounter itself. See above, pp. 158–60.

[79] See above, p. 155.

when it is limited in the way described in the 5.6s. This point of analogy is implicit in the 5.63s, but it is not developed fully, perhaps because it raises an awkward question about the boundary of the visual field. If the visual field 'has no neighbour',[80] is that not because its contents are sense-data?

The first step in Wittgenstein's argument is taken in a single sentence in 5.63,

I am my world (the microcosm).

This, too, is an allusion to Schopenhauer's identification of macrocosm and microcosm in any subject who confronts the world.[81] It combines two theses each of which will be supported in what follows. Both are negative: I, the subject,[82] do not exist outside my world and I, the subject, do not exist as an identifiable object within it.

---

[80] This is what he says about the world in the passage just quoted from *NLPESD*.

[81] The idea is Schopenhauer's. See *The World as Will and Idea*, Vol. 3 p. 279: 'The understanding of the indestructibility of our true nature coincides with that of the identity of microcosm and macrocosm.' Freud called the feeling expressed by this thesis 'the oceanic feeling … it is a feeling of an indissoluble bond, of being one with the external world as a whole'. (*Civilization and Its Discontents*, The Penguin Freud Library, Vol. 12 p. 252.)

Schopenhauer used the 'identity of microcosm and macrocosm' to exorcize man's fear of death (op. cit., Vol. 1 p. 361): 'But as on the surface of the globe every place is above, so the form of all life is the *present*, and to fear death because it robs us of the present is no more sensible than to fear that we may slip down from the round globe upon which we now have the good fortune to occupy the upper surface.' Freud gives an ironical characterization of this aspect of the 'indissoluble bond': Romain Rolland, in a letter, had described the feeling of this bond as the true source of religious sentiments, and Freud's comment is 'that he means the same thing by it as the consolation offered by an original and somewhat eccentric dramatist to his hero who is facing a self-inflicted death, "We cannot fall out of this world,"' (loc. cit., The reference is to Christian Dietrich Grabbe, *Hannibal*.) Wittgenstein, in the course of his exploration of solipsism in *NB* (11 June 1916–20 Oct. 1916) uses Schopenhauer's idea without making such an ambitious claim for it: 'For life in the present there is no death. Death is not an event in life. It is not a fact of the world.' (8 July 1916: cf. *TLP* 6.4311.)

He also endorses Schopenhauer's equation: 'It is true: man *is* the microcosm' (*NB* 12 Oct. 1916). However, in Schopenhauer's writings this equation is more broadly based than it is in the 5.6s of *TLP*, because it covers the world as will in addition to the world as idea. 'Everyone finds that he himself is this will, in which the real nature of the world consists, and he also finds that he is the knowing subject, whose idea the whole world is, the world which exists only in relation to his consciousness as its necessary supporter. Everyone is thus himself in a double aspect the whole world, the microcosm; finds both sides whole and complete in himself. And what he thus recognizes as his own real being also exhausts the being of the whole world—the macrocosm; thus the world, like man, is through and through *will*, and through and through *idea*, and nothing more than this.' (op. cit. Vol. 1 pp. 211–12.)

[82] The Latin word '*ego*' is more convenient and, therefore, more misleading.

The arguments for these two theses are then developed in several overlapping stages. Wittgenstein starts by taking a Humean line in 5.631:

> There is no such thing as the subject that thinks or entertains ideas.

The German, 'Das denkende, vostellende, Subjekt gibt es nicht', suggests a connection with 'the given'. I, the subject, am not given as an object that is experienced. This does not imply that I, the subject, am zero. For he continues:

> If I wrote a book called *The World as I Found it*, I should have to include a report on my body, and should have to say which parts were subordinate to my will, and which were not, etc., this being a method of isolating the subject, or rather of showing that in an important sense there is no subject; for it alone could *not* be mentioned in that book.

Two comments have already been made on this passage. First, it may seem to be doing no more than endorsing Hume's familiar thesis, that, as a matter of fact, I do not encounter myself as subject. That is, of course, an important point, ignored by Russell in the first theory of the self, which he published in *The Problems of Philosophy*.[83] But Wittgenstein must be going further and endorsing Hume's more interesting point, that I could not conceivably encounter myself as subject. However, what he actually says in 5.631 does not make this absolutely clear. He says that 'it alone could *not* be mentioned in that book', but he does not tell us whether this it because it *could not* present itself as an object, or merely because it *does not* present itself as an object.[84]

The second comment was that the book would not be a book about Wittgenstein's sense-data, because it would include a report on his body. Something can now be added to that. Schopenhauer believed that I have especially intimate knowledge of my will in so far as it is embodied in my voluntary physical movements.[85] So, given Wittgenstein's evident interest in the extent to which my will can control my body, we might infer that he accepted Schopenhauer's view that my voluntary physical movements are in an epistemically privileged

---

[83] See above, p. 161.

[84] See above, pp. 158–60 and 167, where reasons were given for thinking that he could not have treated the ego like an object that happened not to have been encountered. The next section of *TLP* 5.632–5.6331 will show that in fact he did not treat it in this way, and so the final sentence of 5.631 must mean that it is unnameable because it could not present itself as an object.

[85] See Schopenhauer: *The World as Will and Idea*, Vol. 1 pp. 121 ff.

position for me. However, a lot will depend on what the inference means. If it means that my awareness of the movement of my right hand and the pen that it grips is quite different from my awareness of the increase in the length of this sentence on paper, it is correct. In fact, he points out in the *Notebooks* that 'We cannot imagine, e.g., having carried out an act of will without having detected that we have carried it out',[86] and that is the seed which later produced his detailed investigation of my awareness of my own actions.[87] But the inference is incorrect, if it means that the existence of physical objects outside my skin is not given, but problematic. Such a view would be irreconcilable with his whole treatment of solipsism in the *Notebooks*, which relies on the assumption that all bodies exist on the same level, as it were side by side in the world.[88]

One more comment on 5.631 is needed. He says 'that in an important sense there is no subject', and so he is not implying that I, as subject, am absolutely zero. Some kind of door is still being left open. I, the subject, am not being eliminated but only 'isolated'.

This allows for a concession and the next remark, 5.632 indicates what it is:

The subject does not belong to the world: rather, it is a limit of the world.

This has already been explained: the subject is neither a nameable item in the world nor something waiting outside the world for the encounter that would make it nameable.[89] It is the inner limit of the world, a point without magnitude. It is the unplaced, and, therefore, unrepresentable point of view from which I view my world.

The next three remarks develop his argument against the thesis that I, as subject, am an encounterable, and, therefore, a nameable item in my world. They confirm the impression that he is pushing Hume's second criticism, that the thesis is not just false, but absurd. The first move in 5.633 is the issue of a challenge,

Where *in* the world is a metaphysical subject to be found?

This may sound like a question about a new entity, the metaphysical subject, distinct both from 'the subject that thinks and entertains ideas' and from 'the human soul with the psychological properties'.

---

[86] *NB* 4 Nov. 1916.
[87] See e.g. *PI* I §§ 611 ff.
[88] See above, pp. 168–70.
[89] See above, p.167.

But he must be referring to the 'subject' of 5.631 and 5.632 and calling it 'metaphysical' because it is neither physical nor psychological. If this were not so, the sequence of the whole passage would be disorganized. His challenge to his interlocutor to find a metaphysical subject in the world would be out of place if he were referring to a new entity distinct from both the ego and the empirical self. His interlocutor could protest, 'But who said anything about the metaphysical subject?' This interpretation is confirmed by 5.641, which calls the subject 'the philosophical self' and equates it with the metaphysical self.[90]

In fact he puts a different response into his interlocutor's mouth,

You will say that this is exactly like the case of the eye and the visual field,

and he retorts,

But really you do *not* see the eye.
And nothing in the *visual field* allows you to infer that it is seen by an eye.[91]

The point has already been made that he is ruling out mirrors, dished eyes, and, in general, anything that would make it possible for an eye to see itself.[92] A further comment may now be added: this part of his argument is directed against Russell's two theories of the self. The analogy is Schopenhauer's, but, given that the eye stands for the self as subject, the suggestion, that it is seen, will represent Russell's first theory, that the subject is known by acquaintance, and the suggestion, that it is inferred from something in the visual field, will represent his second theory, that it is known only by description.[93]

When 5.631 was taken by itself, it was not absolutely clear that it was pointing to an absurdity in the suggestion that the ego might be encountered as an object. But the next remark 5.632 does make that clear, because, instead of placing the ego beyond the limit of the world, like an object which merely happens not to have been encountered, it says that it actually is a limit of the world. The next three remarks give the argument for this very special treatment of the ego. It is a reductive argument, and the hypothesis reduced to absurdity is that the ego is *not* in this very special position. From this

---

[90] The fact, that the sequence of thought requires 'the thinking subject' and 'a metaphysical subject' to have the same reference, is equally clear in the passage in *NB* where the argument is first developed: 'Isn't the thinking subject in the last resort mere superstition? Where in the world is a metaphysical subject to be found?' (4 Aug. 1916.)

[91] Continuation of 5.63.

[92] See above, p. 159.

[93] See above, p. 161.

hypothesis a dilemma is deduced: either the ego would be encountered in the world, or else it would be in the same position as an object which merely happened not to have even been encountered, and so could only be known by description. But both these Russellian theories are absurd. Therefore, the ego must be treated in the very special way proposed in 5.632.

But what are Wittgenstein's *reasons* for stigmatizing Russell's two theories as absurd? In the case of the theory, that the ego is known by acquaintance, he gives his reason rather too succinctly:

For the form of the visual field is surely not like this[94]

and here he draws the visual field with the eye in its tapered corner. This is really no more than a hint of a possible argument, and the only way to understand it is to cash the analogy and to add a supplement drawn from his later development of this particular line of thought.

In the analogue the eye must be supposed to lack the usual resources for seeing itself. It is not dished, no mirrors are available and, in general, it has no way of identifying itself physically. The point of this deprivation is that it restricts the eye to its own resources within the visual field. How then can it identify itself? In order to appreciate this challenge, we need to add to this part of the *Tractatus* an idea which is really implicit in it, but which Wittgenstein did not develop until later. If the eye were in this predicament, it could only identify itself as 'the geometrical eye', the focal point behind the visual field.[95] Or, more accurately, this is all that the eye's owner could achieve by way of identification. Within the visual field he could not point at the thing that sees, not only because it would not be there, but, more radically, because there are absurdities in the very idea that he might pick out something in the visual field and experiment with it in the way in which he would pick out the physical eye and establish by experiment that it is the thing that sees. 'Pointing' at the 'geometrical eye' does not 'make a connection between what is seen and a person'.[96]

When the analogy is supplemented in this way, it is easier to see how to cash it. The 'geometrical eye' stands for the ego which Wittgenstein is challenging his interlocutuor to identify. His implication is not only that his interlocutor is not acquainted with the ego,

---

[94] *TLP* 5.6331, an expansion of the first of the points that he made against his interlocutor in 5.633.
[95] See above, pp. 59 and 157.
[96] See *NLPESD* p. 297, quoted above, p. 176.

but, more radically, that there are absurdities in the very idea that he might pick out something in the field of his consciousness and establish by experiment that it is the subject.[97]

The demonstration, that Russell's second theory of the self is absurd, is almost equally brief and enigmatic. The argument is again reductive, but this time the thesis to be reduced to absurdity is that the subject is only known by description:

> This is connected with the fact that no part of our experience is at the same time a priori.
> Whatever we see could be other than it is.
> Whatever we can describe at all could be other than it is.
> There is no a priori order of things.[98]

Here Wittgenstein is more than usually inexplicit. He does not explain the connection with what has gone before, and even the reference of the word 'This' is not obvious. It would be normal for it to refer to the immediately preceding remark 5.6331. However, that remark was directed against the theory that the subject is known by acquaintance, and the context of 5.634 shows that it is also directed against Russell's other theory. So the reference of the word 'this' must reach further back in the text to include the whole of 5.633 as well as 5.6331. Against this interpretation there stands the fact that in its original context in the *Notebooks* the scope of the reference of the word 'this' is restricted to the original version of 5.6331.[99] However, there is no cogent reason why its reference in the *Tractatus* should be the same.

Perhaps the best way to identify the argument in 5.634 is to ask what theory about the subject would attribute an a priori status to something that is really experiential. Evidently, this is what is done by any theory that puts an a priori link between a subject and his experience. For if I saw a bird fly past the window just now, it is only a contingent fact that I saw it, and it need not have been included in my experiences today. But we have to be careful here, because the unwanted a priori link might run in either of two directions: a philosopher might attach the subject by definition to a particular experience, or he might attach an experience by definition to a particular subject. Which of these two moves is Wittgenstein criticizing?

But before the question is answered we ought to go back and test the general assumption that Wittgenstein is criticizing philosophers who

---

[97] See above, pp. 159–60.   [98] *TLP* 5.634.   [99] See *NB* 12 Aug. 1916.

attribute an a priori status to something that is really experiential. Why should it not be the other way round? Why not take his criticism to be directed against the attribution of an experiential status to something that is really a priori? This is how P. M. S. Hacker takes it in *Insight and Illusion*:[100] 'No part of our experience is a priori. Whatever we see could be otherwise. But, by implication, that our experience belongs to us and could not belong to another is a priori. It could not happen that we should need to employ some principle of differentiation to distinguish within the flow of experience those experiences that belong to us from those experiences that belong to others.'

However, this interpretation does not really fit the text. It is true that, when Wittgenstein compiled the *Tractatus*, he almost certainly realized that the self-ascription of an experience is not problematic to the person who makes it, because he does not first identify the experience and then face the further task of establishing its connection with his ego.[101] But this can hardly be described as the insight that it is a priori that his experience belongs to him and could not belong to another. In any case, the remainder of 5.634 rules out this interpretation, because it is clearly directed against the a priori gilding of an ordinary empirical lily.

So we must return to that way of taking his argument and try to answer the question, whether it is directed against attaching the subject by definition to a particular experience, or against attaching an experience by definition to a particular subject. Now when I have an experience, it is an empirical fact that I have it, and the readiest way to put an a priori gilding on this fact would be to define my ego as the one that has the experience. The correct way to present the empirical fact is to say that the psychological sequence, which I am,[102] is increased by the accretion of this particular experience. The incorrect way, which is to define me as the subject of the experience, turns the fact into something a priori. The attempt to have it both ways and to *find* an a priori order in things is always mistaken.[103]

---

[100] *Insight and Illusion*, Oxford, 1972, p. 63. (Revised edn., 1986, p. 87.)

[101] See above, p. 40.

[102] See *TLP* 5.542–5421.

[103] The best commentary on this prohibition is his own use of it in the philosophy of science: 'We do not have an *a priori belief* in a law of conservation, but rather *a priori knowledge* of the possibility of a logical form. All such propositions, including the principle of sufficient reason, the laws of continuity in nature and of least effort in nature, etc., etc.—all these are a priori insights about the forms in which the propositions of science can be cast.' (*TLP* 6.33–6.44.)

It would be hard to understand a philosophical reconstruction of the ownership of experiences which ran the a priori connection in the opposite direction. Even if this move were intelligible, it would not be a contribution to the characterization of the subject and so would not be an appropriate topic in this part of the *Tractatus*. These are convincing reasons for taking the theory under attack in the other way, namely as the theory that the subject is attached to the experience by definition. If confirmation is needed, it is provided by the fact that this is precisely what Russell did when he said that the subject can only be known by description.[104] According to that theory, his second one, the subject could only be inferred from things in the field of consciousness, or, translating this back into the analogue, the eye could only be inferred from things in the visual field. But how could the inference ever be justified?[105]

The two final remarks in this section of the *Tractatus*, 5.64 and 5.641 sum it all up:

Here it can be seen that solipsism, when its implications are followed out strictly, coincides with pure realism. The self of solipsism shrinks to a point without extension, and there remains the reality co-ordinated with it.

Thus there really is a sense in which philosophy can talk about the self in a non-psychological way.

What brings the self into philosophy is the fact that 'the world is my world'.

The philosophical self is not the human being, not the human body, or the human soul, with which psychology deals, but rather the metaphysical subject, the limit of the world—not a part of it.

The first paragraph of this summing up is an adaptation of an entry in the *Notebooks* discussed above.[106] Two changes have been made. The reference to idealism, which is the starting-point of the intellectual journey reviewed in the *Notebooks*, is omitted, and the vanishing of the ego from the scene is described more elegantly. But the argument is unaltered: solipsism is empty if, as he put it later, 'there is not connection between what is seen and a person'.[107] Alternatively—the other option in the dilemma—the connection is made, and then solipsism is self-refuting.

The next two paragraphs explain how it is that philosophy can talk about the self in spite of the fact that it does not figure as a nameable

---

[104] See above, p. 161.
[105] 'Nothing *in the visual field* allows you to infer that it is seen by an eye.' (*TLP* 5.633.)
[106] *NB* 15 Oct. 1916, discussed, above, pp. 169–70.
[107] *NLPESD* p. 297, quoted above p. 176.

object in psychology. The first one is adapted from an entry in the
Notebooks, which is placed immediately after this statement.

I objectively confront every object. But not the I.[108]

The version in the *Tractatus* is significantly weakened, because the
Notebooks has it that philosophy can and must talk about the self in this
non-psychological way. The change reflects Wittgenstein's understandable uneasiness about the two levels of language, on one of which
the self cannot be 'mentioned', while on the other it can be 'talked
about'. It would be better to conclude that the existence of the self as
subject is shown by the fact that the self-ascription of experiences is
non-problematical.[109] In the third of these two paragraphs he says
only that the self is 'brought into philosophy'. It is, as he would have
said later, an atmosphere surrounding the self-ascription of experiences. In the *Notebooks* and the *Tractatus* it is presented as the vestigial
ghost of personalization. He cannot say that its existence is shown,
because that would make it too like a named object.[110] So what he says
is that it is brought into philosophy by 'the fact that "the world is my
world"'. He could have written 'Q. E. D.' after this sentence, because,
of course, it picks up the valid point ascribed to the solipsist in 5.62.

The final paragraph is an adaptation of an entry made in the
Notebooks on 2 September 1916. The only significant change is that the
Tractatus omits the explanation which immediately follows in the
Notebooks:

... The human body, however, my body in particular, is a part of the world
among others, among animals, plants, stones, etc., etc.
    Whoever realizes this will not want to procure a preferential place for his
own body or for the human body.
    He will regard humans and animals quite naïvely as objects which are
similar and which belong together.

When this passage was first quoted,[111] it was interpreted as a reference
to my natural tendency to give my own body preferential treatment by
making it the seat of the ego. Wittgenstein's point was taken to be that,
if I give this tendency full rein, it will carry me through solipsism to
realism, because it will empty my solipsism of all empirical content.
That, it was claimed, is one side of the dilemma that he offers the

---

[108] *NB* 11 Aug. 1916.
[109] See above, p. 40.
[110] See above, p. 167.
[111] See above, p. 168.

solipsist. But if this interpretation is correct, it makes the passage an important part of his argument, and its omission from the *Tractatus* becomes very surprising. Perhaps the interpretation is wrong?

There is a rival interpretation, offered by P. M. S. Hacker apropos of a slightly later entry in the *Notebooks*. On 12 October 1916 Wittgenstein picks up the point about 'the human body, my body in particular, and its place in the world 'among others, among animals, plants, stones etc., etc.':

A stone, the body of an animal, the body of a man, my body, all stand on the same level.

Hacker's comment on this[112] is that it can only be grasped if one realizes that Wittgenstein is arguing against Schopenhauer's view that my body stands on a different level from other objects inasmuch as my direct knowledge of my own intentional actions gives me an awareness of my body not merely as idea or representation but also as will.[113] My awareness of my will constitutes, according to Schopenhauer, an awareness of noumenal reality, the underlying thing-in-itself, behind the phenomenal idea. The idea that one part of the world be closer to me than another as Schopenhauer suggests is, Wittgenstein later remarks, intolerable.[114]

It is true that Schopenhauer exalts my body by giving it an epistemically privileged position for me. It may also be true that his exaltation of my body reinforced his tendency to make it the seat of the ego. But Wittgenstein's own tendency to solipsism can hardly have been reinforced by a doctrine which he explicitly rejects. In any case, he points out that the preferential treatment accorded to my body may be extended to all human bodies and even that the world-spirit might be 'common to inanimate things too'.[115] This shows conclusively that the epistemically privileged position of my body for me is not what is at issue in these two important passages in the *Notebooks*.[116] The issue is whether the privilege of serving as the seat of the ego should be assigned to my body or to all human bodies, etc., etc. If confirmation is needed, it is provided by the fact that both passages in the *Notebooks*

---

[112] *Insight and Illusion*, pp. 67–8. This is slightly altered in the Revised edn., 1986, p. 91.

[113] Schopenhauer's view, which was mentioned above, p. 178, is developed by B. O'Shaughnessy in *The Will*, Cambridge, 1980.

[114] *NB* 4 Nov. 1916, paragraph 33.

[115] *NB* 15 Oct. 1916.

[116] The other passage is *NB* 2 Sept. 1916, quoted on p. 168.

are explicitly concerned only with 'the subject that thinks or entertains ideas'. In fact, the second passage, written on 16 October 1916 is immediately followed by this remark, on 17 October,

And in this sense I can also speak of a will that is common to the whole world.

The implication is clear: the discussion on the previous day had not been concerned with the will.

So we are thrown back on the earlier interpretation of the explanatory passages in the *Notebooks*, and confronted again by the question why they are not included in the *Tractatus*. Part of the answer must be that in the *Tractatus* the final paragraph of 5.641 serves as summary and conclusion, and so it would have been inappropriate to keep the explanation which is appended to it in the *Notebooks*. However, there is something more to be said about the omission. When Wittgenstein put his discussion of solipsism into the *Tractatus*, he streamlined it not only be cutting out the illuminating account of the philosophical competition between the different physical candidates for the privilege of housing the ego, but also by cutting out the reference to idealism. There is no need to suppose that this indicates any change in his views. It is much more likely that he merely concentrated his treatment of solipsism on the attempt to relate the limit of language to my ego without supplying my ego with any criterion of identity, and left out the peripheral observations which he had made in the *Notebooks*.

Wittgenstein's treatment of solipsism has now been examined in depth and detail. There were several reasons for adopting this procedure. It is the most fascinating section of the *Tractatus*, but also the most enigmatic one, because solipsism stands at the interesection of many lines of thought in his mind. Some of them would have been difficult to follow even if he had singled them out and developed them separately, and the difficulty is increased when they are woven together in a single text. It is true that this produces a rich pattern in which the appreciation of each part enhances the appreciation of all the others. But it also increases the risks of misunderstanding. So it might be helpful to end this chapter with a list of common misconceptions.

We are now in a position to say that, contrary to popular belief, the *Tractatus* is not concerned with the kind of solipsist who complains that he cannot penetrate the veil of his own sense-data and so cannot establish the existence of the physical world or of other people inhabiting it. The whole argument is concerned with the detachment of the subject from the one and only world. There may be side-glances at the problem of sense-data; for example Wittgenstein may have intended the placing of the word 'allein' in 5.62 to make an additional marginal allusion to issues which are certainly irrelevant to his central interest in 'the only language that I understand'. Also he must have realized that the special character of the boundary of the visual field is connected with these issues. But they cannot conceivably be what he is talking about in the texts that have been scrutinized in this chapter.

Another, fairly widespread, but equally mistaken belief is that in his early writings Wittgenstein admits to being a solipsist. Add this to the first misconception and the result is a gross misrepresentation of the development of his philosophy. He will then appear in the *Tractatus* as a thinker forced into solipsism by his belief that his own sense-data cut him off from direct access to anything else, and only later, and with great difficulty, escaping from this intellectual trap.

The truth is quite different and much more interesting. He does not subscribe to solipsism in the *Tractatus*, because that would commit him to treating it as a theory capable of being true or false. He merely concedes that the solipsist has got hold of a good point of a kind which cannot be stated in factual discourse but only shown: the subject is the inner limit of the world. This is not something which he abandoned in his later writings. He simply changed the way in which he presented it. Instead of putting it on show in Kantian or Schopenhaueresque costume, he traced it back to its origin in ordinary human life and language. This, of course, is an aspect of the general change which his doctrine of showing underwent in his later philosophy.[117]

Nor, of course, is the early Wittgenstein an idealist. He introduces idealism in the *Notebooks* merely as a philosophical theory produced, like solipsism, by letting the subject float free of any physical attachment. This, of course, is only one of idealism's many aspects, and he supplies its aetiology because it is a continuation of the aetiology of solipsism, and in this case too it would be a gratuitous mistake to suppose that he subscribed to the theory.

He is, of course, a realist, as he implies in 5.64,

. . . The self of solipsism shrinks to a point without extension, and there remains the reality co-ordinated with it.

---

[117] See above, pp. 146–52.

But it is important to appreciate that the realism attained by this route embodies only one of realism's many aspects. What Wittgenstein says here can be put in the following way: it is impossible to set any personally limited world in relief against the background of the one and only world. Any limited world, defined by its relation to a single point of view, mine or humanity's, will inevitably collapse back into the one and only world, which contains not only all the thinkers but also all the objects of their thoughts.

The discussion of realism in Chapters 2 and 5 was not concerned with this aspect of it. The question asked there was, how much is contributed to a thinker's picture of the world by his own mind, and how much is the independent contribution of the objects of his thought. That is not a question about the limits of the point of view from which language is constructed and understood, for example, whether it is constituted by a single person, or collectively by a group, and, if so, how widely the group extends. It is a question not about individual minds, but about the general powers of the mind, and so it could be asked from any point of view, solitary or collective. The line taken in Chapter 2 was that Wittgenstein's answer to it in the *Tractatus* was too Platonic, or, perhaps, too Aristotelian, but that he gradually worked his way towards the more sophisticated view that the two contributions, one of mind and the other of the world, could not be separated from one another.

The two aspects of realism are connected in Wittgenstein's early philosophy. In each case, his discussion starts from a criticism of the assumption that a limited world can be set in relief against the background of the one and only phenomenal world. The difference is that the solipsist tries to cut his miniature world out of the background of the phenomenal world, while the Platonist tries to set the whole phenomenal world against the background of a further, noumenal world. When Wittgenstein gives these theories a linguistic turn, solipsism becomes a retreat into a personally limited language, while Platonism becomes an advance beyond the existing limits of language and an attempt to explain why certain candidates succeed in achieving possibility in much the same way that science explains why certain possibilities succeed in achieving actuality.[118] According to him, the two theories commit what is, from a certain point of view, the same error: they try to set a miniature world in relief against the background of a larger world.

[118] See above, pp. 95–6 and 171–2.

However, there is a big difference between the ways in which the two theories commit this error. One does it by making an illegitimate retreat, while the other does it by making an illegitimate advance. One tries to impose a personal restriction on the point of view from which language is constructed and understood, while the other tries to expand the horizon to include candidates for possibility behind the line of possibilities.

More than one commentator has claimed that there is an 'important element of idealism' in Wittgenstein's later writing.[119] If the claim is that there is no way of separating the mind's contribution to its picture of the world from the world's contribution to it, it is true, but it is questionable whether the truth should be expressed in this way.[120] In any case, this is only one of the two aspects of the conflict between realism and idealism. If the claim is based on the intellectual journey described in the *Notebooks*, starting from all humanity's point of view, moving through my point of view, and terminating in realism, it is another misconception. For this journey traverses the other issue between realism and idealism, the question in what person or persons the ego has its seat. This is no longer an issue in *Philosophical Investigations*, and in Wittgenstein's early writings, where it is an issue, there is no possibility of connecting the two aspects of the conflict between realism and idealism except by repeating what was said above: in both areas it is possible to make what is, from a certain very general point of view, the same error. The discussion of these problems will have to be taken up again and completed in Volume II.

---

[119] This is Bernard Williams's way of putting it. See his 'Wittgenstein and Idealism' in *Understanding Wittgenstein*, ed. G. Vesey, Macmillan, 1974, reprinted in B. Williams: *Moral Luck*, Cambridge, 1981. Cf. J. Lear: 'The Disappearing "We",' *Proceedings of the Aristotelian Society*, Supp. Vol. 58, 1984.

[120] D. Bolton argues that it is a mistake. See his *Life-form and Idealism*, cited above, n. 65. He also criticizes (pp. 276ff) other points in Williams' interpretation of Wittgenstein's later work.

8

Review and Prospect

WITGENSTEIN gives his own assessment of his achievement in the *Tractatus* in the Preface, and it is a mixed one:

> If this work has any value, it consists in two things: the first is that thoughts are expressed in it, and on this score the better the thoughts are expressed— the more the nail has been hit on the head—the greater will be its value. Here I am conscious of having fallen a long way short of what is possible . . .
>
> On the other hand the *truth* of the thoughts that are here communicated seems to me unassailable and definitive. I therefore believe myself to have found, on all essential points, the final solution of the problems. And if I am not mistaken in this belief, then the second thing in which the value of this work consists is that it shows how little is achieved when these problems are solved.[1]

The last sentence assesses the importance of the task described at the beginning of the Preface:

> The book deals with the problems of philosophy, and shows, I believe, that the reason why these problems are posed is that the logic of our language is misunderstood.[2]

His estimate of the importance of this task is not just a piece of ironical self-deprecation. He is putting life before analytical philosophy. Life encompasses every human activity, including thought, but not the kind of philosophy that he practised in the *Notebooks* and the *Tractatus*. That is a performance on the outermost edge of what is intellectually possible, and, because it has no field of its own, it looks inwards at all the other manifestations of the human spirit.[3]

---

[1] Preface to the *Tractatus*, pp. 3–5.
[2] Ibid., p. 3.
[3] Cf. his letter to L. Ficker about the *Tractatus*: 'The book's point is an ethical one. I once meant to include in the preface a sentence which is not in fact there now but which I will write out for you here, because it will perhaps be a key to the work for you. What I meant to write, then, was this: My work consists of two parts: the one presented here plus all that I have *not* written. And it is precisely this second part that is the important one. My book draws limits to the sphere of the ethical from the inside as it were, and I am convinced that this is the ONLY *rigorous* way of drawing those limits. In short, I believe that where *many* others today are just *gassing*, I have managed to put everything firmly into

He underestimated the compulsiveness of this marginal activity and overestimated the finality of his own contribution to it in the *Tractatus*. These two misjudgements were connected, because the errors that he came to see in the book drew him back into philosophy in 1929, and the great work that he did in the 1930s led him to the realization that finality is unattainable.[4]

There are two ways of looking at the *Tractatus*. It is a book published by its author as an independent shot at the truth and it is from this point of view that he assessed it in 1918 and the immediately succeeding years. But, taking a longer view, we can see it as an artificial break in a continuous development, like a still excerpted from a film. It must be remembered that he always found great difficulty in putting his thoughts in linear order to make the kind of treatise that is expected from a philosopher.[5] They are interrelated in too many ways for the usual two-dimensional arrangement.[6] That is one reason why he always had to struggle to make a book the natural expression of his thoughts. But there is also another, connected reason: his thoughts live in his notebooks, and form their relations with one another slowly over many years. A work published by him is, therefore, an artificial cut in a continuous process of growth, and, instead of treating either of his two great books as a definitive revelation, we ought to trace their ideas back to their points of germination and then move forwards again, following the gradual process of their growth in their own ecosystem.[7]

The errors of the *Tractatus* should, therefore, be regarded as points at which lines of thought are either discontinued or bent in a new

place by being silent about it. . . . I would recommend you to read the *preface* and the *conclusion*, because they contain the most direct expression of the point of the book.' (P. Englemann: *Letters from Ludwig Wittgenstein with a Memoir*, ed. B. McGuinness, tr. L. Furtmüller, Blackwell, 1967, pp. 143–4.)

[4] Years later he wrote, 'It is not our aim to refine or complete the system of rules for the use of our words in unheard-of ways. For the clarity that we are aiming at is indeed *complete* clarity, but this simply means that the philosophical problems should *completely* disappear. The real discovery is the one that makes me capable of stopping philosophy when I want to.—The one that gives philosophy peace, so that it is no longer tormented by questions which bring *itself* into question. Instead, we now demonstrate a method, by examples; and the series of examples can be broken off.—Problems are solved (difficulties eliminated), not a *single* problem. There is not *a* philosophical method, though there are indeed methods, like different therapies' (*PI* I § 133).

[5] See *PI* Preface, p. ix, where he describes his difficulty.

[6] The *Tractatus* treatment of solipsism is a good example of this. See above, p. 187.

[7] See above, pp. 91–2 There is an excellent account of this aspect of Wittgenstein's work in S. Hilmy's forthcoming book, *The Later Wittgenstein* (provisional title), Blackwell.

direction. The logical atomism of the early system is a clear case of a line of thought that was discontinued. It was not a natural growth in Wittgenstein's mind and it temporarily inhibited his tendency to holism.[8] There are many examples of early lines of thought which changed direction after 1929, but perhaps the most interesting one is the doctrine of showing. In the *Tractatus* this doctrine is presented in the rigid framework of logical atomism. The attachment of factual discourse to the world is achieved *au fond* through elementary sentences, each of which is linked to its own bit of reality and displays the simple possibility which it asserts to be realized. There is no way in which such possibilities can be described or explained; each one is a separate mystery, eluding the grasp of science. In the later system this mystery does not disappear, but, rather, is spread over the whole surface of human language and behaviour.

The survey of this surface by the methodical use of language-games corrected the fundamental error in the theory of meaning of the *Tractatus*. Names do not simply attach themselves to things, and though in a sense it is true that 'logic must take care of itself'[9]—it does not need to be backed up by any theory—there is also a sense in which it is false: we are as it were the drivers, and not back-seat drivers either. Now language-games are human activities, and the best corrective for the negligent Platonism of the *Tractatus* is to describe what we actually do to keep language going. This line of thought led eventually to the anti-Platonic argument of *Philosophical Investigations*.[10]

There is also another way of classifying the errors of the *Tractatus*. Some were points at which he changed his mind about the nature of philosophy, while others were only changes in particular doctrines. The transformation of the doctrine of showing was part of a more general shift in his views about language which produced a new conception of the way to do philosophy. When he abandoned the separatism of his early theory of language, he no longer found that the only way to deal with a philosophical problem was to analyse the far-reaching senses of the sentences that generated it. Instead, he looked for its solution, or, rather, its dissolution, on the surface of language as it is used in daily life, in details that are so close to us that it is difficult to single them out and appreciate their significance.[11]

---

[8] See above, pp. 83–7 and 132–5.
[9] The opening sentence of *NB*, as the text now stands (22 Aug. 1914). Cf. *TLP* 5.473.
[10] *PI* I §§ 140–242. See above, pp. 9–11 and 59–60.   [11] See above, pp. 17–19.

The later development of his ideas about solipsism contains a clear example of the correction of an error of the other kind, local rather than global. Quite a lot of this book has been devoted to demonstrating that he did not identify the objects of the *Tractatus* with sense-data, and that he was not criticizing a solipsism based on that identification. If the arguments used were convincing, they will have eliminated the popular misinterpretation which presents him as a philosopher trapped in a solipsism of sense-data and unable to escape until he had worked out a more sophisticated view of sensations and their properties. However, the alternative interpretation offered here would exculpate him from one charge of error only by representing him as guilty of another. For it was surely a mistake to leave the category of the objects underpinning factual discourse unspecified in the *Tractatus*. In fact, the error is nowhere more evident than in his treatment of solipsism. For how could an argument which deals with the attachment of the ego to its physical seat excuse itself from analysing the concept of *phenomena*?[12] Progress towards a better view could not begin until he faced the question of the categorization of objects.

On the other hand, the appreciation and criticism of the solipsist's position that was achieved in the *Notebooks* and *Tractatus* was an important stage in the development of his later philosophy of mind. The vanishing ego is only a point of view, and I do not have to identify my point of view before reporting my experiences. But the point of view marked by the ego is important, although the ego itself is nothing until it is attached to a body, and then it is still nothing, because it is no longer needed. These insights were left undeveloped in the *Tractatus*, because it was enough to present them in a way which identified the solipsist's good point and explained why he could not express it as a factual thesis, capable of truth or falsehood like a piece of science. They were developed in the work that Wittgenstein began in 1929, and that is why the most illuminating comments on his early treatment of solipsism come from writings that he started in that year and soon afterwards.[13]

However, it was not long before the deficiency in the specification of phenomena in the *Tractatus* began to make itself felt. His first reaction was to identify them with sense-data and to treat sense-data

---

[12] This is a mistake of the kind that he later singled out for severe criticism. See *LWVC* pp. 82–4, cited above, ch. 4 n. 72.

[13] See above, p. 159.

in a way that assimilated them far too closely to objects in the physical world.[14] At this stage, his position could be described like this: he had succeeded in dealing with the subject in a way that avoided the creation of a miniature world set in relief against the background of the world in which we all live our lives,[15] but he had not yet succeeded in dealing with objects in a way that avoided this kind of miniaturized reduplication. That proved to be a long and difficult task, completed in the 'private language argument' of *Philosophical Investigations*.[16]

Underneath the changes that generated his later system out of his earlier one there were certain intuitions that remained constant, and some of them have been identified in this book. He was a thinker whose flashes of insight often reached far beyond the position that he had established by argument,[17] and it is hardly surprising that so many of them occurred in his youth. Some philosophers are like chameleons, but others see too far to be able to change so much.

[14] See above, pp. 45–7.

[15] He puts it like this in *PR* § 58: 'All these languages [with different people as their centres] only describe one single, incomparable thing and *cannot* represent anything else. (Both these approaches must lead to the same result: first, that what is represented is not one thing among others, that it is not capable of being contrasted with anything; second, that I cannot express the advantage of *my* language.)'

[16] *PI* I §§ 243 ff. See above, pp. 48–58.

[17] Cf. his own assessment of *TLP* in the preface which is an overestimation of its immediate achievement, but, on a longer view, and excluding the lines of thought that were discontinued, possibly true.

BIBLIOGRAPHY

A. Works by, or originating from (*) Wittgenstein, which are the most frequently cited sources

* *Ludwig Wittgenstein and the Vienna Circle: Conversations Recorded by Friedrich Waismann*, ed. B. McGuinness, tr. J. Schulte and B. McGuinness, Blackwell, 1979. [LWVC]

Notebooks 1914—1916, ed. G. H. von Wright and G. E. M. Anscombe, tr. G. E. M. Anscombe, Blackwell, 1961. [NB]

Notes for Lectures on 'Private Experience' and 'Sense-data', Philosophical Review, Vol. 77, No. 3, 1968. [The notes taken of these lectures by R. Rhees are published in the journal *Philosophical Investigations*, Vol. 7, No. 1, Jan. 1984]. [NLPESD]

Philosophical Grammar, ed. R. Rhees, tr. A. Kenny, Blackwell, 1974. [PG]

Philosophical Investigations, tr. G. E. M. Anscombe, Blackwell, 1953; 3rd edn., Macmillan, 1958. [PI]

Philosophical Remarks, ed. R. Rhees, tr. R. Hargreaves and R. White, Blackwell, 1975. [PR]

Tractatus Logico-Philosophicus, tr. C. K. Ogden, Routledge, 1922, and tr. D. F. Pears and B. McGuinness, Routledge, 1961. [TLP]

Wittgenstein's Lectures, Cambridge, 1930—1932, ed. D. Lee, Blackwell, 1980. [*CLI*]

B. Other Works by, or originating from Wittgenstein, infrequently cited

The Big Typescript, unpublished. Item 213 in G. H. von Wright's list, *Philosophical Review*, Vol. 78, Oct. 1969, Special Supplement.

The Blue and Brown Books, Blackwell 1958.

Notes Dictated to G. E. Moore in Norway, published as an Appendix to *NB*, q.v.

Notes on Logic, published as an Appendix to *NB*, q.v.

On Certainty, ed. G. E. M. Anscombe and G. H. von Wright, tr. G. E. M. Anscombe and D. Paul, Blackwell, 1969.

Prototractatus, ed. B. McGuinness, T. Nyberg, and G. H. von Wright, tr. D. F. Pears and B. McGuinness, Routledge and Kegan Paul, 1971.

Remarks on Colour, ed. G. E. M. Anscombe, tr. L. McAlister and M. Schattle, Blackwell, 1977.

'Some Remarks on Logical Form', *Proceedings of the Aristotelian Society*, Suppl. Vol. 9; reprinted in *Essays on Wittgenstein's* Tractatus, ed. R. Beard and I. Copi, Routledge and Kegan Paul, 1966.

* *Wittgenstein's Lectures, Cambridge 1932—5*, ed. A. Ambrose, Blackwell, 1979.

Zettel, ed. G. E. M. Anscombe and G. H. von Wright, tr. G. E. M. Anscombe, Blackwell, 1967.

C. Books and Articles on Wittgenstein

ALLAIRE, E. B.: 'The *Tractatus*: Nominalistic or Realistic?', in *Essays on Wittgenstein's* Tractatus [see § B. 'Some Remarks . . .']'.

ANSCOMBE, G. E. M.: *An Introduction to Wittgenstein's* Tractatus, Hutchinson, 1959.

BLACK, M.: *A Companion to Wittgenstein's* Tractatus, Cambridge, 1964.

BOLTON, D.: 'Life-form and Idealism', in *Idealism, Past and Present*, ed. G. Vesey, Cambridge, 1982.

ENGELMANN, P.: *Letters from Ludwig Wittgenstein with a Memoir*, ed. B. McGuinness, tr. L. Furtmüller, Blackwell, 1967.

HACKER, P.: *Insight and Illusion*, Oxford, 1972; rev. edn; 1986.

HILMY, S.: *The Later Wittgenstein* [provisional title], Blackwell, forthcoming.

HINTIKKA, J.: 'On Wittgenstein's Solipsism', *Mind*, Vol. 67, Jan. 1958; reprinted in *Essays on Wittgenstein's* Tractatus [see § B. 'Some Remarks . . .'].

—— J. and M.: *Investigating Wittgenstein*, Blackwell, 1986.

ISHIGURO, H.: 'Use and Reference of Names', in *Studies in the Philosophy of Wittgenstein*, ed. P. Winch, Routledge, 1969.

KENNY, A.: 'From the *Big Typescript* to the *Philosophical Grammar*', in *Essays on Wittgenstein in Honour of G. H. von Wright*, ed. J. Hintikka, *Acta Philosophica Fennica*, Vol. 28, Nos. 1–3, 1976.

—— *Wittgenstein*, Penguin, 1973.

KEYT, D.: 'A New Interpretation of the *Tractatus* Examined', *Philosophical Review*, Vol. 74, No. 2, 1965.

—— 'Wittgenstein's Picture Theory of Language', in *Essays in Wittgenstein's* Tractatus [see § B. 'Some Remarks . . .'].

LEAR, J.: 'The Disappearing "We"', *Proceedings of the Aristotelian Society*, Vol. 58, 1984.

LEWY, C.: 'A Note on the Text of the *Tractatus*', *Mind*, Vol. 76, 1967.

MCGUINNESS, B.: 'The So-called Realism of the *Tractatus*', in *Perspectives on the Philosophy of Wittgenstein*, ed. I. Block, Blackwell, 1981.

MALCOLM, N.: *Ludwig Wittgenstein: A Memoir*, 2nd edn., Oxford, 1974.

PEARS D. F.: 'The Logical Independence of Elementary Propositions', in *Perspectives on the Philosophy of Wittgenstein* [see previous item].

STENIUS, E.: *Wittgenstein's* Tractatus, Blackwell, 1960.

WILLIAMS, B.: 'Wittgenstein and Idealism', in *Understanding Wittgenstein*, ed. G. Vesey, Macmillan, 1974; reprinted in B. Williams: *Moral Luck*, Cambridge, 1981.

D. *Other Books and Articles*

CARNAP, R.: *The Unity of Science*, Kegan Paul, 1934.
CLARK, R. W.: *The Life of Bertrand Russell*, Jonathan Cape and Weidenfeld and Nicholson, 1975.
FREGE, G.: *Grundgesetze der Arithmetik, begriffschriftlich abgeleitet*, Vol. 1, 1893; Vol. 2, 1903, Hermann Pohle, Jena.
HUME, D.: *Treatise of Human Nature*.
KANT, I.: *Critique of Pure Reason*.
KRIPKE, S.: 'Naming and Necessity', in *Semantics and Natural Language*, Reidel, 1972: reprinted by Blackwell, 1980.
PUTNAM, H.: 'The Meaning of Meaning', in *Collected Papers*, Vol. 2, Cambridge, 1981.
RUSSELL, B.: 'Knowledge by Acquaintance, Knowledge by Description', in *Mysticism and Logic*, Longmans, 1918.
—— *My Philosophical Development*, Allen and Unwin, 1959.
—— 'On the Nature of Acquaintance', in *Logic and Knowledge; Essays 1901–1950*, ed. R. C. Marsh, Allen and Unwin, 1956.
—— 'On the Nature of Truth and Falsehood', in *Philosophical Essays*, Longmans, 1910.
—— 'The Philosophy of Logical Atomism', in *Logic and Knowledge: Essays 1901–1950* [see above].
—— *The Problems of Philosophy*, Home University Library, 1912.
—— 'The Relation of Sense-data to Physics', in *Philosophical Essays*, Longmans, 1910.
—— *Theory of Knowledge (1913)*, in *The Collected Papers of Bertrand Russell*, Vol. 7. ed. E. Eames and K. Blackwell, Allen and Unwin, 1984.
SCHLICK, M.: 'Meaning and Verification', *Philosophical Review*, 1936; reprinted in *Readings in Philosophical Analysis*, ed. H. Feigl and W. Sellars, Appleton–Century–Crofts, 1949.
SCHOPENHAUER, A.: *The World as Will and Idea*, tr. R. B. Haldane and J. Kemp, Routledge and Kegan Paul, 1883; 9th imp., 1950.

INDEX